THE BOOK OF PROVERBS IN SOCIAL AND THEOLOGICAL CONTEXT

The book of Proverbs is the starting point of the biblical wisdom tradition. But how did individual proverbs, instructions and poems come together to form the various collections we have today? Katharine Dell explores the possible social contexts for this varied material in the royal court, wisdom schools and popular culture. She draws shrewdly on materials from the wisdom traditions of the ancient Near East, in particular Egypt, in order to bolster and enhance her theories. She argues that Proverbs had a theological purpose from its conception, with God's creativity being an integral theme of the text rather than one added in later redactions.

Dell also shows that echoes of other Old Testament genres such as prophecy, law and cult can be found in Proverbs, notably in chapters 1–9, and that its social and theological context is much broader than scholars have recognized in the past.

KATHARINE J. DELL is a Senior Lecturer at the Faculty of Divinity, University of Cambridge. Her publications include *The Book of Job as Sceptical Literature* (1991); *Get Wisdom, Get Insight: An Introduction to Israel's Wisdom Literature* (2000), and *Seeking a Life that Matters: Wisdom for Today from the Book of Proverbs* (2002).

THE BOOK OF PROVERBS
IN SOCIAL AND
THEOLOGICAL CONTEXT

KATHARINE J. DELL

CAMBRIDGE UNIVERSITY PRESS
Cambridge, New York, Melbourne, Madrid, Cape Town, Singapore, São Paulo

Cambridge University Press
The Edinburgh Building, Cambridge CB2 2RU, UK

Published in the United States of America by Cambridge University Press, New York

www.cambridge.org
Information on this title: www.cambridge.org/9780521633055

© Katharine J. Dell 2006

First published 2006

Printed in the United Kingdom at the University Press, Cambridge

A catalogue record for this publication is available from the British Library

Library of Congress Cataloguing in Publication data

Dell, Katharine J. (Katharine Julia), 1961–
The book of Proverbs in social and theological context / Katharine J. Dell.
p.   cm.
Includes bibliographical references and index.

ISBN 0-521-63305-2 (hardback)
1.   Bible. O.T. Proverbs – Socio-rhetorical criticism. 2.   Bible. O.T. Proverbs – Theology.
I. Title
BS1465.52.D45 2006
223'. 706–dc22
2005024191
ISBN-13 978-0-521-63305-5 hardback
ISBN-10 0-521-63305-2 hardback

Contents

Preface

This book on Proverbs has taken shape (and changed shape) over a number of years, and I have used some of my earlier ideas for a more ambitious project in articles that link up with the ideas represented here. Early work on this material was done at the Church Divinity School of the Pacific in Berkeley, during a sabbatical there, and my thanks go to Donn Morgan, in particular, for making me so welcome and exchanging many ideas about wisdom over lunch. I am grateful to the University of Cambridge for sabbatical terms and summer vacations in which I have completed this work. I am particularly grateful to Cambridge University Press for giving me extended time on which to work on this book and for their patience in my delay in producing a final manuscript. During the time of writing this book I have both got married and had a child, and it is to my husband, Douglas Kinnear Hamilton, and to our son, James David Kinnear Hamilton (born 4 February 2003), that I dedicate this book with love.

KATHARINE J. DELL
Cambridge, April 2005

Abbreviations

AB	Analecta Biblica
AOAT	Alter Orient und Altes Testament
BETL	Bibliotheca ephemeridum theologicarum lovaniensium
BHT	Beiträge zur historischen Theologie
BKAT	Biblischer Kommentar: Altes Testament
BS	*Bibliotheca Sacra*
BTB	*Biblical Theology Bulletin*
BZAW	Beihefte zur Zeitschrift für die alttestamentliche Wissenschaft
CB	Coniectanea Biblica
CBQ	*Catholic Biblical Quarterly*
CBQMS	Catholic Biblical Quarterly Monograph Series
DLZ	*Deutsche Literaturzeitung für Kritik der Internationalen Wissenschaft*
EJ	*Encyclopaedia Judaica*
EQ	*Evangelical Quarterly*
ET	*English translation*
EvTh	*Evangelische Theologie*
FAT	Forschungen zum Alten Testament
FTS	*Freiburger Theologische Studien*
HAT	Handbuch zum Alten Testament
HBT	*Horizons in Biblical Theology*
HUCA	*Hebrew Union College Annual*
IDB	*Interpreter's Dictionary of the Bible*
ICC	International Critical Commentary
IOSOT	International Organization for the Study of the Old Testament

JAAR	*Journal of the American Academy of Religion*
JAARS	Journal of the American Academy of Religion, Supplement Series
JAOS	*Journal of the American Oriental Society*
JBL	*Journal of Biblical Literature*
JBR	*Journal of the Bible and Religion*
JCS	*Journal of Cuneiform Studies*
JNES	*Journal of Near Eastern Studies*
JNWSL	*Journal of Northwest Semitic Languages*
JR	*Journal of Religion*
JSOT	*Journal for the Study of the Old Testament*
JSOTS	Journal for the Study of the Old Testament Supplement Series
JTS	*Journal of Theological Studies*
NF	Neue Folge
NS	New Series
OBO	Orbis biblicus et orientalis
OBT	Overtures to Biblical Theology
OTL	Old Testament Library
OTS	*Oudtestamentische Studien*
PTMS	Princeton Theological Monograph Series
RB	*Revue Biblique*
RHPhR	*Revue d'Histoire et de Philosophie Religieuses*
SBL (DS)	Society of Biblical Literature (Dissertation Series)
SBS	Stuttgarter Bibelstudien
SBT	Studies in Biblical Theology
SJT	*Scottish Journal of Theology*
SPAW	Sitzungsberichte der Preussischen Akademie der Wissenschaften
TB	*Tyndale Bulletin*
TBAT	Theologische Bücherei, Altes Testament
Trudy	*Transactions of the 25th International Congress of Orientalists*
TS	*Theological Studies*
UF	*Ugarit-Forschungen*
VT	*Vetus Testamentum*
VTS	Vetus Testamentum Supplement Series

WMANT	Wissenschaftliche Monographien zum Alten und Neuen Testament
ZÄS	*Zeitschrift für Ägyptische Sprache und Altertumskunde*
ZAW	*Zeitschrift für die alttestamentliche Wissenschaft*
ZB	Züricher Bibelkommentare
ZTK	*Zeitschrift für Theologie und Kirche*

Introduction

> Some parts of the Old Testament are far less clearly expressive of Israel's distinctive understanding of reality than others, some parts (and one thinks of such a book as Proverbs) seem to be only peripherally related to it, while others (for example Ecclesiastes) even question its essential features.
>
> (Bright, 1967: 136)

Wisdom, both as a phenomenon and as a distinct literature, has often been treated by scholars as separate from the rest of the Old Testament.[1] Its context has been seen to have more in common with its ancient Near Eastern neighbours than with its mainstream Israelite institutions, and its theology has been seen to offer little contribution to the overall picture of Old Testament theology that is positive. This marginalization of the place of wisdom by scholars is, however, slowly changing in the light of recent interest in wisdom and attempts to understand its place in Israelite thought.[2] The last forty years have seen a great revival of interest in the wisdom literature in its own right.[3] Recent decades have also seen an interest in wisdom as a unifying feature of texts as employed by later redactors.[4] However, despite such attempts to define and understand

---

[1] Clements (1992) discusses this in the opening chapter of his book entitled *Wisdom in Theology*.

[2] Few Old Testament theologies written today would not at least contain a chapter on wisdom. However, in that by Preuss (1995–6), wisdom's relative absence is striking.

[3] A trend begun by von Rad's magisterial work *Wisdom in Israel* (1972).

[4] For example, in relation to the Psalter, the question of overall redactional intention was raised by Wilson (1985), who saw wisdom as having an important role, especially as it appears in Psalm 1. While wisdom influence can be found in the Psalter, evidence of systematic wisdom editorial activity throughout the Psalter is, as Whybray (1996) demonstrates, almost impossible to prove.

wisdom, there is much work that still needs to be done in the area of its integration with the rest of the Old Testament. I maintain that, with a few exceptions in recent scholarly work, the separateness of wisdom that characterized older Old Testament scholarship is still maintained by many today in their attempts to understand the thought-world that gave rise to the wisdom phenomenon and in their overall characterization of its theology and of its affinities with other Old Testament material.

I am intending in this book to focus my concerns on three areas that continue to be at the centre of scholarly discussion, notably wisdom's social context, its theological identity and its relationship to other parts of the Old Testament. The question of social context has been raised as a result of a number of recent scholarly works that have challenged seemingly established conclusions.[5] The question of how to characterize wisdom's theology has been raised almost afresh in recent scholarship,[6] in that the theology of the wisdom literature was not taken seriously enough, particularly in relation to other parts of the Old Testament, which forms my third area of concern. Proverbs has rightly been seen as containing little that could be regarded as substantial influence from other thought-worlds of the Old Testament, but this observation has led to a tendency to treat wisdom completely separately.[7] In the third area of concern I will look at the echoes of other texts in Proverbs and ask whether this separation of both social context and theology on such grounds can really be maintained. Related to this, in my second area of theological concern, is the issue of whether God is extensively represented in Proverbs and whether he is to be identified with the same Yahweh who led the people of Israel out of slavery in Egypt.

I shall be limiting my discussion to the book of Proverbs when looking at these key areas of social context, theology and links with other Old Testament material. This is because it is within Proverbs that most of the oldest and more traditional wisdom of Israel is preserved, both in its maxims and sayings and in its sections of more

---

[5] Weeks, in *Early Israelite Wisdom* (1994), contested many established conclusions about Egyptian influence and the Solomonic enlightenment. More radically, P. R. Davies (1998) views wisdom as almost entirely a scribal function from the later Old Testament period.

[6] Perhaps most excitingly by Perdue, (1994; Perdue et al., 1994).

[7] This is particularly true in discussions of wisdom's theology; see the next section.

theological reflection. The question of how different sections of the book came together, both in relation to oral origin and literary formulation, will be seen to raise the major issues of social context with which scholars are concerned. An examination of the theology of the book of Proverbs gives us an insight into the way a distinctive wisdom worldview developed. The links of Proverbs with other Old Testament genres, although generally seen to be limited, will give us an indication of its relationship to other thought-worlds existing alongside its distinctive worldview and will give us further clues to what kinds of social and theological connections were made by the sages of Israel.

SOCIAL CONTEXT

Any attempt to provide some social and historical background to Proverbs is fraught with peril. (Perdue, 1997: 79)

We have in front of us a biblical book that purports simply to consist of 'The proverbs of Solomon, son of David, King of Israel' (Prov. 1:1). At face value, then, it is no more than a collection of the wise proverbs of a king, known from elsewhere in the Bible to have the gift of wisdom (1 Kings 3:16–28; 4:29–34) as well as being famous for building the temple in Jerusalem. One might assume that this king spoke some or all of the sayings and that they were perhaps recorded by scribes at his court. The Rabbis tell us that Solomon composed the Song of Songs in his youth, Proverbs in middle age and Ecclesiastes in old age (*Baba Bathra* 15a).

This simple picture of the social context of Proverbs has been challenged from every side and I am not about to promote it! In the critical period, the Solomonic attribution has been questioned. There is no doubt that Solomon was famed for his wisdom[8] and that he may have had an interest in collecting proverbs and even promoting the exercise. He may have even coined one or two proverbs himself. But the consensus of opinion is that the attribution is both

---

[8] Alt (1976) stresses the role of Solomon as portrayed in the Deuteronomistic history as collector of wisdom traditions, regarding the influence from the ancient Near East and also the distinctiveness of the Israelite version of wisdom as promoted by him.

honorific and a matter of authority. Brueggemann[9] has recently
stressed afresh the importance of Solomon as a figure of legitimiza-
tion for wisdom. The name of a great king renowned for wisdom
gives authority to a mass of material that may well have had a much
more diverse origin. Solomon is also attributed with Ecclesiastes[10]
and the Wisdom of Solomon, both books that he is unlikely to have
written and that represent different periods of thought and of the
development of ideas.[11] Proverbs is the most likely book to which
Solomon might have had a historical link, but this link was probably
of a limited character. The attribution to Solomon is not the only
one in the book of Proverbs; there are attributions to Hezekiah in
Proverbs 25:1 (whose 'men' are said to have 'copied' proverbs of
Solomon) and to Agur and Lemuel in Proverbs 30:1 and 31:1 respectively. This suggests that different portions of the material were
gathered under different authoritative names, and that the super-
scription in Proverbs 1:1 may be a later attempt to place the whole
book under the name of the greatest wise king, Solomon. However,
the important aspect of the Solomonic attribution is that it places
Proverbs at the heart of Israelite wisdom literature and gives voice to
Solomon's renowned 'three thousand proverbs' (1 Kings 4:32).

Once scholars in the critical period, which effectively began at the
end of the nineteenth century, started to look at the literary, historical and theological features of the text, the conclusion was drawn
that Proverbs was unlikely to be the work of one author – Solomon
or otherwise – and that it is in fact a collection of collections, in that
different parts of the book of Proverbs were probably composed
separately.[12] When the forms and content of the material were
examined more closely, the characterization of the contents of this
book as 'sayings' was quickly seen as oversimplified; in fact, there are
within its pages longer pieces of instruction, poems about wisdom

---

[9] Brueggemann (1990) is concerned to maintain that the tradition is remembering a connection between Solomon and wisdom rather than inventing one.
[10] The genre of 'royal autobiography', which takes its inspiration from Solomon, is a key
   aspect of this work, but it is likely to be a retrospective technique by the author of the book.
[11] The Song of Songs is also attributed to Solomon (see discussion in Dell, 2005). I would
   argue, however, that the nature of this attribution is rather different, connected as it is with
   other references to Solomon in the body of the work.
[12] Consistently maintained by Whybray in his work, e.g. 1994a; 1994c.

and short pieces of narrative as well as the staple genre of the pro-verb.[13] As well as the quest for genres, much scholarship has focused on the process of accumulation, that is, of the gathering together of ideas and their collection into 'books'.[14] There is also a distinction to be made between oral stages of transmission and the writing down of material, so that this may be a book that has come together as a written text as a result of a long process of collection, adaptation and emendation.[15] And then there is the question of the book's relation-ship to other books in the Old Testament, notably to the other wisdom books within the canon (Job, Ecclesiastes) and outside it (Ecclesiasticus and the Wisdom of Solomon),[16] and its place within the broader framework of historical and theological developments that took place throughout the period in which the Old Testament came together.[17] There is also recent concern with the book both as material gathered together from oral and written origins and as a written text within a canon of scripture.[18] A further area of scholarly interest is the book's relationship with the 'wisdom' of other nations, particularly that of Egypt. The close relationship of part of the book with an Egyptian 'Instruction' (*Amenemope*) has made this particularly fertile ground when addressing the question of the origins of ideas and literary genres.[19]

One effect of the scholarly enterprise in relation to Proverbs and the wisdom literature in general has been the ease with which Prov-erbs, Job and Ecclesiastes have been hived off into a category of their own, that of 'wisdom literature'. This has been partly on the basis of form, in that the predominant forms of wisdom appear in these books sufficiently for them to be so categorized. Even if a few wisdom forms are found in other literature, that is explained as wisdom 'influence' spilling over from one genre to another. The separation of the

---

[13] For a useful overview of the different genres used in Proverbs (and other wisdom books) see Murphy, 1981b.

[14] This accompanies a stress on the canonization process and is seen, for example, in P. R. Davies, 1998.

[15] See Niditch, 1996, for an interesting recent discussion of this issue.

[16] An issue aired in any good introduction to the wisdom literature of the Old Testament, e.g. Crenshaw, 1981b; Murphy, 1990; Dell, 2000.

[17] See Dell, 1997.

[18] Childs (1979; 1985; 1992) has pioneered such concerns in reference to all biblical books.

[19] Many scholars have pursued this line. See discussion in Chapters 1–3.

wisdom genre has also been on the grounds of content in that there seem to be particular concerns in this literature, notably in retributive justice, moral behaviour, training of the young and the relationship between human beings and their creator God, who is known through the medium of Wisdom (a personified, feminine concept), that are distinctive to this literature. Again, aspects of these ideas found elsewhere in the Old Testament have been seen as wisdom 'influence' from an essentially self-contained theological agenda. Perhaps most strikingly in the area of social context, wisdom has been seen as the preserve of a small group of 'the wise' (חכמים) (mentioned in Jer. 18:18) who produced the book of Proverbs and members of which, be they all protesting voices on the edge of the mainstream, produced Job and Ecclesiastes. The question whether there was a separate 'class' of sages in Israel has been much debated (Whybray 1974;[20] Weeks, 1994). The separation of wisdom has also been achieved by the close relationship perceived between this material and that of the ancient Near East, which has led many to wonder whether it is home-grown Israelite material, and, even if it is a kind of Israelite version of both Egyptian and Mesopotamian models, whether it fits in with the rest of the Old Testament and with the theological worldview of the Israelites.[21]

I am concerned in this book, then, with the wider issue of wisdom's separation and integration. Especially when discussing questions of social context, there has been a tendency to separate Proverbs (and indeed wisdom as a whole) off into a side-path when speaking of its place in the rest of the Old Testament. The model I have just outlined above prefers separation of the genre – its forms and contents – and hence of the social context. The function of the Proverbs is largely seen as education and moral formation; and wisdom is seen as an area clearly distinct from other concerns of Israelite life such as law, worship, prophecy and story-telling. The

---

[20] Whybray (1974) argues against 'the wise' as a separate class and shows how wisdom thought becomes integrated with other parts of the Old Testament as time goes on.

[21] See discussion in Chapter 1. This kind of view sounds dated nowadays in a context in which Old Testament studies fully recognizes the much greater influence that ancient Near Eastern myths and ideas had on the Israelite corpus. In fact, this broader recognition of 'foreign influence' ironically makes the wisdom literature less out of place within the Old Testament as a whole.

educational, administrative suggestions that owe much to the ancient Near Eastern parallels have also had this effect. While this separation provides a helpful way of categorizing material, one wonders how far it was a reality in people's lives. Personal experience tells us that we interact with all the different 'genres' of life almost without thinking about it. While there might be establishments that deal with certain areas, such as schools for education, even there, other aspects of the formation of the young are taking place at the same time. The other side of the coin is integration. Some of the suggestions regarding context have had a more integrative effect, notably ideas about family wisdom as a broader context for wisdom's earliest roots, arguments that the proverbial material indicates a wider ethical concern for all beyond simply the education of young men, and the changing evaluation of the role of Yahweh in the material in a more integrative direction.

This links up with a wider debate about the 'distinctiveness' of wisdom. Was there a separate group of sages with concerns separate from the rest of Israelite life? Or are there hints of more integration with wider Israelite life? This question of wisdom influence comes in here. Some scholars have stressed this aspect more than others,[22] but it may be that because of scholarly attempts to separate, the majority have been too ready to sideline evidence of integration and to try to make sense of a more complex social world in which different genres were constantly being used and reused in ever new and changing contexts. As I say, I shall be focusing here on the book of Proverbs, but one might equally well extend the argument to all the wisdom books. In fact, the later wisdom books of Ecclesiasticus and the Wisdom of Solomon have long been acknowledged to show much more integration with more traditional aspects of Israelite life, and scholars have spoken of a striking development of wisdom into this new, more unified direction. This is no doubt the case, but are scholars in fact failing to notice the seeds of integration at an earlier stage?

---

[22] Crenshaw (in a useful collection of all his wisdom articles, 1995a) has consistently shown unease with finding too much 'wisdom influence' in texts outside 'the wisdom literature' proper and is concerned about a dilution of the definition of wisdom itself.

WISDOM'S THEOLOGY

It is the wisdom literature which offers the chief difficulty because it does not fit into the type of faith exhibited in the historical and prophetic literature. In it there is no explicit reference to or development of the doctrines of history, election or covenant. (Wright, 1952: 103)

One of the oldest reasons cited for keeping wisdom separate on a theological level is that there is in wisdom no reference to the saving history. There is no mention of Yahweh's self-revelation in the exodus, in the promise to David or in the election of Israel as the covenant people. Wright's comment (above) characterized the mood of the 1950s in which scholars largely dismissed the inclusion of wisdom in a wider estimate of Old Testament theology because 'in it there is no explicit reference to or development of the doctrines of history, election or covenant' (1952: 103). The title of his book, *God who Acts*, indicates that it is in the saving actions of history that Wright believes that God is revealed, not in the everyday, pithy saying. Wisdom seems to some scholars to be a misfit even within the cultic context of Israel's worshipping life, despite the presence of some wisdom psalms. Dentan, for example, sees wisdom as lacking the corporate concern of other material, notably of cultic material. Rather, it satisfied a need for concern for the individual and showed closest links with ancient Near Eastern ideas. Dentan also notes the lack of concern with the covenant, and writes, 'The complete absence of covenantal terminology from the Wisdom Literature is notorious' (Dentan, 1968: 8).

In fact, while it is true of the earlier canonical wisdom material that there is no historical reference (although attributions seek to historicize), it is not true of Ecclesiasticus and the Wisdom of Solomon, in which history is the arena in which wisdom is revealed through the Torah. It also becomes problematic when looking for wisdom ideas outside the strictly wisdom books, since historical and wisdom elements are often very mixed – in psalms on the borders of being included in the definition of wisdom literature, for example, such as Psalm 22, which contains material very similar to Job, but which also recalls God's action on behalf of Israel. If the influence of wisdom can be found elsewhere to be more than just a literary influence and to have been formative in the growth of material outside the wisdom literature as well as within it, then wisdom's separate mooring comes adrift and the evidence points towards integration, even if within the wisdom books themselves the more historical concerns were mainly left aside.

A second reason for wisdom's separateness is that in the attempt to construct an Old Testament theology, with finding a centre at the forefront of scholarly concern, wisdom sits uneasily alongside the main historical development of concepts such as covenant, election and salvation history. Brueggemann, in speaking of the place of wisdom in relation to the salvation-history scheme, writes, 'The unspoken counterpart to that commitment has been the notion that wisdom didn't count, that it really was an unwanted child, if not a bastard in the family of faith, that is unchristian, unbiblical, and not worth our time' (1970b: 5–6). He argues that it is in the broadening out of the quest for wisdom theology into other parts of the Old Testament, such as the Joseph narrative (Gen. 37–50) and the Yahwist's (J) creation account (Gen. 2–3), that a fuller appreciation of wisdom's place can be found.

Childs (1985) has argued that one of the more exciting aspects of Old Testament studies in recent years has been the theological discovery of the wisdom literature. Despite its not containing the revelatory deeds of history, he says that increasingly wisdom has its own theological integrity and cannot be associated with a secularization of religion or restricted to a late influence. It has influenced all parts of the canon in various ways. He writes, however, on its previous marginalization: 'The rebirth of interest in Old Testament theology which began in the 1920s and reached its first high-point with the theologies of Köhler and Eichrodt in the 1930s also had very little interest in wisdom. The reason for this lack of attention is also clear. Theology was thought to be grounded in the great acts of God in Israel's history and therefore it focused on the development of the traditions of election, covenant, people of God and Davidic covenant' (Childs, 1985: 210–12).

Before the 1920s the existence of wisdom literature alongside other parts of the Old Testament was accepted on the assumption that it was a late group of texts that presupposed other Old Testament Literature. So Driver wrote in 1891 that 'the wise men took for granted the main postulates of Israel's creed, and applied themselves rather to the observation of human character as such' (1891: 393). However, once the patently false idea that the wise simply presupposed the rest of Israelite religion is taken away, the problem starts to emerge.

Interest in writing Old Testament theologies began in the 1920s and peaked in the 1930s with the publication of the theologies of Köhler (1936) and Eichrodt (1961–7 [Ger. 1933–9]). Eichrodt was engaged in the quest for a 'centre' of the Old Testament, which Eichrodt himself found in the covenant idea, and so it is hardly surprising that wisdom literature was marginalized as a result of this focus. According to Eichrodt, 'For a long time the wisdom of God made virtually no contribution to Israel's religious understanding. Clearly God was the possessor of the highest wisdom . . . for Israel's central concerns, however, the fullness of divine life and the divine self-communication in spirit and word were far more important than wisdom' (Eichrodt, 1961–7: II: 80–1). He saw wisdom as a predominantly post-exilic phenomenon, as did many earlier scholars. He viewed wisdom writings as having been brought under the shadow of the covenant as their 'cosmopolitan and religiously neutral worldly wisdom . . . changes into a means of obedience to the unquestionable divine command, teaching that true wisdom lies in the fear of God' (Eichrodt, 1961–7: II: 23). Wheeler Robinson saw wisdom as subordinate to prophecy and went as far as to define the wisdom movement as 'the discipline whereby was taught the application of prophetic truth to the individual life in the light of experience' (1946: 241). As Day, Gordon and Williamson write in the introduction to *Wisdom in Ancient Israel*, 'For too long wisdom had been a casualty of the long-running quest for a theological centre in the Old Testament which had seen a variety of potential unifying themes proposed and wisdom almost invariably marginalized in the accompanying discussion. Since the wisdom texts paid little attention to cult and even less to covenant it was virtually inevitable that, as long as the quest persisted in this form, wisdom would be on the sidelines' (Day, Gordon and Williamson, 1995: 1).

Therefore the characterization of Israelite theology that has long held the field in Old Testament study is that what distinguished Israel from its neighbours was the belief in a God who worked in history. This was how the Israelites defined themselves in the face of the cyclical, nature religions of their neighbours. This is what made them 'special'.[23] So the place of creation was played down in the overall scheme of Old Testament theology.[24] This is now seen as a mischaracterization of Israelite religion, and of ancient Near Eastern religion, for that matter, too. Albreckson (1967) has pointed out that history was not divorced from ancient Near Eastern religion and that the nature/history divide has been overcharacterized. In a study of Sumerian-Akkadian gods and those of Mesopotamia, he points out that certain gods have areas of control outside nature; for instance, Enlil is the storm god but is also responsible for the defeat of enemies. Such gods are able to influence historical events, punishing transgressors and issuing curses for those who do not do their duty, including the king. History may have a more primary place in Israelite cultic confession, but it is not entirely lacking in ancient Near Eastern thought. Wright (1952) was suspicious of any part of the canon that had links with the religious and moral approach of other faiths; it seemed to him to take away from the distinctiveness of Old Testament religion.

A fresh approach to Old Testament theology is beginning to emerge in certain scholarly quarters, which gives a more central place to creation theology whereby historical and ahistorical elements of Israelite faith are being recognized. A new emphasis on the importance of creation theology is being made, and ways in which wisdom might be linked up to the rest of the Old Testament through that channel, and others, are being explored. Therefore the possibilities for theological integration and the place of creation theology within that process merit further exploration, and this links up with the third area of concern, which is the relationship with other parts of the Old Testament. It is hoped that looking for wider links with both other Old Testament traditions and other expressions of Yahwism will enhance rather than diminish our conclusions about social context.

---

[23] See the work of B. W. Anderson (1987), who still maintains the primacy of history despite an appreciation of the role of other, less historical religious patterns in Old Testament thought.

[24] For example, by Wright (1969).

RELATIONSHIP WITH OTHER PARTS OF THE OLD TESTAMENT

In a sense, wisdom literature can be labeled an orphan in the biblical household. Virtually ignored as an entity until the beginning of this century, 'wisdom' suffered the indignity of judgment by alien standards and the embarrassment of physical similarities to non-Israelite parents . . . Perhaps it was inevitable, then, that this special orphan would be queen for a day, and possibly even Queen Mother. (Crenshaw, 1995a: 90)

Wisdom has been separated from other parts of the Old Testament on grounds of form, content and context.[25] It has been thought to be easy to define a distinct corpus of material as wisdom literature, characterized by forms, such as the proverb and instruction; content, such as the attempt to control reality by drawing comparisons between unlike phenomena and discussion of the doctrine of reward and retribution; and contexts, such as that of reflections by the wise or teaching material in schools. However, when one tries to define the limits of the wisdom literature, it becomes difficult to know where to draw the line because of the considerable presence of wisdom elements in other literature.[26] So it becomes easier to speak of wisdom as an influence or as a distinct style. This is all very well, but once wisdom is not maintained within its own separate corpus, it becomes less plausible to try to separate it from the rest of the Old Testament in terms of context. Once many books are seen to have been imbued with wisdom influence, the possibility is opened up that this is a more widespread influence.[27]

Two particular reasons can be found for the marginalization of wisdom in terms of context. First, wisdom's context is often seen to spring more from its parallels with ancient Near Eastern texts and contexts than from its place within the Old Testament

---

[25] See Dell, 2000, for an arrangement of material in all the Israelite wisdom books under these headings of form, content and context.

[26] See discussion in Chapter 2 of my book on Job (Dell, 1991), on the problems of defining wisdom.

[27] See Morgan (1981), who finds wisdom influence in most biblical books. The work of Wolff found wisdom in many varied contexts (e.g. his *Joel and Amos*, 1977), especially in the prophetic books. In the process, the definition of wisdom becomes hard to contain and the wisdom corpus hard to distinguish as a result.

itself.[28] Parallels with ancient Near Eastern material have suggested to many that wisdom is the 'foreign element' in Old Testament thought and was generated in contexts outside the mainline orthodoxy of Israelite religious developments. This is supported by the lack of reference to the saving history or covenant in the wisdom literature. Second, wisdom's supposed production by a specialized social group of sages adds weight to the impression that it was a rather separate venture, outside the grasp of many and outside the concern of other social groups in Israel.[29] While such views are changing in the recognition of the broader contexts in which wisdom may have flourished[30] and the influence of wisdom on other parts of the Old Testament, it is still true to say that wisdom is regarded as an exercise taking place in one corner while prophecy or law are taking place elsewhere.

The idea of wisdom's being a more widespread influence has led to interest in the influence of wisdom in other parts of the Old Testament – the prophets and Psalms and in parts of the Pentateuch and narrative books (Morgan, 1981). Yet despite this work, one still finds this separation of wisdom from other contexts that I have outlined above. The reason for this is because wisdom is seen primarily as a literary influence and mainly as a late, literary phenomenon at that.[31] Therefore as well as being sages, those figures engaged in wisdom become scribes. Wisdom as a literary influence, then, has tended to focus on the work of educated redactors, scribes, editors or 'schools'. Wisdom becomes in this context a means of expression, a genre in itself that is able to exist alongside, and even assist in the formulation of, other genres. As a result, little Old Testament literature is unaffected by the wisdom tradition in its literary form and yet the possibility of wisdom's having been a more

---

[28] This was particularly promoted following the noting of parallels with Egyptian texts, most famously the parallel between Proverbs 22:17—24:22 and the *Instruction of Amenemope*, which was seen by many as borrowing by the Israelites (e.g. Heaton, 1974).

[29] This mainly presupposed the idea that there were schools in Israel following the ancient Near Eastern pattern, see discussion in Heaton, 1995.

[30] See Whybray (1974), who emphasizes the breaking down of such groups in the later post-exilic period.

[31] Demonstrated well in discussions of the 'wisdom psalms', where the influence from wisdom is mainly seen as later, largely redactional, and a literary, non-cultic shaping. See Dell, 2004b.

formative earlier influence is left out of account.[32] Either way, it is seen as an outside influence imposed, often secondarily, on the literature.

Therefore, despite the opening up of interest in the possibility of different forms and content of wisdom being found outside the wisdom literature, the refusal to see it as any more than a literary influence has led to wisdom's continued separation in terms of context. It has also led to a crisis in the definition of wisdom. This solution has not fairly represented the evidence from non-wisdom texts in the Old Testament and it is clear that the evidence needs to be considered afresh in order to be true to a definition of wisdom in the context of Old Testament institutions, thought and theology.

There has been much concern among scholars to retain the distinctiveness of wisdom, and of Proverbs in particular, in order not to 'water it down' so that it becomes undefinable and unremarkable. Crenshaw[33] has been a major proponent of this concern, which is a real one. He complains (1995: 590) about the watering down by some scholars of the distinctiveness of biblical wisdom by enlarging its corpus 'with an appetite resembling Sheol's', of which he disapproves. However, it would be hard to deny wisdom influence on other material in the Old Testament in the light of the many studies that have been done in this area.[34] In my view, not enough attention has been given to hints within Proverbs itself of wider contextual links. This has been done in reference to the ancient Near East, but perhaps to the neglect of looking at certain integrating connections with other Old Testament texts and contexts. It is odd that wisdom might have had influence outside, but never itself been influenced from outside. Maybe, it has been argued, if wisdom is primarily an

---

[32] Childs (1985: 210–12) points out that increasingly it is being realized by scholars that wisdom has its own theological integrity and cannot be restricted to being a late literary influence. Rather, its influence spans earlier and later and extends to all parts of the canon.

[33] The quotation cited at the start of this section, which alludes to wisdom becoming 'queen for a day', refers to the upsurge of interest in wisdom in the period between 1924 and 1936 when *Amenemope* was found and there was fresh interest in the genre. However, I believe that wisdom's 'day' has not been and gone, but that it goes on steadily making progress into the mainstream, maybe at a 'snail's pace' (Crenshaw, 1995a: 96) – but then the tortoise did outrun the hare in the end!

[34] E.g. Wolff's extensive work on wisdom influence in the eighth-century prophets (1974; 1977; 1981).

educational activity, it is not so surprising that its forms appear elsewhere – for example in the prophet Isaiah, because a prophet like Isaiah was probably trained in a wisdom school.[35] It is also argued that shared language is inevitable, but not an indication of shared context. I wonder, however, how realistic this idea of a completely separate worldview is. How realistic is it to think of a group of sages in one corner, with prophets, law, story-tellers and so on in completely separate corners?[36] These issues lead us back to social context, and it will be seen that the three areas into which I have divided my discussion thoroughly overlap and that the division has been made only for ease of discussion.

I have argued elsewhere that the book of Proverbs is best understood when divided into different sections (following Whybray, 1994a).[37] Whybray argues that one should not try to posit just one social context for the whole book of Proverbs, because each of the sections has a different character, and hence different social and economic situations are revealed by the different speakers. These divisions are found in most commentaries and are generally accepted by scholars, namely Proverbs 1–9; 10:1—22:16; 22:17—24:22; 24:23–34; 25–9; 30; 31. I shall therefore follow these divisions of material in this book, dealing in Chapter 1 with Proverbs 1–9, in Chapter 2 with Proverbs 10:1—22:16 and in Chapter 3 with Proverbs 22:17—31:31, subdivided into its various sections. In each of these chapters the first areas of discussion will deal with the various scholarly suggestions regarding social context in relation to the book of Proverbs. Some of these suggestions have been applied to the whole book, but, although there is overlap, most suggestions are more readily understood if they can be considered in relation to one part of the book of Proverbs at a time. It will become clear that the many different suggestions do in fact spring from just this fact that the forms and content of Proverbs are actually quite diverse, and this diversity is shown in a comparison between the characters of the different sections.

---

[35] A. Anderson (1960) argued in favour of this, but not to the exclusion of other roles. See also Whedbee, 1971.
[36] This is demonstrated in a recent book by Blenkinsopp (1995b), in which he maintains the separateness of the three groups and in which wisdom is still something of a poor relation.
[37] Dell, 2000, Chapter 2.

In the first three chapters, then, I will focus on the various scholarly suggestions regarding social context in relation to the book of Proverbs and will then move in to look more closely at relevant texts. This area of social context is one in which there has been a huge variety of scholarly views, and the uncertainty surrounding it has led to considerable divergence of opinion concerning the real function of the book. I do not claim to be able to solve this problem, but I wish to air the debate and then suggest possible directions in which our attention may turn to illuminate this issue. How one views the character of the different parts of the book of Proverbs and their interrelationship will be seen to be an important issue. The first fresh direction is to look at the mention of Yahweh in the different sections of the book[38] and at the significance of these references (Chapter 4), and the second is to explore echoes of other Old Testament texts in the material (Chapter 6). In Chapter 5, I will focus on the question of how to characterize the 'theology' of Proverbs, which will also involve wider discussion of wisdom's place within the Old Testament and the place of creation theology within that scheme. This, too, is a question that has exercised many scholars, and different emphases have led to varying opinions. This also links up with the issue of the place of Yahweh in the book of Proverbs and in the overall theological scheme. In Chapter 6, I will pick up on the echoes of other texts that emerge in the book of Proverbs and look at scholarly discussion of possible links and at the wider contextual implications of these findings. I will concentrate on the links indicated from within the book of Proverbs itself rather than looking at material outside the wisdom literature that might be included in the wisdom corpus. Wisdom's interactions with other areas of concern may well in turn influence our overall evaluation of social and theological context in the book of Proverbs, which is the subject of this work.

The pre-exilic period has all but faded away in the minds of some recent scholars, who focus on the post-exilic period in which texts were redacted (and some say created[39]). This study is in part a

---

[38] Generally regarded as secondary redaction, notably and consistently by Whybray (1965; 1979; 1994a; 1994c). See discussion in Chapter 4.

[39] E.g. P. R. Davies, 1998.

reaction against this tendency. In a paper given at the IOSOT conference in Cambridge in 1995, I argued for the uncertainty of dating different developments within the proverbial material until they reached a more literary and fixed form.[40] However, this was not to deny the significance of pre-exilic developments, and in this book I wish to join the ranks of scholars who express an increasing concern to affirm an interest in the nature of early Israelite life and belief.[41] There has been an emphasis on later wisdom redaction of material among recent scholarship, accompanied by a questioning of traditional contextual conclusions that has led to uncertainty about the wisdom input into the context of pre-exilic Israel. I wish to affirm the important place that the wisdom enterprise and its thought had in the early formation of Israelite belief, while not denying its essential role in the shaping of texts and post-exilic thought.

[40] Published as Dell, 1997.
[41] See Dell, 2004a.

CHAPTER I

Social context(s) in Proverbs 1–9

> Proverbs is a slice of a tradition that preceded ancient Israel
> and continued beyond it. This tradition comprised the cre-
> ation, reshaping, and transmission of wise sayings and teach-
> ings about how to live a righteous, productive, and happy life.
>
> (Fox, 2000: 11)

The opening chapters of the book of Proverbs are often regarded as
an intentional introduction to the rest of the book. There is what
appears to be a mature reflection on the nature of the wisdom
enterprise itself that has a character very different from the simpli-
city of the bulk of sayings contained in the body of the Proverbs
text. It is usually regarded by scholars as composed later than the
main sayings section, largely because of its more developed theological stance. However, some have argued for an earlier dating for
the section, or at least for the presence of older concepts, genres and
material within it. I have already mentioned that an important
distinction needs to be made, when dealing with the book of
Proverbs, between oral and written stages of material. Because of
the nature of the book as a collection or series of collections, the
likelihood is that some material may have existed and had a context
before the one in which it now appears. The quest for the context
behind the text in its oral stages has preoccupied some scholars,
while others have shown more interest in the later stages of the text's
formation–that is, the written stage(s)–and its possible social context
among scribes.

There is a range of criteria that scholars apply to texts–and not
just wisdom texts–to gain an understanding of the text's character.
The first is a literary analysis, and it is immediately apparent when
dealing with Proverbs 1–9 that there are predominantly two genres

of material. There are ten 'instructions' or 'lectures' (as Fox (2000) has recently termed them). These are longish sections of text that hold together as a piece of advice usually given from father (and sometimes mother too) to son. They have been termed 'instructions' because of the close parallels to Egyptian 'instructions'. There is then a group of poetic discourses or 'interludes' (Fox, 2000), that is, speeches largely concerned with the description of a female figure of Wisdom and her relationship with God and with that of her counterpart, the strange or foreign woman.

A second criterion applied to most biblical texts is the sense that any book, as a whole or in parts, must in some way belong to a historical and theological development of a religion that took place within a time-frame of history. Although many ideas may be ahistorical and timeless, nonetheless, because its ideas evolved in communities within history and were written down within a historical time-span, this is a question of concern. The hints in a text regarding attribution are one aspect of this, but so are questions of dating and of relationship to other texts from both within and outside the Old Testament. This is where suggestions for a later dating for Proverbs 1–9 in relationship to other parts of Proverbs have come from. Scholars have looked at theological developments within the book and outside it and have found the maturity of theological reflection in Proverbs 1–9 to belong to a period during or after the Israelite exile. This has to be reconciled, however, with Solomonic connections and consequent dating claims and with the fact of oral transmission of material, which could have gone on over a long historical period before material was put in writing and possibly reflected upon at that later stage. Some scholars have attempted a very precise dating for Proverbs 1–9, based on knowledge of the countries outside Israel that dominated the political landscape after the exile in order to find a social context for Proverbs 1–9.[1] However, the problem has always been that a characteristic of the whole book of Proverbs, and of the wisdom literature generally until we get to Ecclesiasticus, is that it does not mention events or characters from Old Testament history either within Israel or outside it. Also, because of its self-contained nature and particular moral and ethical

[1] For example, Perdue, 1997.

concerns, Proverbs has a timeless quality that makes it difficult to relate to particular circumstances. So a more fruitful line in this area has tended to be the quest for theological developments.

A third criterion applied to wisdom literature in particular, but also increasingly across the whole Old Testament, is comparison with the ancient Near East as a whole. The discovery of the close parallel between Proverbs 22:17—24:22 and the *Instruction of Amenemope* in the early 1920s (Budge, 1922, 1924; Erman, 1924) led to great excitement in the scholarly community and to much comparison of the literary forms, theological expression and social context of Egyptian wisdom with Israelite. Proverbs was the most fruitful wisdom book in this area, Job and Ecclesiastes having more in common with Mesopotamian wisdom; and within Proverbs 1–9 the 'instructions' were eagerly analysed for their links with Egyptian material of that genre. The instruction form was an old one, which raised questions regarding the dating, not just of Proverbs 1–9 as a whole, but of this particular genre of material within the text. Could these instructions have had an older context before they were placed here in Proverbs? Egyptian instructions such as *Amenemope* were used mainly as school texts in fairly well-to-do circles, while others were presented as the advice of a dying king to his son and successor. Was this a window into the original social context and purpose of the wisdom enterprise itself?

A final criterion was comparison with other parts of the Old Testament, and this was not always seen as such a fruitful line of inquiry because of wisdom's separateness. Before the discovery of *Amenemope* and the resultant interest in the international context of Proverbs, older scholars saw Proverbs as a rather isolated book in terms of genre and context, but some saw it as essentially in line with the ideas presented in the law and the prophets, its contribution being a more ethical emphasis.[2] It was almost universally regarded as late literature by scholarship of that time. Ironically, after the wave of interest in the Egyptian context and the recognition of earlier and more international roots for wisdom, some scholars dismissed wisdom for a different reason; it was now seen as a foreign element in the Old Testament and thought less deserving of study than other

---

[2] For example, Toy (1899), who saw Proverbs as post-exilic.

parts. This is to raise the question of wisdom's place in the theology of the Old Testament as a whole, which will be addressed in Chapter 5. However, it also raises the question of its relationship with other parts of scripture, both in its historical context as the genres were formed, used and written down, and in its final canonical form as an influence on the final editing of other texts and on the formation of books that succeeded it historically.[3]

In relation to Proverbs 1–9 alone, there have been manifold suggestions as to social context. While some of the suggestions have been broader than just this section, such as the 'school for training courtiers' idea based on Egyptian parallels which was regarded by many as a 'key' to unlock the whole book, it is helpful to look at each proposal in relation to the principal material in any one section that prompted the parallel. So, for example, Proverbs 1–9 and 22:17—24:22 are the chief sections of concern to those drawing Egyptian parallels. In looking at the various suggestions, it is important to recognize the variety inspired by differing emphases on particular parts of the material, such as a focus on the 'instructions' or on the figure of Wisdom in Proverbs 1–9; and I would reiterate the point about stages of compilation. In particular, one is trying to make a distinction between original contexts for the material, possibly in an oral prehistory (or in a written one consisting of small units) and the stage at which the material was gathered together in written form. One may then need to distinguish an editorial stage(s) before arriving at the written form of the text as it stands in front of us. Of course, there is the further complication that the text of Proverbs as canonized and the one before us may not be one and the same, given the issue of transmission of a text and because of the existence of different translations and versions; but this concern is outside the scope of this book.

---

[3] It is highly likely that Proverbs was known to Ben Sira, given their similar views of God and the world. Compare Prov. 15:11 and Ecclus. 39:19; 42:18 on God's omniscience, and Prov. 10:27; 15:33; 16:6; 22:4 and Ecclus. 2:7–9; 15:17 on the fruits of fear of the Lord. There is strong adherence to the doctrine of retribution in both, e.g. Prov. 10:25, 30; 11:17, 25; 13:6 and Ecclus. 7:1–3; 29:11–13; 40:12–17, and the view of the moral attributes of the wise person is close in the two. Ben Sira also shows self-awareness of the role of a wisdom teacher in Ecclus. 38:24 and of his part in that in Ecclus. 51:23–30.

Turning, then, to Proverbs 1–9 in relation to suggestions regarding its social context, there is one further point to note. It is widely agreed in recent scholarship that the primary context of Proverbs 1–9 is an educational one. This relates particularly to the instructions, which clearly have the nature of teaching ostensibly from parents to son (although a teacher–pupil model has also been proposed), regarding how to make choices in life and find the right path of wisdom and 'life' rather than the path to folly and 'death'. The poetic discourses can be regarded as a kind of expansion upon this educational purpose, providing a wider and more theological context for the instructions. Yet they do highlight a second context within Proverbs 1–9, which is the theological/religious context of faith in Yahweh and interest in the divine origins of the wisdom enterprise. The precise nature and interplay of these educational/religious contexts has, however, led to considerable debate among scholars, as I shall attempt to outline in this chapter.

THE 'INSTRUCTIONS' AND EGYPTIAN PARALLELS

The educational context as self-evident from the text, namely that of the family, was quickly dismissed in the light of the discovery of the close parallel between the Egyptian *Instruction of Amenemope* and Proverbs 22:17—24:22 and consequent emphasis on Egyptian parallels. The context of court or school teaching seemed to provide a more attractive alternative, based on links drawn with Egyptian models. The advantage of the Egyptian parallel was that Proverbs was suddenly no longer isolated in literary terms, but could be seen as part of a wide and significant international tradition. The key aspect of Egyptian instructions is that they are the product of a professional class of scribes; they belonged essentially in educated circles based at court with close connections to the king and were the work of the few who could read and write in a society that was mainly illiterate. A point often glossed over by scholars, however, was that the instructions of Egypt were a very varied group of texts, each with its own different context,[4] and so it is in fact quite difficult

---

[4] See discussion in Dell, 2000: Chapter 7.

simply to extrapolate an Israelite context directly from the contexts of these texts. However, this problem was sidestepped in part by the focus on the *Instruction of Amenemope* as the closest parallel, which, because of its nature as a school text that had been copied over and over from one generation to another, led to emphasis on the possibility of a court school. Another problem, particularly in relation to the later Egyptian instructions such as *Amenemope*, was the pietistic stance of the text, which seemed much more pronounced than in the instructions of Proverbs; it seemed that educational and religious purposes were intertwined, whereas in the instructions of Proverbs references to Yahweh were few.

In relation to Proverbs 1–9 in particular, parallels were drawn between the ten instructions in Proverbs 1:8—7:27, i.e. 1:8–19; 2:1–22; 3:1–12; 3:21–35; 4:1–9; 4:10–19; 4:20–7; 5:1–23; 6:20–35; 7:1–27 (Whybray's model[5]), and Egyptian instructions. The criteria of form and content were used to find some striking similarities, notably the introductory call to the one receiving the instruction to 'hear' and 'obey' the teacher. The emphasis on the 'heart' as the centre of the human will was also similar. Kayatz (1966) stressed both similarities and differences between the instructions of the two cultures, and saw particularly close links between Proverbs 1:1–6 and the introductions to some Egyptian instructions. However, she did note that references to 'my son/sons', which abound in the Israelite examples, are lacking in the Egyptian texts, as are references to a mother's teaching; and the Egyptian instructions are much longer than the examples in Proverbs. Formal dependence on Egyptian models was not claimed in relation to these instructions (unlike Proverbs 22:17—24:22 and *Amenemope*), but close contact in terms of literary genre was posited and it was generally felt that Egyptian literature provided the models that Israelite wisdom had in turn imitated and made distinctive.

The genre of instruction was seen as very different from the sentence literature of the bulk of Proverbs, and thus the social context of each section of Proverbs was viewed very differently. McKane (1970) saw the instruction as an international genre probably introduced into Israel with the expansion of the Israelite state under the monarchy, notably under Solomon. This idea linked up very neatly with the Solomonic attribution of Proverbs and with his reputation for wisdom. McKane considered that there had subsequently been a 'Yahwehization' of the instructions which had been essentially pragmatic and educational–what he called 'a way of inculcating Yahwistic piety' (1970: 10). Von Rad (1966a; 1972) proposed the view that there was a cultural expansion under Solomon that could be likened to the Enlightenment in Europe many centuries later, which led to an interest in literature and education that had hitherto been impossible because of the lack of existence of a court life and of a class of the educated. McKane (1970) specifically saw the parallel in terms of the need for administration and a civil service under Solomon (cf. Heaton, 1974) which, he believed, led to a need to establish a school for the training of officials. This neatly brought together the two contextual conclusions drawn from Egyptian parallels–the court context and the educational one. However, McKane (1970) did acknowledge that, although the instruction in Israel originated in a court school setting, it subsequently broadened out in its concerns. He recognized the limitations of interpreting the instructions solely in relation to the training of administrators. In fact, the broader exhortation to young men towards an ethical life did not quite fit the stricture of this model and in this lay the weakness of the proposal.

There is also the related question of whether these were a unified collection of instructions; most scholars have felt that they are not. Whybray (1994c) argued that the instructions in Proverbs 1–9 belong to a common genre, but do not follow a rigid pattern, and show that they are not unified or from the pen of one author because of their repetitive character. Then there is the question of the family: why, if they were intended for the education of officials or even as school instruction, was the primary address from father (and sometimes mother – Prov. 1:8; 6:20) to son?

THE SCHOOL

Even if the idea of a court school, centred on Jerusalem and with the primary purpose of training an educated elite, has fallen from favour in recent years, the idea of an educational purpose for Proverbs 1–9 and hence for a school setting of some kind has persisted. There is a reference in Proverbs 5:13 to 'teachers' in the context of the foolish pupil who did not listen but instead had to learn from bitter experience. 'Father' and 'son' in the instructions have been seen to refer to teacher and pupil and the context may have been wider than just the court. This opens up the question of how widespread education and literacy were. In Egypt and Mesopotamia proper school systems had been instituted and education was not confined to the court, although schools were used mainly for the training of scribes and other officials. Was this not a possible model in Israel? There is a feeling that parental education would not have been enough; there must have been at least some families of scribes who ran local schools, or gave personal tuition at the very least. There seems to be some evidence of prophetic schools in 2 Kings 6:1, in which Elisha's disciples complain that 'the place where we sit before you is too small for us', but can this evidence be applied to wisdom groups?

And what about the writing-down process? The production of literature such as Proverbs would be beyond family learning. It is known that Egyptian schools taught hieroglyphic script, whereas the Hebrew alphabet was much more quickly mastered. Demsky (1971) gives this as his reason for being cautious of using extra-biblical parallels. He stresses the importance of alphabetic writing for the history of education: 'It ushered in a break with the traditional scribal cultures of Egypt, Mesopotamia, and second-millennium Canaan. To be literate was no longer the identifying and exclusive characteristic of a class of professional scribes and priests, versed in the abstruse cuneiform and hieroglyphic scripts' (1971, c. 391). He also emphasizes the importance of stages of learning and of the different levels reached by different groups, so that, for example, quite a number of people might be able to learn the alphabet and copy short texts that may have been learned by heart and practised at home, while far fewer would reach the level of the compilation of administrative documents or the composition of written texts. This might mean that limited education was quite widespread, but that more specialized work was still the preserve of a small scribal group probably based at the court. Baines (1983) has also argued that, even in ancient Egyptian society

– the model on which scholars are largely basing these conclusions about the situation in Israel – few people were actually fully literate, the exceptions being mainly state officials. This seems to point back to the court, administrative setting once more for the penning of texts such as Proverbs.

What about archaeological evidence? Lang (1979; 1986), Lemaire (1981; 1984) and Jamieson-Drake (1991) among others tried to harness archaeological evidence such as inscriptions, fragments of alphabets, ostraca and so on as evidence of writing exercises such as would have been done by schoolboys. Lemaire (1981), after a detailed analysis of such evidence, postulated the existence of schools on a grand scale, even in villages. He envisages a chronological progression from schools modelled on the Canaanite system to schools for professional scribes at the courts of David and Solomon, inspired by the Egyptian model, and, in other major cities, to schools for the general populace by the eighth century. Lemaire argues strongly for the professional scribal school as the context for most biblical writings, but not necessarily of their oral antecedents. He argues for the existence of royal, priestly and prophetic schools in pre-exilic times, with only the priestly schools surviving into post-exilic times. He is generally felt to have overstated the case, and Golka (1983), who prefers to speak of scribal apprenticeship within families, is particularly critical of the school hypothesis.

There is evidence for literacy, but does this translate into evidence for schools? After all, learning alphabets is a far cry from the sophisticated literary artistry of texts. One should perhaps bear in mind Demsky's point about levels of education. He notes, for example, that 'learning the letters of the alphabet by repetition of the abecedary and accompanying exercises was basic for a general urbanite's education. It would have been of particular use for artisans, who introduced writing into their craft–for which there is evidence from potters, ivory joiners, and builders' (1997: 366). The lack of any firm archaeological evidence proving the existence of schools has been aired by Haran (1988) and Puech (1988). Lemaire's answer is to point to the perishability of papyrus and the vagaries of archaeological discoveries. The weight of archaeological evidence seems to come from a slightly later period than that of Solomon in the ninth century BC, possibly supporting the idea of a move towards writing down at the time of Hezekiah or after.[6] G. I. Davies (1995) cautiously affirms the evidence for schools, but not on such a widespread basis as Lemaire, and probably to be restricted to capital cities and administrative centres. He notes that this activity may have been on a more limited scale until the eighth century. He finds evidence of Egyptian influence on Israelite education. Attention might also be drawn to another ancient culture–the Sumerian–which also provided evidence of local school life with mention of a tablet taken home by a schoolboy and read to his father.[7]

There have, then, been some scholarly attempts to move away from positing court schools for the training of administrators as the only possibility for the promulgation of education in Israel. There is no direct mention of schools in the Proverbs or in the Old Testament as a whole; if they were so widespread, this lack is surprising. A school context is first mentioned in the apocryphal wisdom book of Ben Sira or Ecclesiasticus (Ecclus. 51:23). Education 'at the gate' is hinted at, with the figure of wisdom standing at the city gate in Proverbs 1:20ff., combined with the fact that we know that other social dealings, such as the administration of justice, took place in that location.[8] Some scholars have consistently preferred the idea of more informal education by scribal families.[9] Crenshaw, for example, is against any widespread school system, such as posited by Lemaire, and sees the discussion over whether there were schools

---

[6] Jamieson-Drake (1991) argues along these lines, but is criticized by G. I. Davies (1995) for not having taken proper account of earlier inscriptional evidence from the ninth century and even before that.

[7] See Kramer, 1958; 1961, and discussion in Dell, 2000, Chapter 7.

[8] See Hayes, 1980.

[9] Crenshaw (2000) remarks in a footnote that in my 1997 article 'On the Development of Wisdom in Israel' I failed to nuance his view on the issue of whether there were formal schools in ancient Israel. I acknowledge his criticism that, in seeking to find a 'standard' view of a particular period of scholarly opinion, I chose his *Old Testament Wisdom* (1981b), which did not agree in every detail with the picture that I wished to redraw. However, the choice of his work implied a compliment rather than a criticism, because it seemed to me to sum up, in a way that other introductions of the period did not, the state of scholarly argument of the time on a whole range of issues. I see running through his work a consistent thread that is cautious of a formal school setting, but also note that in *Old Testament Wisdom* (1981b) he was more open to the possibility of a court school than his later work indicates. Hence I drew attention in my footnote to his changing perspective and willingness to engage with changing scholarly opinion, which he expressed to me verbally and which is reflected in his more recently revised edition of *Old Testament Wisdom* (1998).

or not as somewhat of a red herring. He writes:[10] 'The evidence clearly points to the existence of literate persons at an early period in Israel. What remains unclear, however, is the place where that literacy was acquired' (1995: 238). He goes on to say in the conclusion to the article: 'In short, considerable diversity characterized education in ancient Israel; a scholarly preoccupation with the existence or non-existence of a school threatens to obscure this significant fact' (1995: 249). In a later work, *Education in Ancient Israel* (1998), Crenshaw concludes that there were probably guilds of scribes, as there were for other trades, some of whom were used in royal service, others of whom were employed in drawing up official documents, and yet others who were employed in the copying of religious texts. Some scholars, however, hold on to the idea of a central, court school where sophisticated literature was produced. There should perhaps be a greater recognition of the archival function of the court, for which there are also parallels in ancient Sumer and Mesopotamia (in which there were three types of scribe: functionaries dealing with economic administration, learned poets and writers, with a major function of writing up court records and so on, and diviners). This raises again the question of how far one can reconstruct the situation in Israel from ancient Near Eastern parallels (a method employed cautiously by Crenshaw (1998) in his quest for clues about educational practice in ancient Israel) as well as how much one can extrapolate from later periods within Israelite history itself.

I have so far avoided any discussion of an actual historical context for Proverbs 1–9, but many have suggested the exilic or early post-exilic period. Perdue (1997) argues for placing Proverbs 1–9 in the early Persian period and relates it to a hierocratic party in post-exilic Judaism. Whether or not one agrees with this, the key point here is that it may enable one to posit schools in a later period. Perdue argues that in this section there is evidence of theological and ethical materials from a school setting in the early half of the Persian period, in which there may have been temple schools as well as family guilds and/or civil academies. The temple schools may have existed for educated scribes to assist priests in interpreting the Torah.[11] Guilds

---

[10] See also, in more depth, Crenshaw, 1998.
[11] See Doll, 1985.

(essentially family households) may have existed for training scribes for service in the government or temple (1 Chron. 2:55). Scribes would also have been needed at central and provincial levels to carry out administrative leadership and bureaucratic tasks. Perdue writes, 'Traditional sages sought through their writings and educational system to promote the interests of the prevailing social and religious order' (1997: 89). I quoted from Perdue earlier when he said that 'any attempt to provide some social and historical background to Proverbs is fraught with peril'. He goes on, 'The few scattered references to historical data are themselves ambiguous, while concrete mentionings are absent from most of the collections' (1997: 79). Is he in danger of not heeding his own warning here? This is a possible reconstruction for how wisdom was reinterpreted in a Persian context, but it is unlikely in my view that Proverbs 1–9 as a whole originated there. Blenkinsopp (1991) argues also for a location in the Persian period for the taboo against foreign wives that manifests itself in the figure of the foreign/strange woman in Proverbs 1–9.

In both the discussion of the possibility of a school context and in discussions about the nature of the literature and its theology, a few scholarly suggestions have from time to time indicated pre-exilic roots for either the institutions or the forms. Those who posit any kind of wisdom school–on a limited or grand scale–are predominantly concerned with the pre-exilic period, whether it be the time of David, of Solomon or of Hezekiah. Arguments for post-exilic school structures, perhaps linked to the temple, seem to be more widely accepted. On the literary side, there have been those who have stressed the antiquity of the instruction form in Proverbs 1–9 (such as Kayatz (1966); McKane (1970)) or those who have stressed the antiquity of some of the theological ideas and even of the figure of wisdom.[12] Such arguments may not be entirely conclusive, but they create an unease about simply placing Proverbs 1–9 within the post-exilic period, lock, stock and barrel. It may well have been completed later on in a historical time-frame (certainly later

---

[12] See the arguments that regard the figure of Wisdom as a vestige of an earlier goddess idea, as aired in particular in Lang, 1986.

than Prov. 10:1—22:16), but are some of its literary roots and theological ideas earlier? Such questions remain and will be addressed in this book.

I return full circle to the evidence from the text of the instructions being from father or mother to child and hence to the idea that education was primarily done in the family setting. An example is Proverbs 1:8: 'Hear, my son, your father's instruction, and reject not your mother's teaching; for they are a fair garland for your head, and pendants for your neck.' Is this too obvious a method of education to be plausible? Are father and son found here in a scribal family alone, or is the context more general than that? Lang (1979) argued that although there was enough evidence to postulate the existence of schools in Israel, the original oral setting of education was in the family, so that the instruction texts had a broader designation than the education of officials; they were for all or any who would benefit from them. Steiert (1990) emphasized the role of father or teacher in the proverbial instructions, seeing the references to Yahweh as being designed to inculcate the 'fear of Yahweh' in the pupils. Fox (1996) has argued that teaching and learning are the main tasks being treated in Proverbs 1–9, (see especially Prov. 2), and regards the religious aspect as secondary. He writes: 'Education commences with the father's teaching and its rote incorporation by the child, but this must be complemented by the learner's own thought and inquiry. *Then* God steps into the picture and grants wisdom' (1996: 76–7). I will go on to consider the family setting more fully in the next chapter, but these comments about Proverbs 1–9 are of interest in relation to whether primary and secondary purposes for the material can be found.

The family setting is argued against by Whybray in *Wealth and Poverty* (1990), who argues that the discourses (instructions) presuppose an educated readership. He assumes that father and son refer to teacher and pupil and that these two both belonged to a social stratum superior to that of the ordinary farmer of the sentence literature, though not necessarily to the governing class. This thesis widens the gap in social context between Proverbs 1–9 and 10:1—22:17. He opts for an urban context and argues that there is a significant paucity of references to agricultural labour in this section (the exception being 3:9–10). Nor are the poor or poverty mentioned here, a theme that is so prominent elsewhere in Proverbs. Of course, 'family' does not equal 'poor family', and this material could reflect the upper-class family situation. In fact, that is Whybray's conclusion: that the pupils addressed were of high social standing and that this represented education for the privileged. This needs to be borne in mind in any consideration of social context in these chapters.

A related matter is the oral/literary question. Fox (2000) argues that speech and writing co-exist in Proverbs in that there is quite an emphasis on spoken discourse, with injunctions to 'hear', 'give ear' and 'pay attention', and direct evidence of a father's instruction in Proverbs 4:3–4 (cf. the instruction to Lemuel in Prov. 31:1). Fox maintains that at the same time, however, a reading audience is in mind, with the image of wisdom as 'written' appearing in Proverbs 22:20: He writes:

The Wisdom tradition is self-consciously literary, but it uses a genre setting (*Sitz im Leben*) that was originally oral, namely, parental advice, the most fundamental form of education. That does not mean that these texts were ever declaimed by the authors to their children, but that this setting is the way the authors want their teachings understood. Writing makes the teachings available to all, but it does not cancel out their familial use, for a literate man may write a book for his family's future edification. (Fox, 2000: 75)

Fox stresses the familial educational setting over many other scholars. Ingenious as the idea that the material was both written and oral at the same time is, I think that Fox is trying to have it both ways here. The picture is probably a different one for each section of Proverbs and so it is important that here the focus is particularly on Proverbs 1–9.

This discussion of possible social context(s) for Proverbs 1–9 has raised a number of recurring issues that lie behind the various suggestions made. The first is the purpose of the material, notably whether its prime purpose was educational with religious elements as secondary, or whether the two elements of educational and religious existed alongside each other as a dual purpose. Related to this is the second issue, whether any elements of this text were originally oral or whether this was a written text from the start. It is possible that each separate genre (instruction or poem) was either oral or written before it was worked into the wider written context of Proverbs 1–9, so this oral/written issue is not a simple one. Related to this is whether the instructions in particular are to be treated either individually or across the section as forming any kind of unity. Finally, there is the dating issue, not in absolute terms of trying to find a specific historical context for the material, but in terms of the nature of the literature.

THE INSTRUCTION TEXTS IN PROVERBS

I shall take a preliminary look here at the instruction texts in Proverbs 1–9. I will also include two passages (introduction and bridging passage) that are not instructions, but share much in common with instruction texts. I am not going to focus on Egyptian links, not because they are not important and fruitful–which they unquestionably are–but because the subject has been well worked, and my concern here is to look at the structure and contents of the texts as products of Israelite wisdom literature. An emphasis on homegrown connections between texts and ideas will, I think, provide an engaging counterbalance to the usual discussion. I shall leave the wisdom poems for discussion in Chapter 4, as also the more theological debate about the place of the mention of Yahweh in both instructions and poems.

Turning to the text of Proverbs 1–9, the four issues mentioned at the end of the last part of this chapter need to be borne in mind. The question of purpose will first and foremost at this stage establish the educational nature of the material. The indicators of an educational context would be reference to father/mother/son or teacher/pupil and exhortations such as 'hear', 'learn'. The possibility of education either in the home or in the school (or both) is left open in looking at this context. The religious question will be addressed in Chapter 4, when the structural integrity and purpose of the Yahweh references will be examined. However, an ethical content will be seen to be a primary element of an educational context; nearly all the instructions contain ethical injunctions or exhortations that need not be confined by a teaching context but, as they are placed now in the body of the content of instruction texts, form a part of the wider educational context. I will go on to discuss whether the religious aspect is similarly integral. The second issue of oral/written distinction is hard to decide, but I will consider whether the main sense gained from the text is of a written context or an oral one. Even if some of the genres used are ancient, that does not necessarily mean that they were oral before coming into written form. This is related to the question of social context in that we know that school texts tended to be written so that they could be copied for the purposes of learning to read and write. Related to this is the issue of structural unity, for if the instructions or poems seem to stand as cohesive, well-formed units in their own right, that may well suggest written units of text. Finally, the question of relative dating of the various genres that make up Proverbs 1–9 is of interest, but I do not want to dwell on this issue at this stage. Other conclusions will be established first. This discussion of Proverbs 1–9 is inevitably influenced by the issues that scholars have brought to the text, and within that debate those of purpose and of structural unity come to the fore, the latter in reaction to the attempts of earlier scholars to carve up the texts more than now seems necessary. In this survey of the texts in Proverbs 1–9, then, I shall look here for indicators of structural unity within each instruction, but not attempt to find uniformity across the whole section, as I am chiefly concerned with finding inner consistency within each instruction.

The emphasis that one chooses to place on the structure of a text can often affect the evaluation of its meaning. The introduction to the book in Proverbs 1:1–7–which I will also include in the discussion here–is generally seen as a unit, but it is variously carved up by scholars. Sometimes verse 1 is separated off and treated as a heading, and often verse 7 with its mention of Yahweh is handled separately (Whybray, 1994c[13]). However, both can be treated as integral parts of the section, and my view is that it is better not to carve the text up without good reason. Verse 7 has been seen as the climax to the passage by some (e.g. Clifford, 1999; see discussion in Chapter 4 below); others have placed the emphasis elsewhere; for example,

---

[13] Whybray (1965) separates off verses 6–7.

Brown (1996) has raised the possibility of verse 3b being a centre point in the structure of the concentric circle formed by verses 2a, 2b and 3a as against verses 4–5, 6 and 7, which would mean that the ethical injunction in verse 3b was being deliberately stressed. Wherever one chooses to find the climax, the unit does have inner consistency and cohesiveness. The emphasis in this section falls upon learning and teaching, which indicate an educational context (verses 2, 3a, 5, 6), but there are important emphases also on the ethical (verse 3b) and the religious (verse 7).

The first of the 'instruction' texts in Proverbs comes in 1:8–19 and is generally thought to be a structural unity, only verses 8 and 9 having been regarded as a separate introduction by some, largely on the grounds of the repetition of 'my son' from verse 8 in verse 10. The focus here is on parental instruction and its value (verses 8–9) and on watching out for evildoers who might entice one away from the straight path with the promise of ill-gotten wealth (verses 10–19). Whybray (1994c) notes that, while there is no personification of wisdom in this passage, the reference in 1:9 to a 'fair garland' and 'pendants' in connection with parental instruction contain strong anticipatory overtones of the description of wisdom in Proverbs 4:9 and hints at the important link between the authority of parents and that of Wisdom, figures which are often interchangeable. The admonitory tone of verses 10–19 would make little sense without the introduction that sets the scene for the advice, and hence the instruction has inner consistency. Although the instruction is more single-themed than some, it has a unity as a piece of specific advice that one can imagine fitting the context of parental or school education.

The second 'instruction' comes in 2:1–22 and is quite dissimilar to the first (although verses 12–14 have echoes of the evil men warned of in 1:10–19). It spends the first eleven verses in exhortation to the pupil and then proceeds with a 'theory of learning' (Fox, 2000: 125) rather than learning proper; namely the protection that will result from following the advice of the first half of the instruction. This emphasis on praise for the search for wisdom and its rewards has led some commentators to see the instruction as unstructured, but this is to use the criterion of the content of other instructions (which could be seen to contain more practical advice) to judge this particular instruction. There is a programmatic quality about this instruction, too, in that themes are introduced that will be expanded on further in later instructions (e.g. 2:1–8, cf. 3:1–12; 2:9–11, cf. 3:13–26 and 4:1–9; 2:12–15, cf. 4:10–27; 2:16–10, cf. 5:1–23 and 6:20—7:27). This might suggest a broader unity of thematic structure, linking up with themes elsewhere in Proverbs 1–9, as Fox suggests, or it might be coincidental. Structurally, the piece is a whole as it is an acrostic with twenty-two lines (matching the number of letters in the Hebrew alphabet), though using only two letters of that alphabet, aleph and lamed, at the beginning of stanzas. The movement from aleph to lamed at verse 12 also marks a break in theme in that verses 1–11 are about wisdom and its advantages, while verses 12–22 concern different 'ways' on offer and the dangers from which wisdom can preserve her advocates. It has been pointed out, furthermore, that the whole forms one long, but continuous, sentence (A. Meinhold, 1991) which Whybray (1994c) calls 'cumbersome' and 'repetitive', but which others (e.g. Clifford, 1999; Fox, 2000) have seen as further evidence of unity of structure and content. While Whybray (1994c) and others argued that there had been expansion from a core,[14] and McKane (1970) also argued for considerable reinterpretation within its lines, seeing it as having been worked over by later moralistic editors who gave it 'a diffuse, rambling style of preaching' (1970: 279), more recent scholars have argued for unity on the grounds mentioned above.[15] The use of the acrostic might suggest an educational context–even possibly an oral stage when mnemonics such as acrostics might have been used (although some have argued that acrostics are essentially literary plays with letters and words). The exhortatory tone is in line with an educational context too.

The third 'instruction' is contained in Proverbs 3:1–12 and is notably more theological. The section makes an integrated whole

---

[14] Whybray (1994c) suggested a core of verses 1–9 and 16–19; Michel (1992) suggested a core of verses 1–4, 14–15, 20.

[15] Murphy sums up recent scholarly uncertainty with this 'carving up' approach: 'Such an analysis is fraught with hazards; it tears apart the clearly unified structure of the text on the basis of later hypothetical views. Such hypotheses are simply not compelling. What is the likelihood of three later hands creating the alphabetic structure . . . that is the framework of the chapter?' (1998: 15).

with five four-line exhortations each containing mention of a benefit or reward that good behaviour brings. The pattern is broken only thematically, not structurally, with a sixth and last four-line section which suggests that discipline is sometimes employed by Yahweh in the manner a father would use to reprove a wayward son. Fox (2000) points out that in verses 1–2 there is no mention of the pupil's needing to hear the teaching, but just of remembering it; and argues that this instruction represents a more advanced stage in the learning of wisdom, rather like the last instruction in Proverbs 2. The use of תורה in Proverbs, he argues, does not refer to law in the sense of ordinances, but to authoritative injunctions nevertheless.[16] The first two verses echo the beginning of other instructions, but then take the subject of the instruction into a more 'spiritual' domain, with references to God abounding in this chapter (see Chapter 4 for the structural significance of the mention of God here). Verses 9–10 are the only verses in Proverbs that actually recommend giving liturgical offerings to God (see discussions in Chapters 3 and 5);[17] sacrifices are mentioned in Proverbs 7:14; 15:8; 21:3, 27, but this is the only time there is an injunction to make a sacrifice. Giving of the first fruits of one's crops and a portion of one's wealth to God will assure that they and the giver are blessed (cf. Exod. 23:19; 34:26; Deut. 26:1–11; Lev. 23:10–14). Fox notes that 'wisdom in no way repudiates the sacrificial cult, though, like the prophets and the Psalms, it gives priority to ethical behaviour (21:3; 21:27; sim. Qoh. 4:17b; 8:10), a ranking that even priests could accept' (2000: 152). In this, then, wisdom is in line with other Old Testament tradition and there is no obvious avoidance of cultic concerns, albeit that the number of references is small (see Chapter 6 and discussion of Perdue's work, *Wisdom and Cult* (1977), there).

---

[16] Fox (2000) sees תורה and מצוה as virtually interchangeable terms here in Proverbs 1–9, both denoting 'authoritative injunctions'. Since there are no specific commands in this section, he argues that this shows that the author of this instruction is aware of other instructions which do contain them. I maintain that there is a difference in terminology here, deliberately made in an echo of other texts (see Chapter 6), and that it is not necessarily the case that other instructions are being thought of here.

[17] Whybray (1994c) argues that in the emphasis on material goods in these verses there is a hint that the pupil being addressed is well-to-do, which, he suggests, may betray an urban setting, possibly a landowner away from his lands. I wonder, though, if one can really make such suggestions on the basis of such scarce evidence.

There is a fascinating broadening out from a strictly educational purpose here, not just into religion but also into ethical behaviour in relation to the cult. These points will need to be evaluated further.

The fourth instruction is found in 3:21–35, the boundaries of which have been disputed, with some scholars wanting to make section divisions at verses 13 and 27. However, verses 13–20 make sense as a unit, as seen above, and also 'my son' in verse 21 marks a section beginning as there is now an addressee.[18] Although verses 27–32 form a sub-unit of five prohibitions on the topic of treatment of others, especially one's neighbour, they make sense in the context of an address, and fill out, in terms of specific situations, the more general exhortations of the earlier part of the section (in verses 21ff.).[19] The argument for unity is therefore, in my view, plausible and preferable to considerable carving up.[20] The theme of this whole section can be seen as engendering good social relationships. In fact, the structure can be viewed rather differently without a break at verse 27. Verses 21–4 can be regarded as an introduction, much like other similar introductions in Proverbs 1–9 which suggest an educational context. Then it is perhaps more plausible to take verses 25–32 as a unit containing six negative admonitions, ending with a general comments on the fate of the wicked and foolish in contrast to the righteous and wise. Again the introduction provides the necessary context for the admonitions later in the chapter and suggests structural cohesiveness and inner consistency within the instruction.

In Proverbs 4:1–9 the fifth instruction calls attention not just to the father's teaching, but to that of the father's own father; this is its unique feature. Through such teaching the pupil is led to walk in the right way of Wisdom and her benefits are bestowed. The section forms a unity, with verses 1–3 containing the call to attention and

---

[18] Fox (2000) argues that a verse may have been omitted by a copyist here, one along the lines of Prov. 4:20.

[19] Fox (2000) argues that in verses 27–31 there are five separate proverbs collected by the author to serve his purpose.

[20] There are also evocations of the first half of the chapter (verses 1–12) in the prohibitions section which emphasizes relationships with neighbours rather than with God. These evocations suggest a wider unity. Fox (2000) agrees that these two sections are unlikely to have been redacted.

introduction. Verses 4–9 contain the father's citation of his father's teaching, but the transition is made in verse 6 to Wisdom, which becomes the active agent here in bestowing her gifts. No specific admonitions are made here; it is mainly introductory. This has led Whybray (1994c) to wonder if it is a fragment of a longer piece and whether in fact the introduction has itself been expanded.[21] Verses 1–4 appeal to tradition, not in general here but to the specific teaching of the father's father. This arguably recalls 'appeals to tradition' as found in Psalm 78:2–6 and Job 8:8–10. Appeal is made in verse 1 to 'sons' (בנים), rather than to a singular son as elsewhere, although this is not unknown (cf. Prov. 5:7; 7:24; 8:32–3). It could suggest a wider teaching community–a school rather than a family, although the possibility of more than one 'son' under instruction within a family should also be borne in mind. In verses 3–4 we are perhaps reminded of Solomon as a child in 1 Kings 3:7–9, when he asks God for the gift of discernment. The early teaching of the mother is also mentioned here, paralleling that of the father and suggesting a family setting. 'Keep my commandments' (שמר מצותי) in verse 4 is a call to remember authoritative commands. In verses 4–9 there is the quotation of the words of the grandfather. Verse 5 marks the father/Wisdom transition point, which indicates the close relationship between the two authoritative teaching figures and which also points to the uniting feature of the instruction. Verse 7, in its repetition of verse 5, has often been regarded as an addition, interrupting the description of Wisdom in verses 6 and 8. However, the repetition of this popular phrase may be for effect or emphasis. The phrase 'Get wisdom' is a common one, found twice here and in Proverbs 16:16; 19:8 (cf. Ps. 111:10 for a more religious version of the sentiment).[22] In verses 6, 8 and 9 Wisdom

---

[21] Fox (2000) takes this to signify that this instruction is presupposing the contents of others, so showing the ten instructions to be a unity. He demonstrates signs of cross-instructional unity more convincingly in the earlier instructions than in the later, and I remain unconvinced of overall authorial unity in the written form of the instructions.

[22] The frequency and significance of this phrase inspired me to use it as the title of my introductory textbook on wisdom, *Get Wisdom, Get Insight: An Introduction to Israel's Wisdom Literature* (2000). Fox (2000) points out that there is a problem in that the beginning of wisdom is to 'get' it (rather than, say, to fear God), and explains it as a reference to a youth acquiring wisdom before understanding its true value, which is the first step before an understanding of its value is gradually taught and acquired. I wonder if this nuance of meaning is in fact found here.

is referred to in the third person and described in the manner of her self-presentation in 1:20–35 and in chapter 8 (see Chapter 4) with hints of the personification to come. The educational context is clear here– and it is unusually found without a specific ethical content. Again parental (even grandparental) instruction is being spelt out here and closely aligned with Wisdom's own authority – a link which gives structural unity to the section.

Instruction number six is to be found in Proverbs 4:10–19 and presents two ways of living life, about which there is a choice, with definite consequences on either side. It falls into three parts: an introduction in verses 10–12; a main section with subsequent motive clauses in verses 14–17 and a conclusion in verses 18–19. Distinctive here is the emphasis on 'the way', that is, 'the way of wisdom', paralleling 'paths of uprightness', which is the goal of the quest in contrast to the figure of Wisdom herself being the prize here. This choice of ways in life is a familiar theme in Proverbs (e.g. in Prov. 1:15; 2:7–9, 12–15; 3:6, 23; cf. Ps. 1:6) and often provides an alternative to either the parent or Wisdom herself as the authoritative figure. As with the last instruction, however, with the father's words leading to the giving of Wisdom's benefits, here the father's words put the son on the right track and then, being on that track, lead to the conferring of benefits, such as long life (verse 10) and the gift of 'instruction' (verse 13). There is still an integral relationship between the instructing father and the benefits of Wisdom, a relationship which serves to unify the passage here. There is a fleeting personification of 'instruction' in verse 13 (McKane, 1970), which I see as referring to woman Wisdom but simply using poetic variation. Verses 18 and 19 are sometimes re-versed by scholars.[23] This does not, however, detract from the unity of theme in the section of verses 14–19 and the overall educational purpose of the piece.

Proverbs 4:20–7, the seventh instruction, is on the importance of vigilance. It begins with the father's exhortation, and the reason given is that his words will lead to life and health in a physical and mental sense. The unit mentions seven organs of the body and this

---

[23] E.g. Whybray, 1994c, but Fox (2000) sees no need for this if it is a distinct concluding unit.

mention has the effect of unifying the section.[24] The heart, eyes and feet are mentioned twice. In verses 20–23 attentive listening and keeping words in the heart could refer to memorization of teaching (McKane, 1970) and indeed to an oral context. The heart is the key organ here; it stores up teaching (verse 21) and from it spring decisions as to appropriate action (verse 23).[25] In Hebrew thought here the heart denotes both the mind of a person (including the intellectual mind) and his or her basic orientation in terms of desires, emotions and attitudes. The faculties of ear and eye take in the teaching in the first part of the instruction, while those of speech, seeing and walking in the second part are the means of expressing that teaching with appropriate restraint. The introduction (verses 20–2) is followed by five admonitions and no general conclusion, unless one takes verse 27 as a kind of conclusion (so Fox, 2000). In verse 20, all the words are found in other introductory sections to instructions and the vocabulary is becoming the familiar prelude within the instruction form. In verse 22, 'life' (pl. חיים) includes physical health as well as material prosperity. This forms a bridge with what follows in that in verses 23–7 the attainment of practical goals in order to achieve 'life' is enjoined, using the language of the physical body and seeing fulfilment in terms of restraint and discipline. Reference to the process of teaching is significant here alongside the more usual exhortations. This confirms the educational context, and the ethical content of the instruction is confirmed by the admonitions, suggesting an overall unity.

The eighth instruction in Proverbs 5:1–23 is generally agreed to be a unity, although scholars have suggested additions, omissions, a shorter original with redactions and so on. Verses 21–3 contain the only reference to Yahweh (see discussion in Chapter 4). Whybray (1994c) imagines a shorter original instruction consisting of verses

[24] Reference to many different parts of the body is found in Ps. 115:5–7, but for a different purpose.
[25] Fox (2000) argues that נצר לבך ('keep/guard your heart') in verse 23 is virtually synonymous with 'guard your mouth', referring to wrong speech, itself the product of wrong thoughts as expressed in verse 24. I differ from his opinion on this point. In the second half of verse 23, the heart is portrayed as a water source from which life erupts, and so in this context it would seem more likely that the reference is to general restraint, allowing for controlled 'springs' rather than chaotic waters. Verses 24ff. then are illustrations of that restraint.

1–6, 8 and parts of 21–3 which have been subsequently expanded. Fox shows a certain impatience with such theories when he writes, 'Dissections like these presuppose arbitrary rules for unity and fragment any unit that does not meet them' (2000: 206). He is in favour of unity and even adds a reconstructed verse after verse 1 to give a motive for the exhortation as in other instructions. The instruction divides into four subsections: verses 1–6, 7–14, 15–19 and 20–3. Units beginning 'my son' can be located in verses 1, 7 and 20, indicating new sections, and one could argue that it is missing from verse 15 and would naturally belong there too (Clifford, 1999). The repeated refrain seems a good marker for unity. The young man being addressed here is inexperienced and yet also, surprisingly, married. The educational tone has a quite individual quality to it here.

The eighth instruction opens with the teacher's exhortation, as usual in these instructions. In verse 1 there is an unusual reference to 'my wisdom' and 'my understanding' on the part of the teacher, as opposed to the usual more universal presentation.[26] The instruction takes a fresh turn with the reintroduction of the loose woman in verses 3–14 (already encountered in 2:16–19 and coming back in 6:20–35 and chapter 7) and then with the introduction of a new character in verses 15–19, the wife of the addressee's youth, who fulfils the same role to a point as Wisdom/Yahweh/'the way' in other instructions in being the counterpart to bad choices. In verses 3–4 reference is made to the smooth lips of the seductive woman that drip honey, suggesting that her speech is insincere.[27] The contrast is therefore being drawn, in the instruction as a whole, between the choice of the wrong kind of woman and the choice of the right kind. There is an underlying contrast also between the dangers from outside (which may well sap a man's strength and resources) and the security from inside, in that a good wife is a protection against such dangers and safeguards a man's seed (verses 15–19).

---

[26] Fox (2000: 190) comments on this usual universality: 'For the most part, then, the author wishes to imply the universality of the wisdom he is teaching (it is not his alone) while claiming possession and authorship of the words and instructions whereby wisdom is conveyed.'

[27] This recalls the dangers of smooth speech noted in Ps. 55:21, where the image of butter is used. It also recalls 'lips dripping honey' in Song 4:11, although in this latter passage sweet kisses are being referred to in a positive manner.

The dangers of adultery are mentioned in verses 9–10: loss of reputation and health (verse 9), loss of wealth (verse 10), and hence finding oneself on the inevitable path to death and destruction bewailing one's lack of discipline (verses 11–13). In verse 13 the reference to 'teachers' and 'instructors' has been taken as evidence for a school setting for this instruction. In verse 14 Whybray (1994c) notes that 'the public assembly' refers to a meeting of assembled citizens, the only reference to such in the Proverbs. He finds it 'a national reference never found elsewhere in Proverbs' (1994c: 84). However, a few hints of communal reference have featured before (e.g. in Prov. 2:20–2 and 3:9–10), and this does not seem to me to be as specific a reference as Whybray makes out. It is nevertheless unusual in the way it appears to ground the wisdom instruction in the arena of a wider Israelite public life. In verse 15 the reference to drinking water from one's own cistern is thought to have sexual overtones.[28] Wells and cisterns tended to be private property for one's own water usage, images contrasted with the common property of streets and squares where the seductive woman roams. Again the contrast is made between inside (at home) and outside in the streets. In verse 19 the language of hind and stag recall the love poetry of the Song of Songs in which the woman swears by the hinds of the field (Song 2:7; 3:5) and the man is likened to a young stag (Song 2:9, 17; 8:14). In verse 22 'his iniquities' (עוונותיו) and 'his sin' (חטאתו) are terms that do not occur elsewhere in Proverbs 1–9 and Whybray (1994c) sees them as specifically religious terms that do not fit here. However, he himself acknowledges that the terms appear elsewhere in Proverbs as a whole and so his argument is not strong, and it is interesting in itself that other contexts are possibly being recalled (see discussion in Chapter 6). This section brings closure to the chapter in its general statement of retribution for all evildoers, not just adulterers. This instruction is rather different with the presence of new characters, but there is expansion of a more general point into areas of personification which opens the context out rather than suggesting disunity. The broader context is that of being out in the world and meeting 'types' rather than being in the

---

[28] References to cisterns are found, for example, in Isa. 36:16 and Song 4:15.

safer environment of home or school. Still, the context is ultimately an educational one with a strong ethical element.

Proverbs 6:1–19 is a section that has caused difficulties for interpreters, as it is not an instruction and it is not a wisdom poem; it just seems to be an interlude that has more resemblances to themes found in Proverbs 10–31 than to other parts of Proverbs 1–9.[29] It consists of four short pieces in verses 1–5, 6–11, 12–15 and 16–19, loosely held together by the theme of personal traits that become obstacles to the acquisition of wisdom and lead to poverty (in contrast to the perils of seductive women and evildoers in the last chapter, perhaps). However, each section is distinctive and each could have had an independent existence before being placed in this context. Fox (2000) believes that there are close links between the first and second sections of the piece (on grounds of shared phraseology) and between the third and fourth sections (on grounds of content). He believes that the third and fourth sections were composed sequentially by the same author in dependence upon other sections of Proverbs. In fact, he argues that all four epigrams are built around sayings and ideas from other parts of Proverbs, which, when one looks at the evidence, appears to be the case. Verses 1–5 begin with 'my son', but there is no exhortation to keep the father's words as in other instructions. Some commentators describe it as an instruction of a kind, but generally it does not fit the mould of the genre or its characteristics. It contains more of a description of certain 'types' and a statement of what is the case rather than having an exhortatory teaching tone or being full of ethical injunctions. Therefore an educational context is not obvious, aside from its broader place in the midst of the instruction texts. The section is concerned with avoiding standing surety for someone outside the family, a major concern of Proverbs 10–31 (with references in 11:15; 17:18; 20:16; 22:26 and 27:13). In verses 6–11 we meet a well-known 'type' of Proverbs, the sluggard (cf. 24:30–4 (24:33–4 are in fact identical to 6:10–11); 26:13–16, as well as numerous individual sayings, e.g. 10:5). Here the emphasis is on the community's welfare at the time of harvest, which is threatened by the actions of the

---

[29] There are certainly few connections to the end of the previous chapter, Proverbs 5.

sluggard; significantly, the communal dimension comes in again here. The foil to the sluggard here is not the diligent, as elsewhere (Prov. 12:24, 27; 13:4), but the ant, which represents hard work (again in a communal context).[30] In verses 12–15 another 'type', the wicked person, makes an appearance, expanding on sketches found in Proverbs 1:8–19; 2:12–15 and 4:14–19). All his activity is represented by reference to his different body parts (making an interesting contrast to Prov. 4:23–7).[31] Fox (2000) points out that 6:12–15 draws particularly on Proverbs 16:27–30, and in fact that the parallels extend into verses 6:16–19. In verses 16–19 there is a numerical saying comparable to such sayings in Proverbs 30:7–9, 15–17, 18–19, 21–3, 24–31.[32]

Proverbs 6:20–35, the ninth instruction, is on the dangers of adultery. It begins with the exhortations of both parents to the young man to follow their teaching and stay on the right path, the one that leads to life. Their teaching will guard the son from the allure of the married woman who is also a temptress (verse 24). The rest of the instruction concerns the repercussions that such behaviour would have. The instruction naturally divides then into verses 20–4 and 25–35. In the second part, two comparisons are made with the act of adultery: the first is with the prostitute, whom one pays for sex and with whom one is advised not to get entangled, but who is preferable to the woman who is already married and 'stalks a man's very life'. The second is with a thief who steals because he is hungry; although he is harshly punished if caught, there is some tolerance of his motive and he is not 'despised'. By contrast, he who commits adultery will be disgraced. Many scholars regard this instruction as a unity, but there have been dissenters such as Whybray (1994c), who regards only verses 20–2 and 24–5 as original, possibly with a small part of verses 26–35 as a conclusion (e.g. verse 32).

The educational context of this instruction is clear from the opening verse. Verse 20 implies a family teaching environment (cf.

---

[30] Cf. similar use of animal imagery in Prov. 30 (see below) and compare references to learning lessons from animals in Isa. 1:3 and Jer. 8:7.

[31] 'Winking the eye' is an image found in Ps. 35:19, also seen as an action done with malicious intention.

[32] 'Haughty eyes' and a 'lying tongue' are known from descriptions elsewhere in Proverbs, but also in Pss. 18:27b and 109:2 respectively.

Prov. 3:1–3 and 7:1–3). Fox (2000) sees much of this as common-places of educational language, namely that teaching must permeate your entire life. Verse 22 is sometimes seen as a misfit, since singular verbs suddenly appear and the most natural reference would be to the 'commandment' and 'teaching' mentioned in verse 20. In fact, the reference to 'commandment' and 'teaching' in verse 20 is picked up in verse 23, where the two are likened to light and lamp respectively.[33] This would suggest that verse 22 also refers back to these. In verses 24–5 the reference to the 'evil woman' (אשת רע) is unusual, as it is not paralleled in any other Old Testament text. This seems to be the same person as the usual אשה זרה (loose/foreign woman or adulteress), who is the subject of the next few verses. At the end of the instruction, Fox (2000) regards verses 34–5 as an appropriate conclusion to the whole with the wronged husband taking revenge on the adulterer in the end, as an illustration of the inevitability of the adulterer's punishment.

Proverbs 7:1–27 is the last of the ten instructions found in Proverbs 1–9 and the fourth of five warnings against the seductive woman. It falls naturally into three parts: verses 1–5 provide the usual introduction to an instruction, verses 6–23 contain an example story, told by the teacher, of a young man who fell under the spell of an adulteress, and verses 24–7 give a conclusion to the instruction. Whybray (1994c) argues that the original instruction would have consisted of verses 1–3, 5 and 25–7.[34] He sees verses 6–23 as a separate moral tale and yet also as an expansion of the adultery theme. There are also close resemblances to the instruction in 6:20–1 and 23–4, except for 7:4, which urges the pupil to make Wisdom his companion. This is the only reference to Wisdom in this instruction, and this is a vital verse presenting Wisdom as the favoured alternative by the teacher before he launches into the moral tale (not, in my view, to be dismissed as an addition, as Whybray (1994c and elsewhere)

---

[33] Whybray (1994c) regards verse 23a as an addition on the grounds that such comparisons are not made elsewhere and are overtly religious 'in a sense not intended by the author of the Instruction' (1994c: 104). McKane (1970) did not see this verse as a later addition, despite the expressions evoking legalistic piety that he found here. A comparison can be made to Ps. 119:105, in which God's word is 'lamp' and 'light'.

[34] Cf. Whybray's remarks (1994c) about the second instruction (in 2:1, 9, 16–19, in his view), which he sees this as strongly resembling.

does). The implication is that, had the young man embraced Wisdom, he would have avoided the snares and deceit of the adulteress. The use of an example story recalls Proverbs 4:3–5; 24:30–4; Ps. 37:35–6; Job 5:3–5; Eccle. 4:13–16. The instruction can, in my view, be seen as a consistent unity.

In the first three verses, which reflect Proverbs 3:1–3, 'apple of your eye' refers to something precious (cf. Deut. 32:10; Ps. 17:3), and in verse 3 there is the exhortation to bind the teachings on the hands (cf. Deut. 6:8; 11:18) (see discussion in Chapter 6). This could refer to finger ornaments, such as a signet ring, which are always in front of one's face, as the teachings are meant to be. The 'tablet of the heart' is also mentioned, which could simply refer to the internalization of the teaching rather than to any actual tablet (cf. Prov. 3:3 and Jer. 31:33). Fox (2000) notes that 'eyes', 'fingers' and 'heart' together represent the whole personality. There is some debate among scholars over whether 'sister' in verse 4 has the overtone of 'bride', as in the conjunction of the two terms in the Song of Songs (4:9, 10, 12; 5:1) or whether it refers more straightforwardly to the close family relationship of brother and sister. The 'intimate friend' (מדע) that parallels it does suggest a relative (Boaz is described as מדע in Ruth 2:1 and 3:2). Murphy (1998) prefers the 'bride' suggestion, while Fox (2000)[35] prefers the family interpretation. The erotic overtones would provide a more balanced opposite to the eroticism of the loose woman, as the description goes on to reveal, but the family interpretation suggests a less distracted type of love that may be more steady in comparison with the short-term sexual lures of the adulteress. In verse 5 the nature of the adulteress as a smooth talker is brought out; this is, in fact, her main weapon (cf. Prov. 2:16; 6:24). In verses 14–15 the adulteress claims to be making a vow and this seems to be the opportunity for the young man to become involved with her. The youth is unaware that he is to be the offering, rather as Jephthah's daughter is the sacrifice in Judges 11. In verse 17 the language of perfuming of the bed with rich spices is ambivalent, in that while the use of myrrh, aloes and cinnamon has sexual

---

[35] Fox (2000) suggests that this verse implies an egalitarian relationship between Wisdom and the 'pupil' here, in contrast to the personification passages in which Wisdom is definitely the superior partner.

overtones, they are also used for perfuming a dead body before a funeral.[36] Perhaps this *double entendre* is intended to warn the addressee of the hidden dangers of his encounter with the seductress. In verses 22–3 the youth is compared to animals quickly ensnared and then slaughtered, unaware, like the youth, that they are about to die (cf. Jer. 11:19a). In verse 24 reference is made to 'my sons' suggesting a wider audience (cf. Prov. 5:7), but then the singular reappears in verse 25. The main point is reiterated in the conclusion: avoid the paths of the seductress and do not imitate the poor, unfortunate, unsuspecting youth of the story. Many have already died at her hands and her house is the gateway to death. This is teaching once more in a broader context; there are significant overtones of Deuteronomic language in the reference to binding the teachings on the hands, which may open the educational context out further (see Chapter 6).

One striking aspect of these passages I have considered is their diversity and different character. Even within the one genre of 'instruction', there is much difference of concern, style and reference, suggesting that each has to be taken on its own terms. And yet, a key uniting context for the instructions is that of teaching and an educational context containing broader ethical concerns. Is that the end of the story, or does the religious element represented by the Yahweh passages have a role to play in determining that context? Clearly, the instructions were composed for a range of different occasions for such teaching, with different emphases being appropriate for different occasions. They have their place in either family or school, either context being plausible for the education of the young men described in the passages.

While the instruction genre may be old in origin, as witnessed by Egyptian prototypes, and while the original context of this material may well have been oral, I suggest that trying to carve up these texts into more original or less, or oral/written, as many commentators have done, is a somewhat futile activity. My survey of these passages has found unity of theme and purpose within each instruction. I have wanted to stress the range of different themes and concerns in

---

[36] 'Bed' can also refer to the place of burial (cf. Isa. 57:2; Ezek. 32:25; 2 Chron 16:14).

the instructions rather than overstressing the links between them, finding the idea that one author composed all ten instructions implausible, but a final editing stage bringing them together as plausible. The consistency of certain elements, such as the very similar introductions, suggests shared genre and context rather than shared authorship.

CONCLUSION

The original use of these instructions in the educational context(s) of either family or school is clear. The religious element will be examined in Chapter 4, but need not in my view be consistently seen as a second layer of redaction (Whybray, 1994c). The key question is how integral the religious aspect is within the educational/ethical context that has been identified. The educational purpose of these texts has tended to be stressed by scholars, with the religious as a more secondary factor. Is this indeed the right emphasis? This educational context needs to be distinguished from the final written context in which the individual pieces are found, which may in turn have had its own purpose, possibly in relation to the whole of Proverbs rather than simply in relation to the rest of Proverbs 1–9 (bearing in mind, for example, the cross-references to Proverbs 10:1ff. in the interlude in 6:1–19). It is at that final written stage that unifying features across the instructions may have been drawn out and deliberately emphasized by use of repetition and overtones of one text in another, but trying to reconstruct this process, of course, rests on presuppositions about the way the material developed over time and so can be seen as a rather circular exercise.

It is fascinating that such a wide range of suggestions regarding social context has been generated from nine chapters of the text of Proverbs! I identified four underlying issues that reappear in these discussions of context and examined two of them in particular in my preliminary look at the instructions–the educational purpose of the material and the issue of structural unity. Another issue was the earlier/later argument, revolving not just around absolute questions of date (which are virtually impossible to answer), but also around questions of the antiquity of material, the priority of texts and their possible interdependence and questions of the nature and place of theological developments. I have aired the possibility of earlier elements within the instruction texts from an educational context of family or school, but have seen also that they generally form unified blocks of material. A further issue that reappears is the related one of oral and literary stages. There is a great deal of uncertainty over how to characterize the material, and whether to posit a long stage of oral development with its own social context(s) or to regard the final written product as the essential stage of development. A few hints of oral context may have been found in the instructions of Proverbs 1–9, but not enough to see that as the primary context here; rather, the hints might betray an older context underlying the present written material. While the writing down of Proverbs 1–9 may have been an exilic or early post-exilic activity (and the issue of link-up with other Old Testament texts will be a factor in deliberating this issue; see Chapter 6), one cannot deny the possibility of earlier elements being incorporated within the final text, and those are perhaps most likely to be early written elements, themselves descended from oral antecedents. The wisdom poems in Proverbs 1–9 (which I have not considered in this chapter but will look at in Chapter 4) have generally been seen as the latest element in the book, a development of wisdom into a more theological arena. And yet, even here, there may be scope for seeing more cohesive roots for the ideas. A crucial factor in this is the place of the Yahweh element in this material and also the interrelationship of the Wisdom motif to a wider thought-world outside strictly proverbial categories.

Having looked at the various scholarly suggestions for a social context for Proverbs 1–9, one comes to realize how open the question remains. However, in Chapters 3 and 5, I am interested to pursue two lines of inquiry that have not hitherto been especially emphasized. The first is the theological nature of the material; there has been interest in this, but largely in the attempt to explain earlier and later theological developments within the material. I wish to take the focus away from this more historical preoccupation to look at whether there is more integration of the theological within the structure of individual sections and whether in fact scholars are justified in doing the kind of cutting and pasting of which some, such as Whybray (1994c and elsewhere), have been so fond. The second line of inquiry is to look at echoes of other texts in the material to see how grounded Proverbs is within Israelite tradition. The wisdom literature is often said to be without reference to wider Israelite tradition and to stand alone (as discussed in the Introduction). I believe that this assumption is questionable in relation to wisdom's influence on other texts, but is it also true of texts such as Proverbs 1–9? It is of interest, therefore, when exploring examples from the text, to focus on these two issues and to see if they shed any light on the question of social context. Before doing that, however, I wish to look at the other parts of Proverbs in the light of the debate about social context.

CHAPTER 2

Social context(s) in Proverbs 10:1—22:16

Wisdom has existed as long as there have been people.

(Westermann, 1995: 135)

The section of Proverbs 10:1—22:16 is usually regarded as a collection of sayings that were originally independent, hence the seemingly haphazard arrangement of one proverb after another, with only a few linkages in subject matter. However, at times, and recently by Weeks (1994) and Heim (2001), there has been an attempt to find longer sections that hang together. This is, once again, to raise the question of oral and literary stages, in that it may be that there has been a more careful placement of these proverbs at the writing-down stage than originally thought.[1] However, in an oral prehistory they were probably of a more independent nature. The stress on the oral becomes greater in this section as the possible social context comes under discussion. There is also the issue of the nature of different proverbs; some have a more popular quality, while others may be the product of more educated circles, and all have a generally ethical character, most the result of observation and experience, some more exhortatory than others, most using ethical categories in opposite types, such as 'wise man' and 'fool' and 'the righteous' and 'the wicked'. Another question that has been raised in scholarly circles is how 'theological' these proverbs are, given that many are maxims on everyday issues such as money, work and communication, and do not mention God specifically. A further question concerns the similarity of this section with

---

[1] Cf. Hildebrandt (1988), who placed an emphasis on the literary nature of the collecting process in which proverbs were gathered into units.

proverbs from a wider international scene and hence the possibility of drawing parallels and positing court (and king) or school
contexts.

THE FAMILY/FOLK/TRIBAL SETTING

The coining of proverbs in everyday speech and life is common to
most cultures in the world and is a natural human inclination.
Features include the drawing of parallels between unlike phenomena
to make a moral point, and warnings and encouragements based on
the fruits of experience and whittled down to pithy sayings. This
kind of 'everyday' context has naturally been suggested for the
proverbs of Proverbs 10:1—22:16. This was an older idea among
scholarship,[2] which fell from favour with the whole international
wisdom debate in which proverbs were regarded as the work of a
more learned group. However, this mantle has been taken up,
especially in recent times, as the simplest explanation of the origin
of these sayings. The question of how 'popular' and generally ethical
these saying are, in contrast to whether they are designed for a
specific educational purpose, has been agonized over by scholars
such as Scott (1961), who found proverbs of both types in the book.
This is an important question: whether the context for these ethical
sayings is primarily of a popular and general nature or primarily
educational. Is there evidence here of pre-literary instruction – an
extension of the instructional idea found in Proverbs 1–9 – of a kind
passed down from father to son? Fox (1996) argues that the locus of
wisdom instruction generally was in the home, but that this does not
prove that it is essentially oral or folk literature. Is there even a legal
aspect to this attempt to give a moral underpinning to society
by using a collection of experiential norms, as Audet (1960) and
Gerstenberger (1965a) suggested? Gerstenberger focused on negative
admonitions in both the ten commandments and the Proverbs and
argued that this legal form and 'family ethic' (*Sippenethos*) form are
closely related and have a common origin. Or are scholars reading
too much into this miscellaneous collection, and should these
proverbs be regarded as simply a collection of broad, ethical sayings

---

[2] E.g. Eissfeldt, 1913.

with no specific contextual reference apart from the general and ongoing moral formation of young and old alike?

Then there is the distinction between oral stages and literary stages; clearly, even if the origin is popular, these sayings were used in the realms of the more educated at some point. Perhaps the 'mother's knee' wisdom for educated and less educated was much the same and these proverbs crossed class barriers. Blenkinsopp (1997) would not agree; he argues that Proverbs 10:1—22:16 and 25–9 contain 'ethics and etiquette for young males from well-to-do families and cannot be taken to reflect the ethical consensus in the whole society' (1997: 83). However, it is clear that folk wisdom was eventually incorporated into a more focused, instructional book (witness the 'preface' quality of Prov. 1–9). Whybray (1990; 1994a) argued that individual proverbs were the common lore of Israelite farmers, but were subsequently and gradually formed into larger groups for pedagogical purposes. This general advice is not addressed to any age group in particular. It is not piecemeal, but links up with individual formation of character and ultimately with societal order.

Some illumination of this issue has come from cross-cultural comparison, not this time with the ancient Near East (although there are significant parallels), but with proverbs as used in primitive tribal societies. Westermann (1971a) suggested that the level of cultural development found in tribal Israel from early times was comparable with that of some primitive African peoples still in existence today. He later did an in-depth study in which he argued that the proverbs reflect the lives of peasants and manual workers. He argued that proverbial wisdom's emphasis on God as creator is a further sign of pre-literate culture and that it was essentially a 'private' rather than a 'public' form of religion. The emphasis on the family and on personal relationships within a small community was a form of regulation of social behaviour. Golka (1993) looked in depth at African proverbs and addressed the particular question of whether a court context was appropriate for some proverbs that mention the king. He decided that a court setting was not appropriate and that proverbs had a popular, folk and tribal origin. Finnegan (1970), an anthropologist, argued interestingly that African traditional proverbs play a part in the administration of justice and are used in argument to influence legal decisions. This brought the legal idea back into focus. Work has also been done by Hamutyinei and Plangger (1987) in collecting together traditional Shona proverbs from Zimbabwe, Africa. Like Proverbs 10:1—22:16, these originated in oral form among a pastoral and agricultural people and cover all kinds of experience. The images and comparisons are drawn from observation of human behaviour, of that of animals, and of the nature of objects in both the natural and cultural environment. In the Shona proverbs, social problems of authority, oppression or power-sharing are treated, as are changes in fortune, both in the domestic sphere and in relation to success in love. There is a written tradition, but the oral tradition exists alongside and so the proverbs are constantly changed to make them more effective in a particular oral context. They often operate on two levels: the obvious meaning and the hidden meaning. There is a clear juridical role for these proverbs as well as an educational one, along the lines that Finnegan (1970) suggested. They express customary law and rules of conduct in life and are used in tribal judgements. They are the fruit of experience, and that experience can sometimes be contradictory. They also contain wit and irony and a richness that enhance speech and language. These offer a fascinating parallel to biblical proverbs and may suggest educational and juridical contexts in which they were used as well as shedding light on the oral/literary dynamic.

Such emphases on the family/folk/tribal served to underline the earliest context of these proverbs and opened up a fresh field of possibility. Westermann found in this section of Proverbs evidence of short, pithy sayings which he saw as representing the earliest oral stages of proverbial transmission within a family rather than a tribal setting. He saw this short form as lying behind more literary forms of the sayings. As to social context he wrote, 'Everything belongs to the experiential realm of normal people living in villages or small towns' (1995: 60). Reference to the wider realm is missing, making it unlikely, he argues, that these proverbs arose in a more highly educated context. Comparisons were also made with the ancient Near East and, although Egyptian wisdom was less fruitful in terms of comparisons (except for the late *Instruction of Onchsheshonqy*, which does contain many 'sayings'[3]), more engaging possibilities were found among Sumerian proverbs, which themselves became part of Babylonian wisdom literature, and also among the Aramaic *Wisdom of Ahiqar*, a document more contemporary with Proverbs (Greenfield, 1995).

Some attempt has been made to place the familial context within the framework of the social and historical development of Israelite society.[4] In the period before the rise of the monarchy there were few public structures and so, it is argued, it is likely that the family had to be self-sufficient, establishing its own rules, patterns of work and so on. There may have been elders from various family groups who gathered together to make larger collective decisions resembling a tribal community, but still the family, it is argued, was primary. Within this unit it was imperative that children (of which there were many in a family, for economic reasons) should quickly learn the skills and procedures for maintaining the household in its mainly agrarian pursuits, and so some educational function is likely on this practical level, coming from both parents (cf. Samson's close relationship to his parents in Judg. 14). However, there was also the need for guidance on a wider range of issues covered by the broader ideal of morality; this is assumed by Perdue et al. (1997) to have been parental, but in my view could also have been for the guidance of all, not only as they took their place in society as youngsters, but also as they continued to live and learn through experience along life's way. Perdue et al. stress that wisdom was not some kind of rarified education, but was simply the basic learning process. It concerned itself with the making of a well-formed individual, but it crucially involved interpersonal and interfamilial behaviour. It was therefore both private and public. It also included relationship with the divine on a very basic level; family religion was pursued, family groups having specific deities often linked to a common ancestor. Households had cult corners and villages had local shrines. It is likely that at the celebration of festivals, mainly agrarian, there were socioreligious gatherings. These would have been celebrated at 'high places' and may have been accompanied by sacrifice and a meal. A fascinating picture is emerging here of the integration of different

[3] See Anthes, 1933, on the different Egyptian instruction texts.
[4] See Perdue et al., 1997.

parts of Israelite life and practice in the family setting, which might indicate that proverbial activity is not so divorced from other concerns, such as the cultic, as practised on a daily basis and from the worship of Yahweh in a religious context. Camp (1985) argues that this family emphasis continued throughout Israel's history and came to particular prominence in the early post-exilic period with the breakdown of state structures.

On this model, the transmission of proverbial wisdom, and in fact of all knowledge and practical skills, would have been oral, as would have been social customs, moral values and religious trad-itions. The simple reason was that most people were illiterate. There may have been some scribal households, probably in towns, where literary arts were transmitted (cf. Judg. 8:14; the young man of Succoth 'wrote down/listed' (כתב) the officials and elders of Succoth). Priests also provided instruction (e.g. Eli to Samuel in 1 Sam. 2–3). How widespread was this literacy? This is a question already encountered when discussing the likelihood of schools in Israel and is clearly a crucial and related issue. This leads on to the question of oral versus literary stages.

THE QUESTION OF ORAL VERSUS LITERARY STAGES

This is a question both of literary form and content and of social context, and so deserves brief mention here. This issue is about the nature of proverbs: are they of a popular oral nature or are they a literary product? The range of opinion on this is telling; both ex-tremes have been claimed and, after a prolonged debate, scholars do not seem to be much the wiser. One method that has been suggested is to look at short sayings from elsewhere in the Old Testament, notably in narrative material and in the prophets.[5] Fontaine (1982) has argued for a parallel between popular proverbs in a number of different contexts, both in their original contexts and their context now in the text. She argues for 'proverb performance' as a vital tradition operational in society at a variety of levels, not just in circles of court sages and scribes. She stresses the practical, utilitarian aspect of the proverbial enterprise and regards proverbs as having been used

---

[5] See McKane's (1970) introduction for this approach.

over and over again during a long time period. An example is Ezekiel 18:2 / Jer. 31:29: 'The fathers have eaten sour grapes and the children's teeth are set on edge', often regarded as a popular saying disputed by both prophets to make a more profound theological point about the non-transference of sin from one generation to another. There has been some uncertainty, however, over whether these different 'proverbs' are related to those in the book of Proverbs. One important point is that most of the proverbs in Proverbs 10:1—22:16 are two-lined sayings rather than pithy one-liners as found elsewhere.

The further question is raised: is the two-lined saying a development from the one-lined? Eissfeldt (1913) put forward the view that short folk proverbs preceded more literary two-liners and was part of a development that saw a change in social setting from oral to more literary and learned. He thought that the pithy forerunners were often to be found in the first half of a proverb, where the second line was not necessary to its meaning. Others, such as Oesterley (1929), took up the idea of development; as the Israelite culture matured, so more traditional sayings took more elaborate forms.[6] This is a parallel to the idea that a folk setting of a general ethical nature developed into a more educational one in more learned circles. Other scholars reacted to the presupposition of development, arguing that different developments might well take place at different times. Egyptian and Sumerian parallels were cited to confirm the point that different types often co-existed and that one type might lead to the development of another type; for instance, a one-lined saying might augment by the attention given to it in an educational context (Scott, 1961). Nel (1981; 1982) argued that both types of saying could well have an origin in a tribal context and that the two-lined saying did not necessarily belong in more educated or educational circles. More recently, Westermann (1995) argued for short sayings as the precursors of longer ones. Against a strict line of development of literacy, Niditch (1996) has recently argued convincingly for an oral/literacy continuum whereby the movement from oral to literary happens at different paces for different sections of material in an ongoing process that cannot be dated in any definitive way. Von Rad (1972) argued in favour of a school setting

---

[6] McKane (1970) particularly pursued this line.

for the proverbs rather than for a popular origin; even in their earliest formulation he thought they were the products of intellectual activity with didactic intention. This leads back to the question of the original purpose of the oral formulation of proverbs: were some educational and some more generally ethical, or was there progression between the two contexts?

Interest has increasingly focused on the way in which proverbs were written down and on the question of whether there are any patterns to be found. This raises the question of when clusters formed: was this, too, part of the oral prehistory or is it a purely literary phenomenon? Hermisson (1968) was the chief proponent of the idea that there were noticeable patterns. A particularly significant contribution came from Whybray (1979), who drew attention to the fact that in Proverbs 10:1—22:16 a number, generally clustered in particular chapters, refer to Yahweh's attitude towards various human activities. He suggested that whoever compiled these proverbs had deliberately placed 'Yahweh-sayings' in prime positions so as to emphasize the theological aspect (see Chapter 4 below). This relates to the question of the place of Yahweh in this collection; many scholars had thought of the proverbs as essentially non-religious. The question was raised: was the collection subjected to a Yahwehizing redaction when written down or was there a religious element to them from the start? Whybray also looked at evidence for independent pairs combined into larger groups by use of 'pivotal' verses. Yahweh proverbs were one group of these, but the category proved to be wider. He made the point in his later work that the Yahwehizing was simply a making explicit of what was already implicit; it was not a correction to previously unreligious material. Whybray thought that the purpose of the groups of proverbs was educational, but that the origin of the sayings was probably more popular.

COURT AND SCHOOL

Basing their discussions on the presuppositions considered in relation to Proverbs 1–9 and Egyptian influence, some scholars have preferred the royal court as a possible context for at least portions of these sayings (see fuller discussion below), notably those that mention the king (Humphreys, 1978). However, the point has also been made that mention of the king does not necessitate a court context (Dell, 1998; Weeks, 1994). This links up with the idea of a group of administrators who needed a formal education and with that of either just a court school or a wider school system. McKane (1965) argued that the Israelite wisdom literature as a whole is a production of state officials, probably from the time of Solomon. However, many scholars have reacted against such a sweeping statement.[7] The question turns on the purpose for which the proverbs in this section were written down. They seem a very diverse group of maxims to fit into an administrative, court setting. The purpose in writing them down may have been educational, but there is considerable mileage in the idea of oral antecedents from a broader ethical setting, which may suggest that the main purpose for writing them down was that they represented important aspects of Israelite tradition and of the heritage of the wisdom enterprise. This marks a return to the question of when they were written down; one might encourage the quest for a written context either at the time of Hezekiah (cf. Prov. 25:1) or later. For instance, Scott (1985) argued for the reign of Hezekiah as the time of a cultural flowering because of Hezekiah's interest in collecting foreign literary works and encouraging a court scribal establishment (see discussion of Prov. 25–9).

A PRELIMINARY OVERVIEW

In Proverbs 10:1—22:16 we are in the heartland of wisdom literature, which is perhaps most strongly characterized, on a formal level at least, by the form of the proverb. The initial impression here is that the material is much more piecemeal and unconnected than the instruction texts were. This has been of concern to some recent scholars, such as Heim (2001), who has sought to find clusters of proverbs linked both thematically and with reference to a principle of co-referentiality, which indicates that there is more continuity of characterization within a given passage.[8] Heim argues for a literary

---

[7] E.g., Murphy, 1967.
[8] So, e.g., in 10:1–5, Heim (2001) suggests that 'foolish son' (בן כסיל) can be equated with 'wicked' (רשעים), so that one can assume a continuity of characterization here. I remain

intention in the clustering of proverbs into units, and so puts a fresh emphasis on the written stage of the text (contra Westermann's (1995) emphasis on the oral), although he also acknowledges the role of proverb 'performance' in oral stages. One problem with the identification of clusters, as Heim acknowledges, is that scholars have often disagreed about the limits of each cluster. With this criticism in mind, Heim prefers to confine his analysis to small to middle-sized clusters as the potential building blocks of larger ones. He has usefully pointed out linkages also within chapters. For example, in chapter 11, Heim finds clusters of proverbs in verses 1–14, 15–21 and 22–31, but further than this he points to interrelationship beyond these prime clusters. He notes the centrality of verse 4 in the first cluster, which speaks of wealth as an object of greed. He argues that this theme is then deliberately taken up in verses 15–21 with sentiments about the dishonest acquisition of wealth, and that this is then given religious backing when the characters depicted here are linked to the divine judgement stated in verses 20–1. The final section deplores self-interest and promotes concern for others with the thought that, ultimately, the latter gain advantage over the former. Heim argues that interconnection is often an enhancement of the meaning of any individual proverbs, although my own view is that, despite this interesting observation, each proverb also stands alone. Heim notes that the strength of proverbs is their adaptability to new situations – but surely this is because of the self-contained nature of their individual meaning. An important point raised by Heim is the strong Yahwistic influence on the clusters in which Yahwistic proverbs appear (see discussion in Chapter 4). There is a certain indigestibility about a series of unrelated proverbs, particularly when read, an indigestibility which is eased by a theory such as Heim's. I would agree with him that there is no 'fixed' meaning for an individual proverb independent of context, especially in the light of the fact that the original context of the saying's first utterance is lost to readership today. Rather, changing contexts may well change the meaning. However, we have to take the text as we have

---

unconvinced by this alignment, as 'the foolish' contrast with 'the wise' and 'the wicked' with 'the righteous' in a consistent manner in the proverbial material, and to align in this way within a section confuses that distinction.

it today and use that as our starting point. Heim usefully counters a tendency to fragment these chapters and to ignore signs of unity of theme, but he is primarily making a literary point about the collection of this material. I will look briefly for signs of purpose and structural unity in these chapters, as I did with Proverbs 1–9.

Proverbs 10 is a series of unconnected, mainly antithetical proverbs, as McKane (1970) and others have held. However, it is clear that the opening three verses provide a kind of programme for what follows. The chapter opens with a sapiential saying referring, as in Proverbs 1–9, to father and mother, the teachers of family wisdom. This immediately hints at that family educational context which may well be prime for many of these sayings, at least when they were originally conceived. Verse 2 contains a predominantly ethical statement and introduces the two major categories of the righteous and the wicked, who will feature strongly in these chapters, alongside the wise and the foolish. Such ethical categories, as well as being characteristic of wisdom, forge a wider link with the broader ethical life of Israel. Verse 3 is where the religious dimension comes in and God is brought into the righteous/wicked equation on the side of justice, the giver of good to those who deserve it and punishment to the wicked. Proverbs 10:1–5 is often seen as a section or cluster, but in fact verses 1–3 form an introduction to the whole chapter (and indeed the whole section) and verses 4–5, with their agricultural theme, are more readily placed together. I would not personally want to overstate signs of unity here, though in its introductory nature the opening of the chapter does bear these marks.[9] In chapters 11 and 12 the righteous/wicked contrast dominates. Chapter 11 was discussed above and, while there are some thematic linkages across the chapter, there is also a diversity of subject matter across the chapter, suggesting the individual, originally oral nature of the sayings rather than their unity. In chapter 12 there is a more unified section in verses 14–25, which are about speech, but other unified sections are less obvious.[10] The 'forced labour' of verse 24 may

---

[9] Heim (2001) finds unity in verses 1–3 and 5–7, with verse 4 as an unrelated saying.
[10] Heim (2001) finds sections in 12:8–12 on the need for diligence alongside intellectual qualities when it comes to work; and in 12:13–23, 25, on speech, and 12:24, 26–8, on actions. He argues that this section also links up with chapter 13 in its emphasis on speaking and listening.

contain an echo of the days of forced labour in Egypt (Gen. 49:15; Exod. 1:11) or of the oppressive policies of Solomon as recalled in 1 Kings 5:13, so linking up with other parts of the Old Testament.

Chapter 13 opens with a verse that resembles Proverbs 10:1 and has led some to suggest the collection from this point was once distinct (but then Prov. 14:1 seems also to open a section afresh). The theme of verse 1 is the obligation to heed instruction. The speech theme is then found in verses 1–3 and references to diligence dominate verses 4–6. In verses 7–11 wealth and poverty are at issue. Verse 12 recalls the tree of life in Genesis 3:24. Verses 13–14 resemble the teaching of Proverbs 1–9 in the emphasis on 'word', 'commandment' and 'teaching' and hence suggest an educational context. In fact, the chapter contains much that is characteristic in subject matter of the Proverbs generally, yet the sayings are individual and do not naturally, in my view, fall into many thematic clusters.

In chapter 14 there is an introductory verse, verse 1, which refers to 'the wise woman', who is in contrast to folly. Personifications of these two featured in Proverbs 1–9, but here the reference is not so developed in that they are not personified as individuals. The reference to the 'house of the wicked' in verse 11 might suggest a small thematic inclusio with verse 1, in which 'the wise woman builds her house but the foolish tears it down', in these verses. Verse 12 is identical to Proverbs 16:25. Verses 15–18 are all concerned with the wise and foolish and 19–21 with social evils. The thematic clusters that are found here are generally fairly short—just two or three verses and not generally as extensive as Heim (2001) maintains. The main impression here is again that of individual proverbs, occasionally brought into small thematic clusters. I will discuss mention of the king in later verses of this chapter in connection with the religious motif in Chapter 4.

In Proverbs 15–16 the references to Yahweh (and royal sayings in the case of Prov. 16) arguably dominate the chapter to such an extent that I shall reserve my comments on these chapters for Chapter 4. There appears to be little arrangement in chapter 17, although the theme of fools and foolishness is prevalent. Heim finds ten statements in the chapter relating to justice, nineteen to relationships, six to speech, and eleven intellectual evaluations. However, these themes are very much dotted throughout the proverbs here. There are small thematic links in chapter 18 on the use of speech (verses 4, 6–8, 19–21, 23), perhaps the most significant grouping, and on the behaviour of the rich (verses 11, 16, 23), the wicked (verses 3, 5) and fools (verses 2, 6, 7), but nothing substantial in the way of an overall uniting theme. Wisdom and prudence are advocated in this chapter and rich and poor are frequently mentioned; the general ethical tone and individual nature of the proverbs here comes across quite strongly.

In Proverbs 19:8, 18, 20, 27, there are four proverbs using the language of education in the manner of the instructions of chapters 1–9. In verse 1 the epithet 'my son' recalls the introduction to an instruction, as in Proverbs 1–9. A number of proverbs are paired in this chapter (e.g. verses 6–7, 11–12), but larger thematic units are absent. There are a variety of forms and yet more solid thematic clusters on the subjects of Yahweh and the king in chapters 20 and 21, likewise best discussed in Chapter 4. There are no major thematic groupings in Proverbs 22:1–16. In verse 14 the loose woman of Proverbs 1–9 is recalled and she is linked with God's anger at those who succumb to her charms. Verse 15 also recalls Proverbs 1–9's emphasis on training and discipline of the young. There is a significant link with Proverbs 1–9 here, but that has been the case at various points in these chapters and so, while a link is there, it is just one of the possible contexts for this material. This may simply be reflecting the language of wisdom and the commonality of educational and ethical purpose uniting the book of Proverbs as a whole.

CONCLUSION

I have surveyed the material looking for indicators of purpose or social context and for signs of unity. I have argued that one cannot simply assume an educational context, and, while that context is hinted at in various places, so also are legal and cultic contexts and often no particular context at all beyond the general ethical one. Structurally, while important clusters of material have been found on thematic criteria, unity has not been seen as the identifying feature of these chapters (despite Heim's protestations and his useful warnings against over-fragmentation); rather, I have found the opposite: fragmentation which reveals oral clusters. Thematic oral clusters would make sense in a primitive society in which much was being memorized. Earlier in the chapter I made the important distinction again between oral and written stages of the material and saw that the likelihood is that much of the proverbial material had oral roots. The emphasis on the family/folk/tribal context for this material has been seen to have a good deal of mileage and would appear to be the most likely origin of the material. However, there must also have been a time of writing down and one needs to make a careful distinction between the two stages. That may not have happened at one sitting, and Heim's cluster theory might well point to an interim stage. However, if there was a decisive time of writing the possibility is raised that it could have been at the time of Hezekiah (mentioned in Prov. 25:1). That possibility is explored below. In Proverbs 1–9 the religious context was marginalized in relation to the discussion of social context. This has been even more the case in reference to the proverbs in this section, and I will turn to the issue of the mention of Yahweh and place of such references in Chapter 4. Also, the issue of broader link-up with the rest of the Old Testament is raised: are we here in the heartland of distinctively Israelite wisdom that had very little to do with any influences from outside? There has been a tendency in scholarship to treat this wisdom in isolation from other genres in the Old Testament and this theory needs to be tested afresh (see Chapter 6).

CHAPTER 3

Social Context(s) in Proverbs 22:17—31:31

These parallels are impressive but do they require a theory of
dependence and an equation of settings?

(Crenshaw, 1995a: 244)

PROVERBS 22:17—24:22

Links with Amenemope

The discovery of the *Instruction of Amenemope* in the early 1920s
changed the face of wisdom studies with the noting of strong
parallels between this text and this section of Proverbs. The question
was whether direct dependence was to be found in terms of literary
comparison, and then the further question was whether one could
extrapolate a similar social context from this Egyptian court and
school text for part or whole of Proverbs. This discovery seemed to
highlight the 'foreign' nature of Israelite wisdom and its dependence
upon international models. In the Proverbs text there is seen to be a
mixing of sentence and instruction forms, and the subject matter
that is very similar to *Amenemope* is in a different order. Scholars
have generally argued for dependence of Proverbs on *Amenemope*
and not the other way around, *Amenemope* probably having been
first produced between 1200 and 1000 BC, but then circulated for
many centuries as a school text. Erman (1924) proposed emend-
ations to the Hebrew text to make it conform more closely to the
Egyptian original. He also found a reference to *Amenemope* in
Proverbs 22:20, in the reference to 'thirty' (interpreting שלישום as
שלושם), arguing that it refers to the number of 'chapters' into which
Amenemope is divided. Gressmann (1924) tried to show that Proverbs

22:17—24:22 also consists of thirty sayings.[1] Some have argued that the main parallels are in 22:17—23:14, following Erman. Whybray (1994b) argued, for example, that there are ten units in 22:17—23:11, but that there are new introductions in 23:12, 19, 22–6 and 24:3–4, 13–14, which rule out the possibility that the wider section is a unitary work. He argued that the thematic parallels end at 23:11 and that it is a miscellany of material beyond that point. Other scholars have played down the links between the two texts, Budge (1924) arguing that the advanced religious and ethical ideas found in *Amenemope* could be attributed to the influence of Semitic ideas on Egypt. This noting of the advanced religious feel of *Amenemope* compared with Proverbs is of interest.

Scholars have also advanced the theories that Proverbs 22:17—24:22 and *Amenemope* might be dependent on an older work of either Egyptian or Hebrew origin, or even that both texts derive from a common source. Perhaps most likely is that the Proverbs section is from a Hebrew translation of the Egyptian source. The uncertainties surrounding this debate make it hard to draw definite conclusions. That there is a close relationship between this text in Proverbs and *Amenemope* is established – but is the Proverbs text just a pitiful remnant of the original (Alt, 1955)? Or has the whole link been overstated and led scholars down a false path (Whybray, 1994b)? Or is there still merit in the suggestion of dependence, albeit with fairly free use by the Hebrew writer of the original source (Emerton, 2001)? If there was an international literary tradition within which borrowing took place from one culture to another, it is credible, in my view, that influence of ideas took place, particularly if this text was copied and recopied by those learning to write and to study wisdom ideas. This does not, however, mean a wholesale 'sell-out' to the Egyptian social context. One is dealing here with a more literary section of Proverbs (the closest comparison to which is Proverbs 1–9), which may well have been used in circles of the educated and formed a small part of their training. The reference in 22:29 to 'a man skilful in his work' has been taken to refer to a

---

[1] Sellin (1924) pointed out that 'thirty' (שלשום) in the Proverbs context refers to the thirty Hebrew sayings, rather than to the thirty chapters of *Amenemope*. However, he argued, the Hebrew writer has been influenced by the *Amenemope* reference to thirty.

scribe or official with a position in government service, since it describes him as standing before 'kings' and not before 'obscure men'.

Returning to the issue of purpose in terms of the social context, this section, in the specificity of the parallel, provides compelling evidence that some of the material in Proverbs was for a specific educational use and is the strongest evidence yet for some kind of school context, even if it be centred only on the training of scribes in the court. It underlines the need for an international approach that takes seriously the contribution of the ancient Near East, but the circularity of the debate also indicates caution in overextrapolating from one context to another. This section provides an insight into the formation of written stages of the book – even if it had an earlier written existence than other parts – in that it indicates that literary borrowing may have taken place and hence that the Israelite wisdom writers were aware of being in a wider educated world, and it gives more fuel to the argument that the whole book of Proverbs, at least in its final form, is the product of educated wise men who were committed to the education of the next generation.

The royal court and school

The Egyptian parallel gave rise to the suggestion that there was a class of 'the wise' in Israel at the courts of kings, who may well have been influenced by international wisdom – perhaps through the mechanisms of international diplomacy – and who had the leisure to write down material as well as acting in administrative roles. This was based on the observation that it was just such a privileged class who had written material in Egypt and elsewhere. For the training of such a class, a court school was posited in Israel, as in Egypt, where scribes would have learnt their art by copying texts such as the *Instruction of Amenemope*, which was used for millennia as a school text. Von Rad (1966a; 1972) tried to give this a historical setting at the time of Solomon. He proposed that during the period of the early monarchy a process of secularization took place in Israel, a move from a 'pan-sacral' faith to a desire to engage with the world on its own terms, to take seriously their own experiences and to acquire new knowledge. Contacts with neighbouring cultures were an important factor in the development of this new critical sense, as well as in the economic successes of the time. Von Rad believed that this new understanding of reality is reflected not just in wisdom texts, but also in narrative texts such as the Succession Narrative (2 Sam. 6 to 1 Kings 2) and the Joseph story in Genesis 37–50. Heaton's influential book *Solomon's New Men* (1974) set out the detail of this possible reconstruction. He pointed to the list of Solomon's officials in 1 Kings 4:1–19 and argued that the account given there of the provisioning arrangements for the palace shows that the Egyptian system was adopted in Israel. He explored the variety of roles played by scribes at the courts of Egypt and Mesopotamia and extrapolated from these to the Israelite context.[2]

More recently, Brueggemann (1972, chapters 3–5) has seen the major time of development of the state as the time of David, but he also maintains that Israel's emergence as a state under Solomon brought about a profound change in the nation and its culture. He writes: 'what von Rad has grasped . . . are the modifications in public life, political power, social organization, ideology, technology, and its management that accompanied, permitted and required a shift in intellectual perspective' (1990: 119). The link to Solomon is clearly stated in the superscriptions of Proverbs (1:1; 10:1; 25:1), and his role in promoting wisdom has been inferred from passages such as 1 Kings 4:29–34: 'Solomon's wisdom surpassed the wisdom of all the people of the east, and all the wisdom of Egypt . . . He also uttered three thousand proverbs . . .'[3] And yet there are other royal attributions and hence other indicators of royal connections, notably the additional mention in Proverbs 25:1 of King Hezekiah and his 'men' who were probably royal scribes, and mention of a queen who gave the instruction in 31:1 to her son, Lemuel. Scott (1985) has especially emphasized the reign of Hezekiah and saw that period, rather than the time of Solomon, as the time of fresh cultural and literary activity in Israel. This was backed up by arguments from archaeology that little written evidence of a great Solomonic enlightenment has been found, most written material having come from a period after that of Solomon.

---

[2] See discussion of parallels between offices held in foreign lands and in Israel in Ahlström, 1982.

[3] Alt (1976) argued that Solomonic wisdom consisted of the enumeration of types, known from Egypt and Babylon, as described in the Deuteronomistic History.

Blenkinsopp (1997), using archaeological evidence and socio-logical analysis, stresses that the basic requisites for statehood, including a minimum level of literacy, were not fully in place until eighth century B C. He too puts an emphasis on the reign of Hezekiah (1995b: 32–4) as the possible historical context for a written stage of the material. This is a move towards trying to date the development of ideas in a manner similar to that promoted by the source critics of the late nineteenth century and yet from a more sociological angle. Blenkinsopp (1995b) makes the point, as does Perdue (1997) in relation to Proverbs 1–9, that ideas and institutions belong together and that they do not exist in a vacuum.[4] In *Wisdom and Law*, Blenkinsopp argues for a large, centralized administration under the monarchy, with scribes, counsellors, secretaries and recorders, who 'had to be educated and socialized into the internationally accepted ethos and etiquette of public life. Much of the instructional and aphoristic material in Proverbs was written with this educational purpose in view' (1995a: 6). He quotes the evidence of Jeremiah 18:18 as suggesting a class of sages and argues for scribal schools to prepare the sons of the well-to-do for public service or life at court.

Royal connections are clearly not anathema to Proverbs, and yet the question remains whether this material belongs to the royal court in the first place and to a court school in the second. Heaton stated, perhaps rather sweepingly: 'Israel soon discovered that a highly centralised state cannot be run without a civil service, and that a civil service cannot be maintained without schools to train its recruits' (1974: 12). Another point is that the diversity of Egyptian instructions shows that wisdom literature was not necessarily always associated with royal scribes; there seems to have been a local and private element to some of them, and by the late period they appear to have been written by fairly lowly scribes, notably the author of

---

[4] Source-critical method has largely fallen from favour in much recent scholarship, in particular the attempt to link different sources, e.g. J, E, D and P in the Pentateuch, to different historical periods in the development of a culture and of its accompanying ideas. However, proponents of a more sociological method assert that ideas and institutions belong inextricably together, so that one cannot speak of a set of ideas without looking for a circumstance or context that gave rise to it. Although the categories are not literary ones, it seems to me that similar links are being made.

Amenemope itself, who was a fairly lowly figure. Some scholars, disheartened by the Egyptian evidence, turned to other centres of wisdom, such as Mesopotamia, where there were court schools and administrators. What is unclear is whether wisdom literature was the preserve of such groups – whether it perhaps passed through their hands at a writing stage – or whether in fact this supposition has led scholars down a false track. It is clear that only educated people could have compiled the written form of the proverbial material, whatever its oral roots, and so fairly elevated circles can be posited. But how far this was a restricted court group is hard to prove. In Mesopotamia, by comparison, it was hard to draw any hard and fast lines between scribes and priests; apparently, religious life was more tied to ethical living, and we know that the lament over the human condition (cf. Job) was a popular form. This raises the further question of whether extrapolation from one cultural context to another is an acceptable method of approach.

Relying on the evidence from Proverbs alone, would such courtly conclusions be obvious? Although there are references throughout the Proverbs to a king or ruler (14:28, 35; 16:10, 12, 13–15; 20:8, 26, 28; 21:1, 30–1; 22:11, 29; 24:21–2; 25:2–6; 28:15–16; 29:4, 14; 30:27–8, 31), some of which are critical of him, it is hard to argue that the whole book is imbued with a court setting. Humphreys (1978) argues for this, propounding a theory of 'the wise courtier' in Proverbs, and Malchow (1938) regarded Proverbs 29 as a manual for kings on the basis of Proverbs 29:4, 14. Whybray (1990) is against an explicit court context. That there was a separate class of 'the wise' who operated at court as argued by McKane (1965), largely on the evidence of neighbouring countries, has also been brought into question (Whybray, 1974). McKane argued that just as Pharaoh had his 'wise counsellors' and Babylonia had its 'wise men', so Israelite scribes had easy access to the king and moved among 'princes' (such as Elishama and others in Jer. 36). He wrote: 'The wisdom literature is, for the most part, a product . . . of men of affairs in high places of state, and the literature in some of its forms bears the marks of its close association with those who exercise the skills of statecraft' (1965: 44). There were clearly wise individuals, but the idea that they formed a distinct class – the most compelling evidence being found in Isaiah (5:21; 29:14) and Jeremiah (8:8–9; 9:23; 18:18) as part of a polemic against wisdom – is still debated in recent scholarship. Weeks (1994, chapter 5), for example, argues against the idea of a class of the wise and shows how the relevant passages from the prophets do not lead to such a conclusion. Blenkinsopp (1995b), following Whybray (1974), prefers to speak of an intellectual tradition, but argues that in later wisdom literature, such as Ecclesiastes 12:9, there is an emerging sense of an intellectual class of teachers.

Having had a more abstract discussion of whether a court context is appropriate for any of Proverbs, it is as well to pause in this section to see whether there is any evidence for this context in this part of the Proverbs text, beyond the possible *Amenemope* parallel context. Proverbs 22:29 praises skill that leads a person to the courts of kings and could be a reference to a skilful artisan. There are possible links, too, with Proverbs 23:1–3, 6–8, which follow and which speak of ways of behaviour in polite society. Proverbs 23:1–3 opens with three admonitions regarding etiquette: 'When you sit down to eat with a ruler, observe carefully what is before you; and put a knife to your throat if you are a man given to appetite. Do not desire his delicacies, for they are deceptive food.' This passage has often been quoted in connection with establishing a court context for at least parts of Proverbs. It certainly seems to indicate such a setting, and yet the moral drawn is a somewhat more general one. The warning is to watch out for someone in a senior position to you who may be out to trick you. There is a reason for his generosity: he wants something from you. Therefore, too much gluttony in his presence might signify a naivety and a willingness to be under his control. The need for restraint when eating is recommended, a theme found elsewhere in Proverbs, but within the wider context of this particular situation. In 23:6–8 the same dinner-party situation as earlier is recalled in reference to a person who seems to be generous, but is not so in reality. Here the status of the person is not stressed. Proverbs 23:19–21 contains another brief instruction concerning the dangers of excessive eating and drinking, but here it is more about the poverty that may well ensue from the laziness that accompanies continuous eating and drinking. This evidence from the text is relatively sparse on which to build a theory of court connections, and yet the educational context is well established, and if that happened to link up with court circles, these few verses may indicate a link between the two social contexts.

This is the strongest evidence yet for a court school context. In relation to the wider debate about a court context for Proverbs, it is less plausible for the whole book, but can rather be seen as an important stage in the scholarly debate which has, to a certain extent, fallen from favour nowadays. However, a court school context is not ruled out in relation to Proverbs 1–9 too.

Links with Proverbs 1–9

Such has been the emphasis on parallels with *Amenemope* that little attention has been given to the link-up of these chapters with other parts of Proverbs. The instructions in this section are very similar to those of chapters 1–9, with a large number of admonitions. The section begins with an extended introduction (22:17–21) comparable to Proverbs 1:1–6. The address is to 'my son' in Proverbs 23:15, 19, 26; 24:13, 21. Proverbs 23:22 and 25 mention father and mother in the same way as Proverbs 1:8 and 6:20. There are also a number of shared words and phrases as well as thematic links, such as warnings against temptation to wicked behaviour in Proverbs 22:22–5; 23:17–18; 24:8–9 and 24:15–16 (cf. Prov. 1:10–19; 3:31–2; 4:14–19). There is one reference against associating with immoral women (23:27–8), which may recall the adulteress figure of Proverbs 7 and 9. Links can also be found here with the main maxims section in Proverbs 10:1—22:16; for instance, Proverbs 23:13–14 stresses parental discipline, a theme found in Proverbs 13:24 and 19:18.

The link between Proverbs 22:17–18 and instruction sections of Proverbs 1–9 is in fact quite striking.[5] Although 'my son' is not found here, it is clear that the educational context of father/son or else of teacher/pupil applies. Although 'the words of the wise' is a general reference, unusual in these introductions,[6] the teaching is

---

[5] For example, 'incline your ear' (הַט אָזְנְךָ) in verse 17 occurs in 4:20; 5:1; 'hear' (שמע) occurs in e.g. 4:1, 10; 'apply your mind to my knowledge' is paralleled (but not word for word) in 2:2; the essence of 'keep them within you (lit. in your heart)' (verse 18) is found in 4:21; 6:21; 7:3.

[6] In fact, the Septuagint amends to 'my words', possibly indicating an earlier version of the Hebrew.

more personalized in verse 17b with the reference to 'my knowledge'. Verse 20, with its reference to writing – the only reference in the entire book of Proverbs – is worthy of comment in that the usual admonition is to 'hear wisdom' as in verse 17. In fact, the process of hearing, memorizing, reflecting and speaking is expounded in verses 17–18, as also in *Amenemope*. Maybe there is a small witness here in verse 20 to the writing-down process; in fact, a link is usually made in this verse to the thirty sayings of *Amenemope* and little is made of the mention of writing by the teacher. We read: 'Have I not written for you thirty sayings of admonition and knowledge, to show you what is right and true, that you may give a true answer to those who sent you?' (verses 20–1). In Proverbs 22:22–3 the admonition is given a motive clause in that Yahweh will protect the poor; in verses 24–5 the warning is against encountering anger, and the (non-Yahwistic) motive clause is in verse 25 (cf. 15:18; 29:22). In Proverbs 22:26–7 there are two verses on the giving of surety which recall 6:1–5 as well as other parts of Proverbs (e.g 11:15; 17:18; 20:16 ; 27:13). Verse 28, on unjustly acquired property, stands in contrast to twenty-eight lines in *Amenemope* on the subject and how it will eventually disappear. Verse 29 praises the skill that leads a person to the courts of kings and could refer to a skilful artisan. There are possible links to Proverbs 23:1–3, 7–9, which speak of ways of behaviour in polite society.

In Proverbs 23:12—24:22 there are four references to wisdom (in 23:23; 24:3, 7; 24:14), in which wisdom is presented as an acquisition to be desired, but she is not fully personified. Proverbs 23:23 associates wisdom with parental teaching in precisely the same words as 4:5, 7; 24:3–7 is solely concerned with wisdom by which 'a house is built'; 24:14 is part of the father's advice to his son that wisdom is a desirable commodity worth finding. The second part of this section, which is less close to the Egyptian parallel (such that some scholars take the parallel only as far as 23:11), has a more distinctively Israelite flavour in its closeness to motifs in Proverbs 1–9.

A new section appears in Proverbs 23:12. It is close in sentiment to 22:17 with its positive commands and parental tone, and its terminology parallels Proverbs 1–9, notably 1:1–7. Again the close parallels within the book of Proverbs itself are striking. Proverbs 23:14 mentions Sheol as the fate that awaits those who do not learn discipline (cf. 1:12; 7:27; 9:18; 15:24). Proverbs 23:15–18 contains a standard address to a son or pupil, which has parallels in Proverbs 1–9 (2:1; 3:1; 5:1, 20; 6:1; 7:1). The reference to 'the way' in 23:19 recalls 4:11 (the way of wisdom) or 6:23 (the way of life). In 23:22–3 there is a separate saying, and again the material is reminiscent of earlier instructions in the book, particularly their introductions. The father and mother are mentioned here, as are the general merits of the acquisition of wisdom (cf. 1:2–5). Verses 24–5 do not appear to be part of the father's speech, however, and express the joy of parents when a son is wise (cf. 23:15–16). In verse 26 there is a similar parental admonition, and in verses 27–8 there are overtones of Proverbs 2:16; 5:20; 7:5 in reference to the loose woman. Importantly, many of the sentiments here are grounded in the book of Proverbs itself in that a number of comparisons can be made within the book without necessary reference to outside.

The first two verses of chapter 24 recall other verses in Proverbs, notably 23:17a and 24:19, and, in Proverbs 1–9, 1:10–19 and 3:31–2. They provide a warning concerning the attractions of evildoers. In verses 3–9 a sentence-literature style recalls other admonitions in Proverbs; for instance, in verses 3–4 the house imagery recalls 9:1–2 and 15:6 in gaining treasure. Whybray remarks that these verses 'show knowledge of various passages in earlier chapters and subtly build on them' (1994c: 344). In fact, God builds the universe by wisdom (Prov. 3:19–20; 8:22–31). Proverbs 24:13–14 goes back to the theme of acquiring wisdom; this abstract calling to observe wisdom in general terms seems to be a keynote of this section. The address in verse 13 is to 'my son'. The instructions of chapters 1–9 are again recalled, as are Proverbs 23:15, 19.

I have deliberately avoided discussion of the links with *Amenemope* in the analysis of these verses in order to find a different angle on the text. It would seem that much of the material is echoed elsewhere in Proverbs, notably in chapters 1–9, and that a characteristic of this section is to muse on the value of wisdom, with hints of its educational value again echoing the instructions of chapters 1–9. This raises the question of the priority of material here. Is this an early or late section, and can one establish any lines of dependence? The Egyptian link, as with Proverbs 1–9, might seem to indicate pre-exilic influence, and yet this is a more literary product that indeed, within its chapters, indicates a scribal context. Might one suggest earlier roots for much of the material, pulled together in more literary circles? Or might one wish to establish priority of this section over other parts? Could this section have provided some inspiration for Proverbs 1–9? Might it have taken some inspiration from older sections of Proverbs as in 10:1—22:16? There is plausible evidence here of an educational context for this wisdom which links up with the instruction texts of Proverbs 1–9. This, like *Amenemope*, may have been a text that circulated for some centuries in a formal school context and was written down in Proverbs only at a late stage in its circulation. One wonders if there is a parallel to be drawn here with the way the instruction texts reached Proverbs 1–9: might they, too, have been used in an original educational environment of family or school for some years before being encapsulated in writing in Proverbs 1–9 and put in a new theological context? I would suggest that this is entirely possible. In the next chapter I will explore references to Yahweh in the material and consider the question of whether religious shaping can be found at an early stage in the material's development. In Chapter 6 I will explore the little-discussed area of possible echoes of other Old Testament texts or ideas. These explorations will, I hope, add some further focus to my deliberations here about social context.

PROVERBS 24:23–34

This is not a main section of Proverbs, but if I am to be thorough in my coverage of the book it deserves a mention. It may be a separate collection because it begins with the heading 'These are the sayings of the wise' (verse 23), and it could be an appendix either to the previous section or to the main section of Proverbs 10:1—22:16. In the Septuagint it is placed after Proverbs 30:14. The attribution to 'the wise' (לחכמים) is unusually general. The section is a miscellany of verses of a generally ethical nature. Verse 26 emphasizes the need to be truthful, and the reference to lips is a reminder of the communication theme in Proverbs. Verse 27 speaks of forward planning, another common proverbial theme – in this case building a house with adequate preparation. In fact, verses 27–9 are the only actual admonitions on the topics of wise husbandry (verse 27), honest testimony (verse 28) and abstention from personal vengeance (verse 29). The background is an agricultural one (in particular in verses 27, 30–4), and there is an overall concern with just utterance (verses 23b–26, 28–9). Verses 30–4 are a moral tale or short autobiographical narrative in the first person singular (like Prov. 4:3ff.); it again echoes a familiar theme in Proverbs, particularly in the main sayings section of 10:1—22:16. Verses 33–4 are virtually identical with Proverbs 6:10–11. There are no references to wisdom or to Yahweh in this section, and this probably belongs best as an appendix to Proverbs 10:1—22:16, where similar themes occur. This section does not take me much further in my discussion of social context, but it does indicate that sayings were originally separate and then were brought together, often, but not always, thematically.

PROVERBS 25–9

Analysis of the section

This is another independent collection, as indicated by the attribution to the 'men of Hezekiah' who 'copied' this material (although not forgetting the mention of Solomon): 'These also are proverbs of Solomon which the men of Hezekiah, King of Judah, copied' (Prov. 25:1). This verse indicates that the collecting process may have been more a matter of copying pre-existent oral or written material rather than of constructing something new. The heading has given another possibility for a royal context apart from that of Solomon, and it is suggested that at this time of national revival under Hezekiah in the seventh century B C there may have been a fresh interest in gathering this material together. This emphasizes once again the written stage. However, the material, as with Proverbs 10:1—22:16, may well have been oral, circulating in family or tribe, before it came to form part of this collection. Naré (1986), in a work comparing the oral proverbs of his people, the Mossi of Upper Volta, with Proverbs 25–9, found considerable formal and thematic links. He also found religious links between this section and the Mossi belief in a universal creator God and made the point that when the Mossi are converted to either Christianity or Islam they are not conscious of encountering a new God, but only of a fuller revelation of the God they already know through these maxims. This possibility of integration with other areas implicitly is an interesting one.

Most proverbs in this section are again of a general ethical type, which indicates possible contexts broader than just the educational one. These may not all be isolated proverbs. Scholars such as van Leeuwen (1988) have attempted to demonstrate the existence of large units or poems with patterns of adjacent couplets in chapters 25–7. There is little evidence in this section for a school context, unless a court reference is taken to mean that there was a school at court at which these 'men' of Hezekiah taught. A wider group of counsellors could be indicated. It would seem from this evidence that the writing down of material was an important court activity and scholars know that this was the case from other cultures (e.g. Sumerian; see Kramer, 1958; 1961). It is possible that scholars have overstated the school context and understated the scribal role of educated courtiers here in relation to the written stage of material.

In structural terms, a subdivision is sometimes made in this section between chapters 25–7 and 28–9 on the grounds that the character of the chapters is sufficiently different to denote two separate collections. Could it be that one is in danger of overgeneralizing with regard to context even here, when speaking collectively of Hezekiah's men? It is true that chapters 25–7 are characterized by the virtual absence of references to Yahweh, by a large number of similes and metaphors, and by the relative absence of antithetical parallelism, while they have a relatively high number of admonitions. Chapters 28–9, on the other hand, possess the contrary characteristics, notably mention of Yahweh, few metaphors and a good deal of antithetic parallelism. Also, there is a preoccupation with the topic of the alternate rise to and fall from power of the righteous and the wicked respectively (mentioned four times in these two chapters and rarely elsewhere). Some scholars have sought to subdivide these chapters even further, van Leewen suggesting that verses 2–27 of chapter 25 constitutes a single 'proverbs poem' with an introduction (verses 2–5), part one (verses 6–16) and part two (verses 17–27). Its subject matter is thought to be advice to courtiers, based on the observation that verses 1–7 refer to kings and the heading in verse 1 states that the proverbs were collected for King Hezekiah by his 'men'. The weakness in this view, however, is that in the rest of the chapter there are no references to kings (except to a 'ruler' in verse 15), and that the proverbs are of a general nature, so that they could refer to anyone, not just courtiers.[7] Chapter 26 seems to have a close structural unity, with three distinct thematically linked sections: verses 1–12 that deal with the fool, verses 13–16 that deal with the lazy person, and verses 17–28 that deal with people best avoided who are a danger to the community. They may have been united by the theme of different types of character that one might meet in a community. Chapter 27 is more disjointed and seems to be a compendium of advice, the topic of friendship playing a dominant role in verses 1–10. Chapter 28 could have been an independent instruction, most proverbs being of an ethical nature, and the word תורה ('teaching' or 'law') occurs frequently–four times in verses 4, 7 and 9 (and elsewhere in the sentence literature only in Prov. 13:13 and 29:18). There are also two references to wisdom: a warning against being wise in one's own eyes in verse 11, and a commendation of the one 'who walks in wisdom' in verse 26. These qualities seem to link the chapter with the emphases found in Proverbs 1–9 that have a connection with law (cf. 3:1; 4:2; 6:20–1; 7:2–3) and reflect on the nature of wisdom. Chapter 29 is particularly repetitious of proverbs that have appeared previously and one gets the feeling that originality is running dry. It is significant that in this chapter there is a proverb that mentions not just law, but also prophecy: 'Where there is no prophecy, the people cast off restraint, but happy are those who keep the law' (Prov. 29:18). I take this to be a veiled way of saying that prophecy is a good thing because it keeps people in check, and that without it they are unrestrained; the law also has this restraining effect. This proverb indirectly links up with the proverbs about discipline found here, but it is both unusual and fascinating that the reference to wider areas of Israelite life is made (see Chapter 6). There is also mention in Proverbs 29:25 of the need to trust God, and other references to Yahweh, in verses 13 and 26, relate to the broader question of how religious this material is (which I will address in the next chapter).

However, even if they were once separate collections, they have been united now under the heading in Proverbs 25:1, which suggests

---

[7] See Dell, 1998, for further discussion of the royal sayings.

editorial unification of these chapters, if rather clumsy. Are these chapters to be aligned with Proverbs 1–9 in some way and regarded as later in origin, or are they witness to the fact that the concerns they display and the topics they treat permeated the proverbial enterprise at all stages? The latter option seems more plausible to me, especially in the light of significant links with Proverbs 10:1—22:16 rather than with Proverbs 1–9, as I shall discuss next.

LINKS WITH PROVERBS 10:1—22:16

Many of the same topics covered in Proverbs 10:1—22:16, such as the nature of kingship, behaviour in the lawcourt, the importance of the spoken word and so on, appear in chapter 25. For example, compare verse 5 with 16:12; verse 11 with 15:23; verse 13 with 13:17; verse 15 with 15:1; verse 24 with 21:9; verse 25 with 13:17a and 15:30; and verse 28 with 14:29, 16:32 and 17:27. Verse 2 associates kings with God and has affinities with other royal proverbs. The reference here is to God as אלהים, which is rare in the book, and it is probably making a general contrast between God and kings; compare Proverbs 2:5, where 'fear of Yahweh' and 'knowledge of God' are parallel descriptions. Verses 11–14 contain four metaphorical proverbs all concerned with the spoken word. Verse 15 concerns the persuasive power of speech; compare Proverbs 11:14 and 15:22 (cf. Hos. 2:16–17). Verse 16 makes a comparison with honey, as do Proverbs 16:24 and 24:13. This chapter contains many echoes of proverbs from the main sayings collection, these being examples. Verses 21–2 concern kindness towards an enemy (cf. Prov. 19:11b; 20:22; 24:17, 19; Lev. 19:17–18). In verses 23–8 paired proverbs are featured. Verse 24 recalls Proverbs 21:9, with which it is virtually identical, and verse 25 recalls Proverbs 13:17 and 15:30. Verse 26 speaks of a righteous man giving way to the wicked (cf. 12:3 and Ps. 55:22 which express the opposite sentiment of the steadfastness of the righteous). Verse 27 recalls 25:15–16, and verse 28 recalls Proverbs 14:29; 16:32 and 17:27.

There are quite a few echoes of other texts in Proverbs in chapter 26. I have already mentioned the three thematically linked sections on the fool, the lazy and those best avoided. Proverbs 26:1 picks up 25:27 and 25:2. Something being 'not fitting' for a fool is found in Proverbs 17:7; 19:10 and 30:21–3. Verse 3 can be compared to

Proverbs 10:13 and Psalm 32:9. Verse 4–5 are two proverbs put together, containing contrary advice, recalling this kind of technique in Ecclesiastes. Verse 6 recalls Proverbs 10:26, and in verses 7b and 9 the second line is identical. Verse 8 recalls verse 1 of the same chapter (and the imagery of stones is also found in Isa. 8:14). Verse 12 contains the phrase 'wise in his own eyes', which is a kind of leitmotiv in this chapter, occurring in verses 5 and 16 also. It can be used of the fool, but its use is not restricted to him alone (cf. Prov. 3:7; 28:11). Verses 13–16 treat the sluggard, also wise in his own eyes (verse 16) and so a close relative of the fool. Verse 13 is a variant of 22:13, and verse 15 of 19:24. Proverbs 26:22 recalls 18:8.

In chapter 27, friendship is the most treated topic. Verse 7 mentions honey (cf. 16:24; 24:13; 25;16, 27). In verses 11–22 a young man is addressed as 'my son' and an educational context is again indicated. Proverbs 27:11a strongly resembles 23:15; in fact, of eleven verses in 12–22, four are variants or reminiscences of proverbs occurring in earlier chapters of the sentence literature. Verse 12 recalls 22:3; verse 13, 20:16; verse 15, 19:13; verse 21a, 17:3a. Verse 15 speaks of a contentious woman, recalling not only 19:13 but also 21:9, 19; 25:24. Verse 21b is paralleled in 12:8a.

In chapter 28, where law and wisdom feature, there is a similar pattern of repeated proverbs or parts of proverbs. In Proverbs 28:6 the first line is identical with 19:1a and the second is a variant of 19:1b. In verse 7 the law is associated with wisdom in that the one who keeps the law is wise (cf. 10:1; 27:11; cf. Deut. 21:18–21). Verse 10 expresses the doctrine of just retribution, the second line being a variant of 26:27a. The mention of a 'goodly inheritance' recalls 3:35. In verse 11 the rich/poor contrast is paralleled in 10:15 (in Prov. 18:11, another parallel, just the rich are mentioned). Verse 12 is a partial variant of verse 28 (cf. 29:2), and the reference to glory (תפארת) recalls 17:6 and 20:29. In verses 15–16 the rule of the wicked is described, following verse 12b (cf. Ezek. 32:2; 1 Sam. 17:34–5, 37; Amos 5:19). This recalls other proverbs critical of oppressive rulers, in 17:7; 29:4, 26. In verses 18–20 the theme of the consequences of acceptable and unacceptable behaviour continues. Verse 19 is a variant of 12:11, while verse 20 can be compared with 13:11 and 20:21. In verse 21 the first line is a variant of 24:23b, while in verse 23 comparisons can be drawn with 9:8; 19:25; 25:12 and 27:5. The expression 'flatter with his tongue' recalls the 'smooth words' of the loose woman in 2:16 and 7:5. In verse 24 parallels can be drawn with 19:26 and 20:20 (and the use of 'companion' recalls Isa. 1:23; Ps. 119:63). In verse 25, the context of the 'greedy man who stirs up strife' is given (a description applied to the hot-tempered man in Prov. 15:18), and then he is compared to the one who trusts God, a line found in 16:20b and 29:25b (cf. Hab. 2:5). In 11:25 the 'liberal man' will be enriched and in 13:4 the 'diligent' is the referent. It looks as if phrases are starting to be used interchangeably. In this section greed is the theme and so the greedy man becomes the main referent. Verse 27 can be compared to 11:24–5; 19:17; 22:9. One wonders from whom the curse proceeds; God is a possibility (as in 3:33), or perhaps the poor themselves. Verse 28 is paralleled in 29:2 and 29:16.

There is a wide range of subject matter in chapter 29 and it is somewhat repetitive of what has gone before. Alonso-Schökel (1968) observed that in this chapter almost all the sayings are repetitions or variations of proverbs that have appeared previously. This is a slight overstatement, but it gets the point across. As in other parts of Proverbs, here is an unconnected string of maxims with no obvious link in subject matter; there has been little concern on the part of editors to unify them in a thematic way. However, clusters of related subject matter can be found, as in the other main section of unconnected maxims in Proverbs 10:1—22:16. There is concern with opposites: the stubborn person whose stubbornness is broken (29:1), and love of wisdom versus love of prostitutes (19:3), for example. Quite a few are single-line or single-thought sayings rather than double, and they do not involve a contrast; rather they make an observation, as in 29:5: 'A man who flatters his neighbour spreads a net for his neighbour's feet', and verses 9–10, 12–14. Discipline seems to be a minor theme of the chapter in verses 1, 15, 17, 19, 21, with a bearing on the education of children in verses 15 and 17 (also verse 3). Contrasts, on various subjects, between the righteous and the wicked feature (verses 2, 6, 7, 16, 27), and closely related to this are contrasts between wise and foolish behaviour (verses 3, 8–9, 11). One area of wise and foolish behaviour is in the administration of justice, which is a particular concern here (verses 2, 4, 7, 9, 12, 13–14, 16, 26). There are also a few proverbs on anger (verses 8, 9, 11, 22). There are three references to the poor in verses 7, 13 and 14. The rest simply stand alone in their treatment of a subject. The references to the king in 29:4, 14 are of interest in connection with the discussion of social context; it is also noteworthy that they contain a questioning note about the possible behaviour of the king, unlike more submissive and admiring references elsewhere.

The finding that many of the proverbs in Proverbs 25–9 are repeats of other proverbs or close variations on them provides a fresh angle on the role of the 'men of Hezekiah' mentioned in 25:1. It is said that they 'copied' 'other proverbs of Solomon' – one keynote of this section is unoriginality! This may suggest that they had more of an editorial than a creative role and it may indicate that they collected together more than just this section (although there is no actual evidence for this). What is likely, however, is that the proverbs contained in 10:1—22:16, and certainly those quoted in these lines, preceded those in chapters 25–9. The only other possibility is oral variation. There are here some hints of issues raised in Proverbs 1–9 too, suggesting that we are seeing wisdom at a point of development between the original oral proverbs and the collecting and writing-down process. McKane's (1986–96) image of a 'rolling corpus' (a phrase coined in reference to Jeremiah and the process of Deuteronomic redaction) comes to mind here in that the different sections of Proverbs are revealing various stages of a complex process of oral to literary, and literary in various stages, that is almost impossible to reconstruct with any certainty, but which would seem to be evidenced by overlap between the different sections.

PROVERBS 30

Proverbs 30:1–14

The title of this section is 'The words of Agur, son of Jakeh of Massa' (verse 1a). Scholars do not know to whom these names refer and the likelihood is that they are not Israelite. The designation 'of Massa', probably the north Arabian tribe mentioned in Genesis 25:14 and 1 Chronicles 1:30 as a son of Ishmael (alternatively translated 'the oracle'), would seem to confirm this. It is significant that this section is introduced as the wisdom of a particular person. It is sometimes pointed out that it is a strange omission that

Proverbs 22:17—24:22 is not so introduced, and yet its Egyptian parallel, *Amenemope*, is so designated. However, it is not clear how much of this chapter is from Agur; only the first three verses seem to relate specifically to the experience of an individual. This section has been seen as a series of unrelated short pieces or as a dialogue between more orthodox and less orthodox positions (i.e. scepticism in verses 1b–4, orthodox reply in verses 5–6, conclusion in 7–9[8]). There are several allusions in these verses to other Old Testament texts (see Chapter 6). Verses 10–14 have the nature of warnings to those who perpetuate wrongdoing, and they contain a number of lone proverbs. Verse 4 echoes the rhetorical questions of Job 38 when God appears in the whirlwind to challenge Job; and verses 7–9 have a more religious character than most of the proverbs and resemble theological discussion, as in Job, on the nature of the relationship between God and man. It may be that this passage is later and reflects some concern about how wisdom is regarded in the canon (Moore, 1994), echoing the insufficiency of human knowledge of wisdom and stressing the God-given nature of real knowledge. The social context is almost unfathomable; it has the character of a personal reminiscence by a foreign wise person, although its nature as dialogue and its theological maturity bring it in many ways closer to the later wisdom books of Job and Ecclesiastes than to the book of Proverbs. The prayer in verses 7–9 seems to reject both wealth and poverty as likely to corrupt and instead asks for a bare sufficiency; this does not sound quite at home in royal circles!

Proverbs 30:15–33

This section is different again, consisting almost entirely of short numerical proverbs that list unlike phenomena (cf. Prov. 6:16–19; cf. Amos 1:1—2:16). They form a series of relatively unconnected clusters of sayings, the only uniting feature being the numerical aspect. They do not appear to be in any particular order, and examples from natural phenomena are intermingled with examples

---

[8] E.g. Gemser, 1938.

of human behaviour; in two examples, references to animals reach a climax in the final human item (verses 18–19 and 29–31). Roth (1965) saw these verses as graded numerical sayings and compared these proverbs with Solomon's knowledge of trees and animals as described in 1 Kings 5:1ff., and one might also draw comparisons with the listing of animals in the divine speeches of Job 38–41. They might be seen in connection with an international list-making tendency, which resulted in texts known as 'onomastica'. These Egyptian and Mesopotamian texts sought to list and classify phenomena in an encyclopaedic fashion in order to understand the world. The question is raised about the purpose of these verses. Are they a pre-scientific attempt at ordering? Are they for entertainment purposes[9] or educational ones? Or do they serve to stress that God is ultimately in control of ordering an apparently disorganized world? Of course, one must remember that the original purpose of these verses might have been different from their purpose as a collection. Are they an Israelite version of another ancient Near Eastern genre? Or are they simply observations about human character in relation to nature and animals, perhaps with a note of wonder at the implicit order behind completely unlike items? The questions remain, but it is of interest that the religious dimension is not lacking in that, implicitly, the thread that holds these verses together is the idea of God's control of the order of creation. The social context here, at least in its final form, is possibly collected material for use by the educated–by scribes or in schools if such existed – but these proverbs may well have circulated in an oral pre-literary form.

PROVERBS 31

Proverbs 31:1–9

Like the last chapter, this chapter falls into two halves and there is a sense of increasing fragmentation of the book of Proverbs. This may well suggest that these last two sections are later additions or at least

[9] Scholars have noted the playfulness and irony in this section, especially in verses 29–31 (seen by McKane [1970] as social satire); in verses 24–8, with the description of a lizard as found in king's palaces as wise; and in verses 29–31, with the description of a king's self-important striding before his people.

that they circulated relatively independently until a fairly late stage. The heading here is 'The words of Lemuel, King of Massa', and this is a king taught by his mother. This is an instruction or set of precepts given by mother to son, and queen mother at that. This social context is spelt out here and provides good evidence of a court context very much akin to the Egyptian instruction context. This instruction could well be from court circles, as it contains a series of admonitions to a young king about his duties, which are primarily of a judicial nature. He is to avoid involvement with women who may exercise a pernicious influence upon him, and keep sober so that his judgement may not be impaired; and, as judge of his people, he is to maintain the legal rights of the poor and helpless, a principal duty of ancient Near Eastern kings. In fact, this has been compared in particular to the *Instruction of King Amenemhet* to his son and to the *Instruction for King Merikare*. The major difference, though, is that this is an instruction from a woman – unique among ancient Near Eastern instructions! This harks back to mention of the role of the mother in education in Proverbs 1–9 and would seem to link up with the second part of the chapter (31:10–31) with its description of a good wife. The only oddity here is verses 6–7, which treat the problem of strong drink, a topic which seems out of place here in an instruction which, in the main, commends the virtues of kings (although there is a warning to Lemuel from his mother not to give his strength to women) – a digression perhaps inspired by the reference to drinking in verse 5. A question that interests scholars about this section is its framing role in the book of Proverbs and possible links with chapters 1–9 in the motifs of a mother's instruction. These possible links with chapters 1–9 are even more pronounced when turning to the second half of the chapter.

Proverbs 31:10–31

This last section of Proverbs is unusual because it is an acrostic poem.[10] It describes the capable wife in twenty-two verses, each beginning with a different letter of the Hebrew alphabet. The

---

[10] Cf. acrostic poems in, e.g., Lam. 3 and in Pss. 25; 119.

description focuses on the worth of the wife and her devotion to her husband and then on the domestic work that she does. However, she is also involved in wider administrative concerns, such as the buying of a field and the planting of a vineyard. She is a real worker, who sells merchandise and works at night. helps the poor, sews and sells her products and, perhaps most important of all, in verse 30 she fears the Lord. The purpose of this section seems simply to be the listing of qualities in a woman that a man ought to look for when it comes to choosing a wife; discussion of good and bad women from a man's point of view runs through the wisdom literature, both Israelite and Egyptian.[11] Or perhaps, as has been suggested by Crook (1954), it is a handbook for marriageable young girls on the ideal towards which they must strive. Another idea (e.g. McCreesh, 1985) is that this ideal figure goes beyond what any real woman could aspire to and so might be personified Wisdom herself. There are close links with the portrayal of Wisdom in Proverbs 3:13–20 in particular. Whybray (1990), on the other hand, sees Proverbs 31:10–31 as a picture of a well-to-do family, neither aristocratic nor royal, which has achieved prosperity and stability through decent and honest hard work, the very ideal strived for in Proverbs 10:1— 22:16 and 28:19–20. He therefore draws closer links with other parts of Proverbs than with chapters 1–9.

The wife figure here has, in recent scholarly study, been seen as an allegory of the figure of Wisdom, especially as portrayed in 9:1–6 (first suggested by Barucq, 1964). This was expanded upon by Jacob (1971), who notes that there are certain points of similarity, such as the references to Wisdom's house (cf. Prov. 9:1; 14:1; 24:3) and to her workmanlike skill (cf. Prov. 8:30 – but only if one reads 'master worker'). The reference to crossing the sea and bringing food from afar may indicate the international nature of wisdom teaching. The references to the husband's prominence in local politics (verse 23) and to his dependence on his wife (although he is important enough to 'sit with the elders of the land'), and the account of her administrative ability, might reflect the claim that Wisdom controls human

---

[11] For example, the *Instruction of Ptahhotep* (third millennium BC) discusses the fact that the choice of a suitable wife was a matter of great importance to a man with regard to both his domestic happiness and his career.

affairs and that kings rule at her discretion (8:15–16). In verse 31 the 'deeds' that praise the wife 'in the gates' are taken to refer to the works of creation. This would give a neatness to its positioning at the end of the book as a kind of summary of the main advantages of Wisdom, paralleling Proverbs 1–9. The main question is why the acrostic form is used. Is this evidence of a mnemonic device for easy learning and hence of an oral piece? Or is this a literary phenom-enon – a game for the educated to see how cleverly they can piece together an acrostic with a consistent theme? One idea of the acrostic is to indicate completeness in the treatment of a topic; ano-ther seems to be authorial skill whether at the oral or written stage, and it has even been suggested that the letters were seen to have magical significance. The genre is old, found in Akkadian literature, a well-known example being the Babylonian Theodicy (c. 1000 B C). An acrostic can have a lack of thematic sequence and a repetitious quality because of the strictures of the form, but this is a particularly good example of thematic consistency.

A fascinating suggestion has been made by Wolters (1988), that this poem is formally a 'hymn' or 'song of praise' according to Gunkel's form-critical analysis.[12] It has the characteristic structure of introduction, with announcement of praise to be given and recipient (verses 10–12); recounting the subject's valiant deeds (verses 13–27); and concluding exhortation to the audience to join in praise (verses 28–31; cf. hymns to Yahweh such as Pss. 145 and 150). These hymns are normally in honour of Yahweh, and so to have a hymn in honour of a human being is unusual; however, if it refers to personified Wisdom it is more in keeping with the hymn of Prov-erbs 8:22–31. The question is raised whether the poem is an allegory of Wisdom or whether in fact the capable wife, as described, should be seen as in herself an embodiment of what it is to be wise. It may have been placed at the end of Proverbs to sum up its teaching, but it may alternatively have had an earlier life. The family described in the poem are clearly relatively well-to-do, but not of the highest class. There is mention of Yahweh in verse 30, which adds a religious note to the poem, but the rest lacks those elements.

---

[12] Gunkel, 1967.

CONCLUSION TO CHAPTERS 1–3

This final section of Proverbs is very diverse in character, but what has been most striking is that Proverbs 22:16—24:22 seems to be closely related to the concerns and images of Proverbs 1–9, and that 25–9 are quite repetitive of 10:1—22:16. The other, smaller, collections stand alone, but each has its own character. These other sections can be loosely aligned contextually, thematically and in terms of character with the main sections of Proverbs, so that one could add to Proverbs 1–9 not just 22:17—24:22, but also chapter 31 with its instruction to a king and its acrostic poem, which could well be the products of the educated and could also relate to the Wisdom portrayal in Proverbs 1–9 and function as an epilogue of a kind. Proverbs 30:1–14 also seems to indicate a court context and has the nature of a more theological debate, perhaps to be compared with the more mature theological reflection of chapters 1–9. Proverbs 24:23–34 can also be ranged together with both 10:1—22:17, and chapters 25–9, since the former section has the same character of independent ethical sayings, possibly formulated in an oral context originally and then collected together later. Proverbs 30:15–33 would also seem to fit in here, although the wisdom more descriptive and of a nature type. These similarities indicate that it would be reasonable to posit at least two distinct social contexts for different sections. The first is more educational, with possible links to school life, taking considerable inspiration from Egyptian circles. The second is the more homegrown Israelite maxim-making from family/folk/tribal settings.

Proverbs 1–9; 22:17—24:22; 30:1–14; 31

The study of these sections has clearly been illuminated by Egyptian parallels, which have stressed, above all, the educational context of the instruction material. That some kind of teaching activity went on is evident, whether that was at home or in a school. Although many of the instructions in chapters 1–9 suggest a home context, with the references to father, mother and son, other parts of the material (30; 31) and the parallel with a school text from Egypt in 22:17—24:22 suggest a more formal educational setting. It may be that one can accommodate both by positing some development from a more informal family setting to the eventual putting down in writing by the educated. But it is probably not as simple as that, and what we have here is evidence of different contexts in which education took place. After all, it was of prime importance that kings and those around them were educated, and the need for written material recording the events of a reign, as well as material for educational and even entertainment purposes, would be great. The evidence of a court context from Proverbs 31:1–9 seems to me to have been underplayed in the discussion by scholars; it provides strong evidence of a court setting for a part of the book of Proverbs. Schooling may have been going on at different levels of home and local community and, in a more high-profile sense, at the court of the king in the training of high-flying young men destined for powerful positions in society one day.

Proverbs 10:1—22:16; 24:23–34; 25–9; 30:15–33

In these sections of Proverbs one gets the sense that one is going back to an older tradition of sayings that may have circulated in an oral tradition before they were set down in writing. This is to tune in, not just to an educational context, but to a broader ethical one that is of interest to any and all as they seek to understand life. There are hints of the treatment of these sayings in more elevated circles, such as the court of Hezekiah, but it is to the copying stage that Proverbs 25:1 refers. In Proverbs 30:15–33 these verses hark back to the kind of nature wisdom in which Solomon was said to be well versed (1 Kings 5), and so may also have retained here an important part of the agenda of those who saw themselves as 'wise'. It was not just kings who could be wise; it was open to all and everyone who sought to better themselves and to tune into God's creative purpose.

With these two distinctions in mind between sections of material in Proverbs and possible corresponding social context(s), I shall move on to more theological concerns and return to the matter of social context in the Conclusion. In the next chapter, then, I will explore the references to Yahweh, and in the following one echoes of other Old Testament ideas in passages in Proverbs.

CHAPTER 4

Mention of Yahweh in Proverbs

> Thus the often assumed 'secular' background of many sayings,
> including notions of theological 'reinterpretation', should
> finally be put to rest.
>
> (Heim, 2001: 316)

PROVERBS 1–9

Theological context

There has been much discussion of how integral a religious and
specifically Yahwistic dimension is to Proverbs 1–9. This involves
both the figure of personified Wisdom and the references to Yahweh
and the 'fear of Yahweh'. Whybray argued (in 1965 and 1994a) that
the literary history of Proverbs 1–9 involves stages of additions. The
original 'instruction' material, characterized by the father/son mode
of address and reconstructed largely with reference to Egyptian
parallels, although definitively Israelite in its concerns, was then
subjected to redaction. Whybray finds two distinct sets of additions,
each made with a particular theological purpose in view. The first
additions were made to the instructions, and the second to the first.
The first layer of the secondary material was added to equate the
'father's' words with that of the figure of Wisdom. The second layer
was to align Wisdom with Yahweh and to remind readers that the
ultimate aim of teaching was to instill into pupils 'the fear of
Yahweh'. Both redactions were an attempt to reinterpret the original
teachings in a more theological manner.

The 'cutting and pasting' method of procedure with texts has
come under a good deal of criticism in recent times. It is perhaps the

90

preoccupation with finding genres – and different genres, such as 'instruction' and 'wisdom poem', can be clearly found here – that has arguably detracted from evaluation of the more religious elements in this section. The identification of genres is an acceptable procedure, but part and parcel of this approach seems to be the positing of redactional layers, and it is in this area that I question how successful the defining of these additional layers has been by Whybray and others. Whybray himself admits that it is difficult to date any of the developments, citing scholars who think that they are late and others who think that they are early. He argues that some of the wisdom poems may have had an independent existence before they were placed in the text as it stands. Further, the additions were sporadic and not systematic. Fox (2000) criticizes Whybray's method of identifying the original instructions as 'procrustean', based on the mistaken assumption that the instructions were uniform to start with. He tries to steer a middle course in his assessment of the formation of Proverbs 1–9 between considerable cutting and pasting and overunification. He criticizes A. Meinhold (1991) for finding too intricate an overall design for the section. Fox writes: 'The present essay argues that there is considerable cohesiveness in Prov. 1–9, but it is not the result of single authorship. The authorship was, in a sense, collective, the work, perhaps, of several generations. The process described here is not simply the assembling of earlier texts by a later redactor, but a process of growth, in which later authors read, learned from, and elaborated the themes of the earlier texts' (2000: 323). Fox does not even see the poetic material in Proverbs 1–9 as of separate origin, but regards them as an outgrowth, in midrashic style, of the instruction material. Fox stresses the educational function of the instruction material, but he is concerned to include the religious aspect of life in the assessment of what wisdom fundamentally is, and so he does not see the need to separate the religious and Yahwistic elements from more secular concerns. He sees wisdom as moral character as well as an intellectual quest. The question to ask here is whether the formation of moral character is as far as the religious aspect of this material goes, and I will suggest in Chapter 5 that, with the emphasis on God as creator, there is an extra dimension beyond the moral context.

When Whybray formulated his ideas about redaction in 1965, a presupposition of his work, as of many other scholars, was that of religious development from one set of ideas to another. This linked up with literary development, so that just as one-limbed and multi-limbed sayings were regarded as having developed one from another (McKane, 1970), so one set of theological ideas was seen to follow another in an orderly manner. This presupposition is open to some debate in that the whole process of theologization may not have happened in a line of development like this, but may well have been a much more piecemeal and 'messy' process. One 'instruction' that caused a problem for Whybray (1965 and 1994a) was 3:1–12, in which he is forced to acknowledge that the teaching is concerned with God and that the references to Yahweh are not subsequent additions but constitute the main theme of the instruction. He finds Yahweh additions, however, in Proverbs 2:5–8; 3:26 and 5:21. His theory presupposes that the original genre of Proverbs 1–9 was 'educational treatise', subsequently remodelled into 'educational and theological treatise' in changing times. The wisdom poems are seen as another group of additions, but again the three do not fit together very well, Proverbs 3:13–20 being, by his own admission, more similar to other wisdom additions in the instructions and in the third person, while Proverbs 1:20–33 and chapter 8 are first-person poems. In fact, Whybray has to subdivide 3:13–20 into 3:13–18 and 3:19–20, because, unlike the rest of the section, verses 19–20 have Wisdom subordinated to Yahweh. Even in chapter 8 Whybray wonders whether the statement about Yahweh in verse 29 is superimposed. Chapters 1 and 9 are both seen as quite composite. An acknowledge-ment of different genres is clearly needed, but one wonders whether, if the sections are treated more holistically, a more integrated view of the Yahwistic nature of this material would come into view. The presupposition of a strictly educational purpose to this material may also have led to distortions. If the more religious aspect were included, the context question broadens out again. Were there reli-gious aspects to the instructional as well as to the poetic material from its inception?

As I have mentioned, interspersed with the instruction texts in Proverbs 1–9 are passages that largely deal with the figure of Wisdom; some describe her in the third person while other speeches come from her mouth. They also include reflection upon the nature of wisdom, the comparison of wisdom and folly, and more overt mention of Yahweh than is found in the instructions. These features have led many scholars to see them as later additions to the earlier instruction material, on theological grounds. A number of scholars have argued for development into this more Yahwistic direction for both instructions and discourses, notably McKane (1970). However, in relation to the poetic discourses alone, Camp (1985), for example, argues that they represent a reorientation from the exilic/post-exilic period by the addition of poems. The passages are 1:1–7 (introduction), 1:20–33 (first speech by Wisdom), 3:13–18 (poem in praise of Wisdom), 3:19–20 (verses on Yahweh and wisdom), 6:1–19 (general warnings and admonitions), 8:1–36 (second speech by Wisdom), 9:1–18 (scenes describing wisdom and folly). As the text reads now, these passages certainly enhance the authority of the instructions, and that may have been their intention. Rather than simply presenting the findings of human experience, the teacher is claiming to be allowing the pupil to tune into Wisdom, the ground and essence of 'life'. Furthermore, Wisdom is an attribute of God, so that 'getting wisdom' means ultimately 'fear of Yahweh'.

Egyptian influence has also been posited in this section. The prologue describing the benefits of wisdom and the purpose of acquiring it was likened to instruction material, and perhaps most essentially the figure of Wisdom was likened to Ma'at, the Egyptian divinity representing order. Kayatz (1966) pointed to affinities between the genre of self-praising speech as spoken by Wisdom and similar 'I' speeches by Egyptian divinities. She also stressed the Ma'at connection, which fits the emphasis on divine order matching societal order well, but had to acknowledge that Ma'at makes no such speeches. This theory did not fit Proverbs 1:20–33, which, Kayatz believed, showed the influence of the teaching of the Israelite prophets (see discussion in Chapter 6). The concept of Wisdom itself is also lacking from Egyptian material, and many of the traits of Wisdom can, she argued, be seen to derive from the character of Yahweh as known from Israelite tradition. One wonders how far the attempt to match the instructional material with Egyptian parallels has taken attention away from that which is especially Israelite in these chapters and in fact led to a diminution of the distinctiveness of Israelite, Yahwistic, wisdom.

Some scholars have taken a different path when considering the figure of Wisdom in Proverbs 1–9, Lang (1986) in particular regarding her as having originally been a goddess figure, a feature toned down by later Yahwistic monotheism. He also posited the idea of a marketplace school, as indicated by Wisdom's presence in the community. He saw the more developed discourses as evidence of scribal school products because of their high poetic quality. By contrast, Gilbert (1979) thought that the family was a plausible background for the poetic discourses, although this is a minority view.

In the more reflective passages of Proverbs 1–9 there is an explicit association made between education and Wisdom and between Wisdom and Yahweh. The whole enterprise, from whichever social context it ultimately came, is arguably made distinctively Israelite by the Yahwistic context that is most explicit in this section of Proverbs. However, the question has been asked: 'Is this the same Yahweh that we encounter in other parts of the Old Testament?' This identification has been denied repeatedly by Preuss (1972; 1987). This needs to be evaluated further. Other questions include: Does it represent a religious recontextualization of what was earlier a more secular enterprise or is the Yahwistic element part of the original development of the material? Does it have the effect of placing the whole of Proverbs 1–9 'late' in terms of dating, or is it plausible that this could be part of the earliest formulation of what wisdom was really about? And what does one make of this move towards Yahwistic piety in Proverbs 1–9? What does it indicate about the nature of such piety and of wisdom's links with the Yahweh of Israelite tradition?

Yahwistic elements

As discussed earlier, mention of Yahweh has often been seen in scholarship as evidence of later addition, and in what follows I wish to avoid that presupposition, looking again at the place of such mention within the context and structure of individual units. I have observed that Proverbs 1:1–7 has often been carved up into separate units, verse 1 sometimes being separated in its nature as a heading, and most notably verse 7 (Whybray, 1994c[1]) also being treated separately as a later addition. However, scholars have generally regarded verse 1 as integral on the level of sense, and verse 7 can convincingly be seen as the culmination of verses 1–7. Clifford (1999) gives three reasons for seeing verse 7 as the climax of verses 1–7. The first is that 'revering Yahweh is an appropriate culmination to the introduction of a book that makes Yahweh the source of blessings' (1999: 34); the second draws the parallel with 22:17–21, where trust in Yahweh (verse 19a) is similarly the goal of instruction.[2] Clifford's third reason is the reprise of the phrase 'wisdom and instruction' in verse 7b, echoing verse 2a and so creating an inclusion. The 'fear of Yahweh' in verse 7 functions as a definition of the status of wisdom; wisdom is therefore equated with the ultimate religious virtue. There is a parallelism in Proverbs between 'knowledge' and 'fear of the Lord', as in 1:7 (also in 1:29; 9:10), and the 'fear of the Lord' is associated with retribution in 10:1—22:16 (also in 10:27; 14:26–7; 15:16; 16:6; 19:23). The relationship of these phrases forms an interesting bridge between the educational and religious contexts. Murphy notes that dating the concept of the 'fear of the Lord' as 'late' does not work, because of its appearance in chapters 10–29, and suggests that the concept cannot be given a 'temporal pigeonhole' (1998: 256). He rejects the work of Preuss (1987), in which it was argued that the 'fear of God' concept was a widespread ancient Near Eastern one – a natural response to a Higher Being who cannot be fathomed – but not a distinctively Israelite one. On the contrary, as Fox notes, 'The importance Israelite Wisdom assigns to the fear of God in motivating behaviour is not paralleled in foreign Wisdom [where] . . . it is one virtue among many . . . Its importance in Wisdom literature is an Israelite innovation and shows the rootedness of Israelite Wisdom in Israelite thought generally' (2000: 71).

The lack of reference to Yahweh in the first of the instructions has often set the tone for scholarly comment, leading them down the

---

[1] Whybray (1965) separates off verses 6–7.

[2] This is an important cross-comparison within the book, Prov. 22:17–21 being part of the section often likened to the Egyptian *Instruction of Amenemope*. This suggests an important link between Prov. 1–9 and 22:17—24:22.

'secular' track in interpreting these instructions as a unit. In Proverbs 1:8–19 there is such lack of reference. McKane (1970), for example, points to a concept of order in the background, but argues that there is nothing explicitly Yahwistic about the way the doctrine of retribution is handled in this passage. Whybray (1994c) notes further that there is no personification of wisdom here, and yet, as already noted, the mention in Proverbs 1:9 of a 'fair garland' and 'pendants' in reference to parental instruction contains strong overtones of the description of wisdom in Proverbs 4:9 (cf. Deut. 6:6–9; Exod. 13:9). Proverbs 1:12 mentions Sheol, the place of the dead, as a point of comparison for what the wicked do to their victims (cf. Prov. 7:27), itself a religious context, albeit an undesirable one!

In Proverbs 1:20–33 the first speech of Wisdom appears, a speech generally held to form a literary unit. There is mention of Yahweh in 1:29b in relation to the fear of the Lord. However, more significantly from a theological angle, Wisdom is aligned with God in this speech. The admonitions of verses 24–31 are couched in the style of denunciations of pre-exilic prophets in that accusation is followed by announcement of judgement and the perfect tense is used as if Wisdom's teaching has already been rejected, making judgement inescapable (cf. Isa. 6:9–13; Ezek. 3:7). I shall go on to discuss the passage in more depth in relation to prophetic overtones in Chapter 6.

In the second instruction, in Proverbs 2:1–22, there is mention of both Yahweh and Wisdom and this has inevitably led some scholars to find additions to an original core on grounds of the development of theological concepts in wisdom. The mention of Yahweh occurs in verses 5–6. There is also reference to God (אלהים) in verse 5b in the context of 'knowledge of God', and to 'her God' in verse 17 in relation to a covenant that the loose woman has broken with her own god (probably the marriage covenant; cf. Mal. 2:14; Hos. 2:20–2). In verse 3 the pupil is told to 'cry out' for insight; this could be seen as answering Wisdom's speech in 1:20–31. The mention of 'knowledge of God' in verse 5 is unusual in that this is a rare phrase,[3] found also in Hosea 4:1 and 6:6. The concept is of importance in

---

[3] In fact, use of אלהים in Proverbs is also quite rare – only five times.

the prophets in particular, and its use here is of interest whether there is any specific influence or not (see Chapter 6). The search for Wisdom leads to a right relationship with God, who in turn bestows wisdom, so clarifying the two-way nature of the wisdom process. Fox (2000) makes the point that in verse 5 – the climax to verses 1–4 – it is not just the finding of Wisdom that is the ultimate goal of everyday human wisdom, but 'religious enlightenment' in the understanding of the fear of the Lord and knowledge of God himself. In verse 6, knowledge and understanding come from God's 'mouth', anticipating perhaps Proverbs 8:22–6. In verses 21–2 there is an echo of Proverbs 1:32–3, where refusing Wisdom's call led to death and obedience to life. Could this be an echo of the earlier call?

In the third 'instruction', in Proverbs 3:1–12, the topic of God is dominant. The divine name occurs seven times (including the reference to 'him' in verse 6b), and the message is that trust in God leads to prosperity for the discerning pupil. However, the warning at the end of the section is that not all is a bed of roses. The last four-line section suggests that discipline is sometimes employed by Yahweh in the manner a father would reprove a wayward son. The message to trust God comes out most fully in verses 5 and 7, and then in verses 9–10 this extends to cultic obeisance. There is a lack of reference to wisdom in this instruction; it is mentioned only in a negative admonition and is not required in the same way that faith in Yahweh is. In verse 4 there is mention of finding favour 'in the sight of God and man', referring to God in a general way (as אלהים) in conjunction with man to denote all that is seen. In verses 5–6 the piety dimension is introduced along with the need to trust God (Yahweh) rather than simply rely on one's own understanding. The theme of trust in God rather than in human beings is well known from the Psalter and is one of the major themes of the prophet Isaiah (1–39). McKane (1970) argued that these verses are an attack on traditional wisdom teaching and a later exhortation to substitute the moral teaching of Yahwism for it. However, traditional wisdom teaching often warns against over-self-confidence, as here, and McKane's 'older wisdom' has the idea of trusting God. The truly wise person knows that there are limits to the understanding that can come through human wisdom, and the person who claims all wisdom is more foolish than a fool (cf. Prov. 26:12; Jer. 9:23). God's role in the ways of humans is a theme found elsewhere in Proverbs, as in 16:9 and 20:24 (cf. Hos. 14:9). McKane argued that 'insight' (בינה) in verse 5 is given a negative meaning here, but there is a question whether this refers to the insight of the pupil or to supposed insight (cf. Isa. 29:14),[4] or whether in fact it refers to divine kindness and insight in a consequential clause.[5] Fox argues that חסד does not denote covenant loyalty in verse 3, but it is thoroughly Yahwistic (which is not the same thing). He writes: 'Yahwism is the framework for various covenants, but it is not co-extensive with them' (2000: 145). This theme of being against self-sufficiency and in favour of trusting Yahweh comes out in verses 7–8 (cf. Prov. 26:12). In verses 9–10 are contained, as already noted in Chapter 1, the only verses in Proverbs that actually recommend giving liturgical offerings to God in a communal sense.

In Proverbs 3:13–20 there is a second Wisdom poem, or perhaps more aptly here 'hymn', but in the third person rather than the first (unlike Prov. 1:20–33 and 8:1–36), and in this it resembles Job 28. Verses 13–20 make up an eight-line poem on Wisdom's benefits and her prestige. Verses 19–20 differ thematically, but are integrally related to what precedes them in explaining why Wisdom is able to be so lavish in her gifts and mentioning her role in God's creation. There is no mention of Yahweh in this passage, rather as there was no mention of Wisdom in the last.[6] Verses 13–15 on wisdom's benefits can be compared to the benefits of a good wife in Proverbs 31:10–31. Furthermore, the phrase 'Happy is . . .' (אשרי, verse 13) often marks the beginning of a psalm, as in Psalms 1:1; 32:1; 41:1; 112:1; 119:1; 128:1. Verses 14–15 in their comparisons of wisdom and wealth use metaphors from the world of commerce, and mention of Wisdom's precious nature recalls Job 28:15–19. Verses 16–18

---

[4] As argued by Whybray (1994c).
[5] As held by Fox, 2000: 144.
[6] This is not seen as a problem by Fox, who argues that, since piety is tantamount to wisdom, there is no contradiction between the passages. He writes: 'The balance and interdependence of these two virtues is [*sic*] a central theme in Proverbs 1–9' (2000: 161). However, other scholars have regarded this poem as an addition designed to counterbalance the first section of the chapter (e.g. Whybray, 1994c).

stress Wisdom's power, and she is described as a 'tree of life' (cf. Prov. 11:30; 13:12), a common ancient Near Eastern image and also reminiscent of the tree of life in Genesis (Gen. 2:9, 16–17; 3:22, 24). The depiction of 'life' in one hand and 'riches and honour' in the other recalls images of Ma'at, the Egyptian principle of order, and such images have royal associations. Verses 19–20 stress that the world was created by Wisdom so that the person who lives in accord with her does so in accord with the structure of the created world.[7] There are many overtones throughout these verses of what is to come in Proverbs 8. In fact, most of the epithets applied to Wisdom in these verses are applied to her elsewhere in Proverbs 1–9 (e.g. 1:28; 2:4; 4:13; 8:1, 10, 11, 18, 19, 35), although some are applied to the words of the teacher (e.g. 3:2, 22; 4:22; 6:23).

In Proverbs 3:21–35, the fourth instruction, there is mention of Yahweh in verse 26 and in verses 32–34, verses which Whybray (1994c) considers later additions[8] on the grounds of later Yahwehizing redaction. However, verse 26 follows on thematically from verses 21–5 in the emphasis on security if the pupil follows the paths of wisdom, which naturally leads on to the idea that security ultimately comes from God, who protects the virtuous from violent crime (cf. Ps. 35:8). Verses 32–4 also stress God's protection of the righteous and punishment of the wicked. As Clifford writes, 'As in the second and third instructions, the pursuit of wisdom soon brings the student to Yahweh, the opening duo of father and son becomes a trio of father, son and God' (1999: 58). The idea of God scoffing, in verse 34, is parallel to Wisdom's scorn of fools in 1:26–7. God has the same role here, in preserving the youth on the way, that is ascribed elsewhere to Wisdom, showing the fluidity of attribution of virtues to each.

No mention of Yahweh is made in Proverbs 4:1–9, the fifth instruction, although, as Fox points out, elsewhere (e.g. Prov. 2:1–6) the father's authority reinforces Yahweh's authority and so the two are often interchangeable. He writes: 'where only one is mentioned the other is not thereby excluded' (2000: 178). In verses 6, 8

---

[7] The image of founding the earth recalls Ps. 18:15.

[8] Whybray (1994c) also describes verse 25 as 'redundant' and verse 26 as a belated introduction of Yahweh.

and 9 Wisdom protects and gives honour to the pupil. There is a question whether the language of love between a man and a woman is being used here, with 'embrace' and 'crown' (which could refer to a marriage crown). Murphy (1998; 1988) is convinced of the 'erotic' nature of this language, with Wisdom as a woman who is to be loved and will exalt her lover in return (cf. Song of Songs). Alternatively, as argued by McKane (1970) and Plöger (1984), Wisdom's actions can be seen as those of a patroness, conferring honours on her protégé, rather than as those of a loved one.

In Proverbs 4:10–19, the sixth instruction, just as Wisdom is not mentioned directly here (except in verse 11 in reference to the father's wisdom), neither is God. There is a possible personification of 'instruction' in verse 13 (McKane, 1970), as discussed in Chapter 1. There is no mention of God or Wisdom here, although in Proverbs 3:3–6 trust in God was associated with direction in the right paths (cf. 3:23), and this motif is strong here. Fox finds it surprising that God is not mentioned explicitly and writes, 'There is no question but that the figure of God/the Lord lurks behind these chapters' (2000: 29).

In Proverbs 5:1–23, the eighth instruction, verses 21–3, which contain the only reference to Yahweh, are variously regarded as an appropriate conclusion (in the way in which these verses generalize theologically away from the specific emphasis on adultery contained in the body of the piece) or as a later addition.[9] Whybray writes, 'The introduction of a reference to Yahweh at the end of a chapter in which there has been no reference to him at all suggests a subsequent attempt at a Yahwistic interpretation of the whole' (1994c: 92). However, in its echoes of earlier formulations used in the instruction, unity is indicated; for instance, Yahweh sees every person's conduct while the seductive woman cannot even see her own path.

In Proverbs 6:1–19, the interlude, there is a numerical saying in verses 16–19. Mention is made of Yahweh here; he cannot abide such malicious behaviour.[10] 'Haughty eyes' and a 'lying tongue' are

---

[9] McKane (1970) and Plöger (1984) for similar reasons, and according to the 'Yahwehizing redaction' theory.
[10] Whybray (1994c) points out that, elsewhere in the Old Testament, conduct which is an abomination to Yahweh includes idolatry and cultic or ritual offences, and also ethical ones.

known from descriptions elsewhere in Proverbs, but also in Psalm 18:27 and 109:2 respectively. In 6:20–35, instruction nine, no mention of Yahweh is made, nor indeed in instruction ten in 7:1–27. In 7:27 mention of Sheol is again made, this time in reference to the loose woman; there are religious consequences in following her path.

The passage that I wish to turn to now is Proverbs 8, a key chapter in the book of Proverbs. This is the second of Wisdom's speeches in which she exhorts all to follow her way, particularly the inexperienced and foolish (verses 1–5). She needs to establish with her audience that she is trustworthy (verses 6–11), and promises riches, honour and the skill of governing to those who follow her (verses 12–21). She describes her presence with God at creation, which gives her special authority (verses 22–31) and urges her hearers to choose her path. The last actual speech by Wisdom was in Proverbs 1:20–33, and there is the same description of the setting, the address to the simple and foolish and the appeal to heed Wisdom's teaching, but this speech is more positive and assuring. Instead of denunciation of those who have failed to heed her (1:24–31), there is a catalogue of Wisdom's virtues and of the gifts that she bestows. Both chapters end with a contrast between the fates of two contrasting types of person. The speech here falls into four parts: verses 1–11, 12–21, 22–31 and 32–6. Whybray (1994c) argues that verses 22–31 could have been a self-contained poem and that it does not link thematically with the other sections, in that the speech would make sense without it. He argues that it could be a later insertion into an earlier poem, trying to make it clear that the Wisdom who makes these claims is Yahweh's own Wisdom. He argues that verses 13a and 35b, both brief references to Yahweh, are also interpolations, an unnecessary carving up of the text in my view.[11]

In verse 1, Wisdom is described in a city setting, that is, in an open square rather than, as the seductive woman, behind closed doors. In contrast to the 'one-to-one' style of the wisdom teacher in the instructions, she is available publicly to all. Her appeal is

---

Lists were compiled of Yahweh's ethical requirements for approaching him in the temple (e.g. Pss. 15; 24:3–6).

[11] Murphy (1998) argues that verses 1–11 and 22–31 could together be an alphabetizing poem of twenty-two lines, but the lines are interrupted by verses 12–20.

universal (cf. Ps. 49:1–3). McKane (1970) notes that she delivers her message in a place where everyday distractions are around and so she gets involved in the daily round of business and political life (cf. Deut. 30:14, where God's word is close at hand). Wisdom, like a prophet, delivers her message even to those who appear unable to take it in (cf. Ezek. 2:3–5; 3:7). In verses 6–11, Wisdom recommends the integrity of her utterances eight times, in contrast to the words of evil men and loose women. In verse 7, wisdom and truth are equated (cf. Psalm 51:6). In verses 8–9, her words are straight as compared to the twisted speech of the seductive woman. In verse 10, she calls her followers to accept instruction; usually this refers to divine instruction (e.g. Jer. 17:23; 32:33; 35:13; Zeph. 3:2, 7), but here it is about acceptance of Wisdom's teaching. Verse 11 has sometimes been seen as a separate proverb; however, Fox (2000) argues that it is not an interpolation but that it works well as a proverb cited to support the preceding advice and round off the first section of the speech. In verses 12–16, Wisdom's loves and hates are listed, comparable to the avowal of associates and disavowal of enemies as, for example, in Psalm 101. Wisdom is associated with kings (cf. links with Solomon in 1 Kings 3:9) and governing (cf. 2 Sam. 14:20b; 1 Kings 3; 4:29–34; 10:1–10). Verse 13 mentions the fear of the Lord, introducing a religious dimension. In verses 15–16, Wisdom is described as the principle of ruling on which good statecraft is dependent – and that includes all nations. Again references to Yahweh and to the king are found in close proximity. Verse 17 describes Wisdom as bestowing gifts that the seductive woman took away. The section of verses 17–21 is framed by 'love'; in verse 17 reciprocal love, and in verse 21 rewarding with wealth those who love Wisdom.[12] In verse 20, the way of righteousness and paths of justice are attributes central to the understanding of God (cf. Isa. 5:16; Jer. 9:24).

In verses 22–6, an elaboration of Proverbs 3:19–20 perhaps, Wisdom's own creation (lit. acquisition) is described (see further discussion in Chapter 5), and in verses 27–31 her relationship with God at creation and her intimacy with him are portrayed. The relationship between Wisdom and Yahweh is very important. She

---

[12] 'Wealth and honour' as a phrase is found in Prov. 3:16; cf. 1 Kings 3:13.

was his 'delight' and she finds joy in watching God create the world (cf. Job 38:7). There is a relationship here between this and other creation passages in Genesis 1:2, Psalm 93; 104; Job 28; 38; Isaiah 40:12 and 45:18, in that there are common features, but not enough to posit dependence. God's crafting of human beings in verse 23, described in the language of weaving in the womb, is familiar from Psalm 139:13b and Job 10:11. In verse 24, being 'brought forth' is used of God's pre-existence to creation in Psalm 90:2 and of creating Israel in Deuteronomy 32:18. Verses 27–9 link up with Genesis 1 and Job 38, but here there is not a complete account of creation; there are no references to heavenly bodies, vegetation or the animal world. In verses 32–4, Wisdom delights also in the human race, mirroring her relationship with God above. She calls three times to people to 'listen' or 'hear', which links her with an educational context. The only element of threat in the piece comes in at the end, in verses 35–6: the choice of Wisdom or not is a matter of life and death (cf. Deut. 30:19; Ecclus. 15:17).[13]

In Proverbs 9, Wisdom's third speech appears in verses 1–6 and 11, followed by an interlude in verses 7–10 and 12, and then by a contrasting speech by woman Folly, who is here personified for the first time. Verses 7–12 consist of five independent sayings, and most scholars move verse 11 to follow on from verse 6 because it naturally reads as a continuation of what Wisdom is saying. Scholars have struggled to find the relevance of the interlude to the two contrasting speeches of Wisdom and Folly that surround them. A. Meinhold (1991) thought that they were directly relevant to chapter 9, arguing that verses 7–9 and 12 form a frame treating scoffer and wise, thereby heightening the inner statement in verses 10–11 on the beginning and fruit of wisdom. Verse 10 is the only verse which mentions Yahweh in this chapter, and is regarded by Whybray (1994c) as an addition with the purpose of linking Wisdom and Yahweh. Murphy (1998), however, argues that these verses (10–11) are arguably at the centre of the chapter in the emphasis on Wisdom and could have carried the other verses with it. Murphy writes against chopping up the chapter as a whole, saying

---

[13] Verse 35b is identical with 18:22b.

of verses 7–12 that 'their immediate join with verse 6 indicates that the figure of Woman Wisdom in verses 1–5 has stimulated this further comment. Although it does not fit into the invitation scene, verses 7–12 are not to be separated from Wisdom' (1998: 61). Verse 12 has been regarded as a separate element in the chapter (e.g. Fox, 2000). The two invitations to a feast by woman Wisdom and woman Folly respectively are often compared, but in fact they have only one verse that is closely parallel, as found in verses 5 and 17. Wisdom builds a house (probably to be taken literally, although it could refer to a temple), and in the act of building there is security and permanence. She prepares a feast[14] and commissions her maids to give out invitations.[15] Wisdom demands a response from those who become her guests; they are called to embrace life (cf. Deut. 30:15–20 for the choice between life and death). The path of folly only leads to death (verse 18); woman Folly trades on the ignorance of her guests. Whybray (1994c) airs views that hold that verses 13–18 are a later modelling by an author based on material from earlier chapters, but decides that possibly the whole of verses 1–6 and 13–18 is a variant based on portrayals in earlier chapters.

During this discussion of sections of Proverbs 1–9, I have erred on the side of structural integration which has the effect of bringing key concepts such as Yahweh and Wisdom back into their wider context, and often into the heart of some units (e.g. mention of Wisdom as 'fear of Yahweh' as the climax of Prov. 1:1–7). It is clear from this kind of approach that the religious elements stand alongside more general ethical concerns and a specifically educational context, suggesting a wholeness of life that is lost in analyses that seek to find theological additions to an original, more secular core. The particular equation of Wisdom with Yahweh in certain key passages forms the heartland of this integration, notably in Proverbs 1:7; in 1:20–33 in which there is a specific alignment of the two; in 2:1–22, in which religious enlightenment is presented as the ultimate

---

[14] Unlikely to be a sacrificial meal, although there is an interesting parallel in Isa. 55:1–3 to giving up evil conduct before eating food in a sacred precinct.

[15] Woman Folly does not build a house or send out maids; rather, she calls to passers-by from her chair. She offers food and drink too – stolen water and bread. Her character here is based on descriptions of the adulterous woman in Prov. 2:16–19; 5; 6:20–35; 7.

goal of the wisdom quest; in Proverbs 9; and most notably in Proverbs 8:22–31, where Wisdom and Yahweh are most closely interrelated as partners in creation itself. In some passages one concept appears to replace the other, almost as if they are interchangeable; so in 3:1–12 mention of Yahweh dominates, while in 3:13–20, as if to counterbalance the previous emphasis, Wisdom comes to the fore; in 3:21–35 there is minor reference to Yahweh; in 4:1–9 Wisdom is emphasized and there is no mention of Yahweh; and in 5:1–23 there is just one reference to Yahweh but with the pupil's wife fulfilling the Wisdom/Yahweh role; in 6:1–19 there is a minor reference to Yahweh, and 7:1–27 minor reference to Wisdom. In other passages there is mention of neither, but background echoes are often found: for example, echoes of the description of Wisdom in 1:8–19; in 4:10–19 the emphasis on 'way' rather than Wisdom or a description of God, and, in 4:20–7, the 'paths' are motifs which are often interchangeable with the role of Wisdom or of God. Furthermore, the father or mother in his or her teaching role often seems to take the Wisdom role, and their teaching is backed up by Yahweh. Therefore, while mention of these concepts is not found in every passage, the presupposition that they are there lies behind most of the material. Both Yahweh and Wisdom are integral theological concepts for a deeper understanding of the purpose of the wisdom quest. This does not prove the early or late origin of either the parts or the whole of Proverbs 1–9, but it does suggest that these concepts are not later redaction but form an integral part of the material. It is not possible to know whether they were integral at a formative stage or as part of the writing-down, contextualizing process, but the number of references and their importance to the sense of the passages suggest that the former option is more likely.

PROVERBS 10:1—22:16

Mention of Yahweh

The question has been raised whether the proverbs in this section can be seen to have had a broader ethical context rather than only the educational one, and that was found to be the case in my preliminary survey of the material in Chapter 2. Linked with that is the question of how 'religious' they are and where Yahweh fits in. Are they to be seen as moral formation in a religious manner (cf. Fox, 2000), or as religious education, or are they simply chance references in a substantially secular set of proverbs of a generally ethical nature? Clusters of Yahweh sayings have been noted by scholars, with a particular cluster in chapter 16. Whybray (1979) has made an in-depth study of the Yahweh sayings in Proverbs 10:1—22:16. He notes that 55 out of a total of 375 sayings are Yahweh sayings. There are four in chapter 10; two in chapter 11; two in chapter 12; none in chapter 13; four in chapter 14 (I count only 3); eight in chapter 15 (I count 9); ten in chapter 16 (I count 11); two in chapter 17; two in chapter 18; five in chapter 19, six in chapter 20; five in chapter 21; and four in chapter 22. Therefore one third of the Yahweh sayings are in chapters 15–16, at the centre of the collection. There is a particular concentration of them, within these chapters, in Proverbs 15:33—16:9 at the heart of the collection, in that nine out of ten verses are Yahweh sayings. Proverbs 16:10–15 consists of royal sayings but integrally links the king and God. Whybray argues that this suggests careful placement of sayings at the writing-down stage, possibly in reinterpretation of another saying, such as Proverbs 15:16 reinterpreting 15:15, 17, and Proverbs 18:10 contradicting 18:11 (although, in fact, many have their own independent meaning too). What Whybray is concerned about in his analysis is placement, although he goes on to conclude that the arrangement indicates a later redaction. In this view he follows McKane (1970), who also thought that the 'Yahwistic' stage was a later one. I agree with Whybray that the placement of these Yahweh sayings is important in this section. However, this does not rule out the possibility that there was a Yahweh element in these proverbs from earliest times.

In later work, Whybray (1994a) changed his mind about a strict line of development from more secular to more Yahwistic. He still thought that there was strong evidence for meaningful pairings, arguing that many of the groupings are of thematic pairs or triads, with non-Yahweh proverbs surrounding a Yahwistic one, and that the proverbs were drawn into a more theological and instructional framework by editors. Yet the frequency and primacy of the Yahwistic emphasis might, he conceded, suggest an origin for these Yahweh sayings in less obvious clusters and in an oral tradition.

This opens up the possibility of a religious tradition in the proverbial oral stage. He believes that the reason for the writing down of these proverbs in clusters was for instructional purposes; once again the point is raised regarding different usages and origins in oral and written stages. Whybray writes: 'The idea of a non-religious "old wisdom" later "baptized", as it were, into the Yahwistic faith is no longer tenable. Rather it was a question of making these collections of proverbs more explicitly theological and specifically "Yahweh oriented"' (1994c: 152).

I have already discussed the work of Heim (2001), who has recently contributed to this debate about the place of the Yahweh proverbs. An important point raised by Heim is the strong Yahwistic influence on the clusters in which Yahwistic proverbs appear, and he puts the final nail in the coffin of the theory that proverbs were once secular and only later put into new theological contexts (see the quotation at the beginning of this chapter). I will go on to discuss his views in more detail in approaching the text. I will say at this point, however, that I see more significance to the 'linkages' stage that Heim isolates in reference to the placement of Yahweh sayings than I saw when simply discussing the structure of chapters without this element (in Chapter 2). This is because there does seem to be some significance in the placement of Yahweh sayings, as will become clear. This demonstrates that the sayings are important both in their own right and within a wider context. This need not mean that they represent a superimposed 'reinterpretation', however. Rather, I shall argue that they are as original as the next proverb and that placement makes them even more integral to the essential nature of the material.

Finally, this discussion raises the further question of how 'Yahwistic' the religion as demonstrated in the proverbs is. Koch (1983) maintained, as did Preuss (1972; 1987), that the Yahweh mentioned here was not the same as the Yahweh of the rest of the Old Testament. Koch argued that this Yahweh lacks most of the characteristics of the God of Israel and that he is basically the great watchmaker, setting the world ticking and making sure that it runs according to the preordained doctrine of retribution. Koch noted that most of the proverbs in this section assume this doctrine without reference to God. However, this is an oversimplification of the case, in that a number of proverbs suggest that there are limits to human knowledge and that God alone is the source of all wisdom. The proverbs that do not explicitly mention Yahweh probably presuppose that he is the dispenser of the justice being meted out. It is, in my view, highly unlikely that we are speaking of a different Yahweh here; the point is surely that the wisdom literature draws out different aspects of the same Yahweh who is found in the rest of the Old Testament (see discussion in Chapter 5).

Yahwistic elements

A move needs to be made from the broader issues raised to a closer look at the chapters that make up this section in relation to the mention of Yahweh and the relationship of such mention to the structure of each chapter. There are four mentions of Yahweh in Proverbs 10 which, Whybray argues, provide signs of a Yahwistic reinterpretation, but which Heim (2001) sees as integral to the understanding of the different sections themselves.[16] Verse 3 is where the religious dimension comes in, and God is brought into the righteous/wicked equation on the side of justice, the giver of good to those who deserve it and of punishment to the wicked. Verse 22, which is the second Yahweh saying, arguably relates to verse 2, suggesting that material rewards as well as other blessings are, like righteousness and wickedness (in verse 3), to be traced back to God. Furthermore, verse 4 states that diligence makes a person rich, which is again attributed to God in verse 22. Heim argues that verse 22 deliberately recalls vocabulary from elsewhere in the chapter,[17] making divine blessing depend on righteous behaviour. He sees this verse as providing a frame with verse 3, but also its message influences the next section of verses 23–30. The two other references to God are in this last section; in verse 27 the reference to the fear of the Lord puts the following two verses in context, and in verse 29 there is a description of the security that God can offer to the

---

[16] As noted in Chapter 1, Heim (2001) is keen to draw thematic linkages across the chapter.
[17] Heim (2001: 126) writes: 'Verse 4 stated that diligence enriches (תַּעֲשִׁיר) while v. 22 states that divine blessing (בִּרְכַּת; cf. vv. 6 + 7) enriches (תַעֲשִׁיר). There is also a connection to vv. 15 (עֹשֶׁר) and 21 (sc. the association "lack of sense" – "enrich").'

upright. However, the presupposition of God's action spreads further: for example, in verse 25 the tempest often refers to God's wrath. In verse 32 one might ask, '"Acceptable" to whom?', and see divine approval as a presupposition of the verse.

In fact, there are a number of verses in this chapter which seem to presuppose the 'behind the scenes' action of Yahweh; for instance, 'blessings' in verse 6 (the Septuagint adds 'of the Lord') have to come from somewhere, and in verse 8 heeding 'commandments' could refer to divine commandments just as well as human ones. In verse 9, 'walking in integrity' recalls 2:7, in which the protection of Yahweh is offered, and 'will be found out' implies 'by God' too. In verse 11, the 'fountain of life' is elsewhere associated with the 'fear of Yahweh', notably in Proverbs 14:27 (cf. Ps. 36:9), as well as with Wisdom herself in Proverbs 16:22. In verse 12, 'offences' could refer to personal ones or ones committed against God. So the Yahweh sayings, notably that in verse 22, can be seen to have influenced that which surrounds them, and, even more significantly, the presupposition of God's action underlies many of the proverbs. Heim argues that this religious aspect is part of the formative structure of the chapter, Whybray that such sentiments represent later reworking. However, the overtones are so extensive that reworking seems to me a less likely option.

In Proverbs 11 there are two mentions of Yahweh – in verses 1 and 20 – and both can be seen to relate to surrounding verses. Verse 1 describes false weights as 'an abomination to the Lord' (cf. Prov. 12:22; 20:10, 23). This recalls Old Testament law and prophecy (see Chapter 5). The message here is that the divine will should reign supreme even in the world of commerce. Proverbs 11:1 can be seen as commenting upon 10:32 in that 11:1 clarifies the idea that moral and immoral behaviour are issues in which God gets involved in judgement and are not simply in the human domain. The catchword link of רצון is also a clue to the linkage. Verse 20 links up with verse 1: acceptable and unacceptable conduct are described. The message is that the whole of human life comes under divine judgement. The consequences of God's approval or disapproval are made clear in verse 21. The references to God, therefore, seem to be quite integral to the chapter and variants on a theme can be seen running through the chapter.

In chapter 12 there are again two references to Yahweh, in verses 2 and 22. The phrase 'abomination to the Lord' in verse 22 is the same as that featured in Proverbs 11:1. Verse 2 is virtually identical to Proverbs 8:35, where Wisdom is the source of favour. Here God confers favour, and it is significant that, as noted in discussing Proverbs 1–9, Wisdom and God can often be used interchangeably. Verse 2 explicates verse 3, making it clear that God is behind the consequences of wicked or righteous behaviour. In verse 22, the fates of the righteous and of the wicked are said to be determined by divine judgement. It has the effect of giving a religious context for the section of verses 13–23 in that God's attitude towards witnessing in court is made clear. So again the Yahweh sayings are related to those around them, and yet this need not mean that they are secondary recontextualization of material. Rather, their presence seems quite integral and they are indicators of more unity in the segments than older scholars gave credit for. Sayings are put into a religious context at key points in the chapter. They belong to Heim's 'collecting' stage, but they also exist in their own right as separate proverbs.

Chapter 13 contains no reference to Yahweh. However, in verse 4 some scholars have seen echoes of Psalms 42:2 and 63:1 in the image of the craving soul. In these psalms the soul craves for God, and the question is raised whether this sense is in the background of this reference. In verse 21, prosperity appears to be personified. Is this just a poetic turn of phrase, or should God be presupposed here as the only one who can dispense rewards?

By contrast, in chapter 14 there are frequent references to God in verses 2, 26 and 27 in the context of the fear of God, and in verse 31 there is a reference to God as Maker. They are all placed in positions where they can be seen to comment on adjacent proverbs. So again the Yahweh sayings are related to those around them. In verse 2 it is made clear that the way of wisdom is inseparable from service to Yahweh, a theme found in Proverbs 1–9. In verse 9, some translations emend to include God in an obscure verse, the only non-Yahwistic reference to God in the section. In verse 22, loyalty and faithfulness are mentioned, which in 16:6 are equated with the fear of Yahweh. Verses 26–8 make it clear that the fear of God guarantees safety and good fortune. It could be a comment on verse 25 to suggest that truthfulness is closely linked with God's ethical demands, as Whybray suggests. However, it could also stand alone. Again, verse 27 could relate to verse 28, which is a royal proverb; it is fascinating that here, as elsewhere, a royal proverb is found in close proximity with a Yahweh proverb (cf. Prov. 14:35—15:3; 15:33—16:15; 20:26—21:3; 22:11–12; 25:2–7; 29:12–14). The main purpose of such juxtaposition seems to be to stress that obedience to Yahweh is particularly important for kings, in whose hands are the lives of all his people. However, in chapter 14 the connection is not so close. In verse 31 the poor person is particularly linked with God, in that God offers protection to the poor (cf. Ps. 41:1–3). In verse 35, the king metes out favour justly, echoing God's justice, perhaps (cf. Ps. 101:6–8), but here acting in his own right, not as God's explicit representative.

In chapter 15 there are nine references to Yahweh, in verses 3, 8, 9, 11, 16, 25, 26, 29 and 33, and so they dominate the chapter. Verse 33 introduces a further group of Yahweh proverbs in 16:1–9. In verse 33, wisdom is fully identified with the fear of Yahweh. Verse 3 acts as a reminder that the whole range of activity is under Yahweh's scrutiny (cf. Ps. 11). Verses 8–11 arguably constitute a small unit dominated by the references to God. Verse 8 refers to specific religious cultic acts of sacrifice and prayer (cf. 15:29; 21:27a; 28:9), which leads to a wider appraisal of moral conduct in verse 9. Verse 10 is the odd verse out in not mentioning God; however, it links to the way of the wicked in verse 9, and verse 11 makes it clear that nothing is hidden before God (cf. Ps. 139:8). These verses arguably connect thematically to other parts of the chapter (Whybray, 1994c), but this does not prove that they are added later on; rather, they may have had a shaping role at any stage in the compilation of the collection. In verse 16, the fear of the Lord is stressed (cf. 16:8, which is almost identical, and Ps. 37:16). Verses 25–33 are another cluster of proverbs mentioning Yahweh. He is again on the side of the underdog, this time the widow. He upholds good against wickedness. In verse 26, ritual purity is again used within an ethical context. In verse 27, bribes are condemned. In verse 29, the fate of the righteous and of the wicked is due to Yahweh's favour or disfavour, in similar vein to psalms of lament. Verse 33 defines instruction in wisdom, as featured in verses 31–2, as equivalent to the fear of the Lord, echoing 1:7

and 9:10. Heim (2001) regards it as a pivotal verse linking 10:1—15:32 and 16:1—22:16 and thereby marking the end of a subdivision within Proverbs 10:1—22:16.

Yahweh proverbs dominate the opening verses of chapter 16. Verses 1–9 contain a reference in each verse except verse 8. There are references to God also in verses 11, 20 and 33 (the last of which echoes verse 1, forming an inclusio, perhaps). It is significant that the verses that follow 1–9, namely 10–15, contain all royal proverbs, except verse 11, which is a Yahweh saying. The close juxtaposition of these two groups of sayings and the intertwining of Yahweh and royal sayings in verses 9–12 might suggest deliberate arrangement. These proverbs also enjoy a central position in the book of Proverbs, 16:17 being in fact the centre of the book, although it is unwise, in my view, to read too much into this observation.

Proverbs 16:1 concerns God's crucial interaction with humans. He is a part of the human thought process itself and human beings need to remember that divine aspect of their decision-making process. Verse 2 moves from thoughts to actions and reminds human beings that God can see into the inner spirit and judge it accordingly regarding purity of motive. Verses 2–3 closely resemble Proverbs 4:26b, while verse 4 stresses God's role as maker of all (cf. Ps. 11:4–7; Exod. 9:16). Verse 5 uses the phrase found a number of times, 'abomination to the Lord', and God's role as judge is stressed. Verse 6 uses the phrase 'loyalty and faithfulness', which can be seen in a purely moral context, but could refer more widely than that, possibly echoing covenantal language. The use of 'atoned' establishes an interesting cultic connection. In verse 7 the advantages of loyalty to Yahweh for human relationships are stressed. Verse 8 closely resembles 15:16 and 17:1 and can be seen as an illustration of pleasing the Lord as featured in verse 7, even though here only righteousness and injustice are mentioned. In verse 9 there are echoes of verse 1, rounding off the section. Here the whole of a person's activity is subject to Yahweh's scrutiny and guidance.

In verses 10–15, diverse royal proverbs are brought together. They all concern the role of the king. Just as verses 1–9 stressed the dependence of humans upon Yahweh, so verses 10–15 are concerned with the king's relationship with both God and his people, as well as with his role as ruler. Verse 10 stresses the king's judicial role (cf. Ps.

72:2). The one Yahweh proverb in verse 11, concerning weights and measures, is perhaps surprising given that this was usually the king's domain. Maybe it is inserted to make the point that God is ultimately the one to whom all, even the king, are answerable. Some statements about the king echo verses 1–9 about God, such as the king as judge in verse 10, while verses 14 and 15 echo verses 4 and 5. In verse 15 it is usually God's face that is described as shining (cf. Num. 6:25), while here it is the king's, another indication of a fluidity of role. The verses from 16 to 23 have an overall wisdom theme which echoes Proverbs 1–9; for instance, verse 16 echoes 8:10, 19, where Wisdom personified is compared in value to silver and gold. There is a Yahweh proverb at the centre of this section, in verse 20, stressing that trust in God should lie behind the wisdom quest. Verse 24 has connections with verses 21–3, but may be a separate popular proverb (cf. Ezek. 3:3). Another small thematic group is contained in verses 27–30, which concern speech and are very similar in vocabulary and theme to 6:12–19. Verse 31 echoes Proverbs 4:9, and verse 33 discerns the will of Yahweh that lies behind the chancier aspects of human decision-making.

In Proverbs 17, there are three references to God, two to Yahweh in verses 3 and 15 and one to 'his Maker' in verse 15. Proverbs 17:1–3 can be regarded as a small unit, with the reference to Yahweh putting them in a religious context. Both strife and questions of inheritance will be settled by Yahweh who tries the hearts. Some have related this subsection to Proverbs 16:33, at the end of the previous chapter, which contains another Yahweh proverb. In verse 5, the phrase 'insults his Maker' is found (cf. 14:31a). In verse 12, the dramatic picture of a she-bear robbed of her cubs echoes other images of bears in the Old Testament, notably of 2 Kings 2:24, in which the bear's appearance is seen as punishment from God.[18] Verse 15 concerns the misconduct of judges and it is Yahweh who judges the conduct of human judges. The phrase 'abomination to the Lord' comes again in this verse. Here divine justice is recalled, whereas in other parts of the Old Testament, (e.g. Exod. 23:6–8; Deut. 16:18–20; 25:1) it is presumed that these offences will be

---

[18] Yahweh is compared to a ferocious bear in Hos. 13:8 (cf. Amos 5:19), and a bereaved she-bear appears in 2 Sam. 17:8; the context, again, is the anger of a she-bear robbed of her cubs.

punished by human judges in a just manner. The section verses 13–15 concerns improper conduct in human relationships and puts such conduct in the context of God's judgement.

In Proverbs 18, Yahweh is mentioned twice, in verses 10 and 22. Verse 10 links up with verse 11 in that the point is made that God is the ultimate strength, more than wealth, and that righteousness is the key to divine favour. The 'name of the Lord' occurs only here in Proverbs (cf. 'name of my God' in 30:9), but in 10:29 God is described as a stronghold to the upright and so the same image is being used. In verse 22, the finding of a good wife is a sign of favour from God. There does not appear to be much connection between these two Yahweh proverbs, which treat rather different aspects of God's action.

In chapter 19, Yahweh is mentioned five times, in verses 3, 14, 17, 21 and 23. Verse 1 is nearly identical with 28:6. Verses 1–3 are linked with the idea of walking in the way, although it is not necessary to see verse 3 as a comment upon the other two; it is closer in sentiment to verse 2 than to verse 1. The sentiment of verse 3 is that folly leads to ruin and to anger against God. Verse 5 parallels a number of other proverbs: 6:19; 12:17; 14:5, 25; 19:9; 21:28 (near doublet). Verse 12 compares the king's favour to dew upon the grass. Elsewhere dew is described as a gift from God (Deut. 33:28; 1 Kings 17:1; Hag. 1:10; Zech. 8:12). Similarly, the description of the king's wrath as like the growling of a lion is paralleled by descriptions of Yahweh as a lion (Hos. 5:14; 13:7–8). There seems to be some interchangeability of images here between the king and Yahweh, which might be to stress their interrelationship or might indicate a tension between the two. In verse 13 the familiar images of foolish son (cf. Prov. 17:25) and quarrelling wife (cf. Prov. 21:19) are found, and in verse 14 there is a contrast of house and wealth, which are human inheritances, with a prudent wife, who is seen as a gift from God. In fact, verse 14 arguably compares the predictability of inheritance with the choice of a wife, which is presumably more unpredictable and is helped by some divine guidance! Verse 17 employs the language of usury; Yahweh will repay kindness (cf. Isa. 59:18, where he repays wrath and requital). In verse 21, Yahweh's direction is needed. This belongs in the context of verses 18–23, which broadly treat issues of education and discipline (cf. 2:1–9). Whybray (1994c) tries to relate the Yahweh sayings here to the verses around them in order to show that they are editorial comment, but even he admits that it is hard in this chapter to find much relationship between verses; he finds three cases where this theory works and two where it does not. This theory of commenting on adjacent proverbs is often slightly forced and one wonders how much can really be built upon it.

There are six Yahweh proverbs in Proverbs 20, in verses 10, 12, 22, 23, 24 and 27, and four royal ones, in verses 2, 8, 26 and 28. Furthermore, chapter 21 begins with three Yahweh proverbs, of which verse 1 is also a royal proverb, and so there is another cluster of Yahweh and royal proverbs as in 16:1–15. Proverbs 20:2 is a variant of 19:12a, another royal proverb. Verses 8–12 appear to be inter-related with the mention of eyes in verses 8 and 12. The all-seeing eye of the king is then recalled in verse 12, with the statement that God has made eye and ear. In verse 9, a statement of the sinfulness of humankind is made (cf. 1 Kings 8:46). True wisdom is attained through Yahweh, who created eye and ear (cf. Prov. 15:31; 18:15; 25:12, on the importance of listening with the ear). In Proverbs 20:20—21:4, seven out of fifteen proverbs are Yahweh proverbs, and there are two clusters of three plus three royal proverbs in 20:26, 28 and 21:1. In Proverbs 20:20–5, relationships between humans and God and between subjects and the kings are explored. In verse 22 it is best if Yahweh, rather than human beings, avenges crimes (cf. Prov. 24:29; cf. Deut. 32:35–6) and in verse 23 Yahweh hates dishonest practices (this verse is a variant of Prov. 20:10; cf. 11:1a). In verse 24 God controls human destinies. This statement counters more positive sentiments about this, as found, for example, in Psalm 37:23, in stating that humans ultimately lack control of their own lives. In verse 26, the king punishes the wicked, while in verse 27, it is God who sees into the innermost hearts of human beings (cf. 15:3, 11; 16:2; 21:2). This tension between roles is apparent again here. In verse 29, loyalty and faithfulness are partly personified as they are described as preserving the king.

In chapter 21, verses 1–3 are Yahweh proverbs and are linked by 'heart' in verses 1 and 2 (also in verse 4). Verse 1 mentions the king as well as Yahweh and makes it clear that the king is subject to God's direction, in contrast to other proverbs which simply describe the power of the king without mentioning God (i.e. 14:35; 16:14, 15;

19:12; 20:2). The reference to a 'stream of water' indicates water channels that can be diverted into any desired direction (cf. Isa. 32:1–2, where the same phrase is used of the beneficial rule of the king). The choice of this phrase indicates that the rule of the king is under Yahweh's protection (cf. Ps. 1:3). In Proverbs 21:2, a variant of 16:2, God knows the truth of the hearts of human beings however hard they may try to justify themselves. This is a common theme among the Yahweh proverbs (cf. Proverbs 15:3, 11; 17:3; 20:9, 27). In verse 3, righteousness and justice are stressed over sacrifice in what sounds like a rather prophetic saying (cf. Isa. 1:11–17; Hos. 6:6; Mic. 6:6–8; 1 Sam. 15:22; 2 Sam. 8:15; cf. Isa. 56:1–2). After verse 3, Yahweh is not mentioned again until verses 30–1, which round off the chapter, although verse 27 implies God's involvement. In verse 27, the Septuagint adds 'to the Lord' after 'abomination', which would bring the verse closer to 15:8. This, then, is arguably virtually a Yahweh proverb. Verse 30 states that human wisdom is weak in comparison to that of Yahweh, and will not prevail over his wisdom. Verse 31 states that nothing can be achieved without the approval and help of Yahweh. Verses 30–1 with 1–3 form a frame for the whole chapter. There is no need to see, with Whybray (1994c), verse 30 as rectifying verse 29.

Finally, in Proverbs 22:1–16 there are four Yahweh proverbs, in verses 2, 4, 12 and 24, and verse 11 is a possible contender too. The king is also mentioned in verse 11. In verse 2, God is described as maker of rich and poor; this indicates that riches and poverty are a fact of life, but that God has equal concern for them both. Verse 3 is virtually identical with 27:12 and contains similar sentiments to 14:15, 18. Verse 4 mentions the fear of the Lord as one of the conditions for reward; I find it hard to agree with Whybray (1994c) that it provides comment on verses 3 and 5. Verse 7 mentions debt and the ensuing slavery of the borrower to the lender, a familiar proverbial theme. Verse 11 does not mention God but does mention the king, and the Septuagint adds 'the Lord' as the subject of the first line. This is not a necessary emendation, however, as the reference is a general one. Verse 12 is a Yahweh proverb closely resembling Proverbs 15:3. God protects those who seek wisdom, but will punish those who use words against faith. Whybray finds possible reference back to verses 10 and 11, and there is certainly a loose thematic link with words and communication. In verse 14, the loose woman of Proverbs 1–9 is recalled and linked with God's anger. Whybray writes: 'The appearance of such a theme here and the way in which teaching corresponding to that of the "father" of the Instructions has been glossed by a Yahweh-proverb confirms the conclusion that both sections of the book (chapters 1–9 and 10:1—22:16) have been finally edited in the same spirit. The fact that these verses occur at the end of the section supports this view' (1994c: 322).

I have commented here on the prevalence of Yahweh sayings, especially in certain chapters. I have argued that in their present context they extend beyond their own confines, so performing a framing and relativizing function. However, this does not necessarily mean that they are a later redaction; they are simply a vital part of a living process of gathering sayings on all topics together. I would argue, therefore, that the sayings already existed independently in an oral context before they were placed in their present context. This was not in the service of a Yahwehization process of otherwise 'secular' or even 'foreign' material; rather, they were placed where they were to reinforce the messages of other Proverbs within a religious context and to give structure to the material as it was formed into literature. The proximity to the Yahweh proverbs of proverbs mentioning the king suggests an integral link of the role of the king with God's role, authority and status.

PROVERBS 22:17—31:31

Mention of Yahweh

In what follows I will continue my survey into mention of Yahweh and the relationship of such mention with the overall structure of each chapter in slightly briefer terms. In Proverbs 22:17–23:11 there are just two references to Yahweh (in 22:19 and 23) and one to a 'redeemer' (in 23:11), which may be an indirect allusion to him. Whybray (1994a) holds that these are later additions, arguing that in 22:19 the first line interrupts the discourse, since verses 19b–21 resume the first-person address found in the previous verses. Proverbs 22:23 could also be an added motive clause;

similarly 23:11. However, in my view, they can just as easily be regarded as integral references.

In Proverbs 23:12—24:22 there are four references to God, three of which are to Yahweh. Two references occur in the section 24:13–22, the first in verse 18, which, Whybray (1994c) argues, is in a motive clause linked to verse 17 and enjoining Yahweh to revenge, an element not original to the admonition in verse 17. The second is found in verse 21, which he also maintains may not be original to the instruction, but may instead be an isolated short instruction, with Yahweh and the king mentioned together as elsewhere in Proverbs. The third reference is in Proverbs 23:17, which occurs in a motive clause again, but the admonition to which it is attached is so short that Whybray thinks it is likely to be original. The reference in Proverbs 24:12 is to God as 'he who weighs hearts' (cf. 16:2; 21:2) and as 'he who keeps watch over you', also considered by Whybray as original.

Proverbs 22:19 links wisdom with trust in God. Whybray argues that verse 19b should be aligned with verses 20 and 21, and that it strikes an unusually personal note in reference to the one receiving the wisdom on offer. One difference with *Amenemope* is the naming of Yahweh in verse 19. This mention is at the centre of this section, which indicates that, far from being an editorial afterthought, trust in Yahweh is the goal of the teaching. In Proverbs 22:22–3, the admonition is given a motive clause (verse 23) with the reference to Yahweh's protection of the poor. He will argue their case and see that justice is done. In verses 24–5, the warning is against encountering anger and the non-Yahwistic motive clause is in verse 25 (cf. 15:18; 29:22). In 23:10 there is a partial doublet with 22:28, except that here in 23:11 the mention of a redeemer figure is given as a motive clause. This figure could refer either to the relative who pleads the case of the fatherless (cf. Boaz in Ruth) or to God as the redeemer of the poor (linking up with 22:22–3). In 23:17 is a mention of the fear of Yahweh, the reference being an integral part of the admonition and linking up with verse 18 about future hope. Avoidance of envy of the wicked is advised here (cf. Ps. 37:1; Prov. 3:31–2; 24:1–2, 19–20). Proverbs 24:10–12 return to an admonitory style. In verse 12, 'he who weighs the heart' may well refer to

Yahweh's retribution. In verses 13–14, eating honey is used as a comparison with acquiring wisdom (cf. 16:24). Verses 15–16 warn against criminal activity, and house imagery recurs; and verses 17–18 warn not to gloat over the fall of an enemy and caution that enemies can rise up again after a fall. These four verses appear to be connected and the judgement of the wicked is presupposed. In verse 18, God is mentioned as the one who sees into the hearts of human beings and judges them accordingly, and this unites the section together. In verses 19–20, there is a close variant of verses 1–2, indicating that evil has no staying power (cf. 3:31; 23:17–18; 24:1–2; Ps. 37:1), and in verses 21–2 a short piece of instruction to fear the Lord and the king. The two are paired here (cf. 1 Kings 21:10), while elsewhere they are often alternatives. In either case the two are integrally related. The message here is to stay well away from either or both of royal or divine wrath!

It is again hard to know at what stage the Yahweh references may have been integral to the material, but there is a sufficient number of references here to indicate that it is difficult to regard them as simply editorial. The references are also essential for the understanding of the purpose of passages in that the religious element is never far away from the instructional/educational context.

Proverbs 24:23–34

There is no mention of Yahweh in this section and so very little to say. In verse 29 the inference is that it is God who repays good and bad deeds and so the meddler here is interfering with divine processes (cf. 20:22; 24:12). There is, of course, no explicit mention of the divine here. However, this small sample does not provide enough evidence to regard the sayings as originally secular with no interest in the divine.

Proverbs 25–9

In these chapters there are six Yahweh proverbs, one in chapter 25, none in chapters 26–7, two in chapter 28 and three in chapter 29. It is clear that chapters 28–9 in particular contain more reflection on Yahweh, on the nature of wisdom and on the connection with law. Notably in chapter 29 there is mention in verse 25 of the need to trust God, and other references to Yahweh in verses 13 and 26 which open up to the broader question of how religious this section of the proverbial material is.

Proverbs 25:2 associates kings with God and has affinities with other royal proverbs. The idea that God remains inscrutable and does not wholly reveal things to human beings, kings included, is a frequent Old Testament belief (cf. Deut. 29:29; Isa. 45:15; Job 11:7–8; 15:8; 26:14; Eccles. 8:17). The reference here is to God as Elohim, which is rare in the book, and it is probably making a general contrast between God and kings; compare 2:5, where 'fear of Yahweh' and 'knowledge of God' are parallel descriptions. Verse 3, although it does not mention God, indicates that he is there in that the statement points to a characteristic of kings that they share with God, namely, they are 'unsearchable' (cf. 1 Kings 3:28; 12:6–15). In verse 22 the Lord will approve; here is the first mention of Yahweh in this chapter and section. Coals of fire usually denote punishment (Pss. 18:8; 140:10; 2 Sam. 22:9, 13), but are not normally found on someone's head! There is no reference to Yahweh in chapters 26 and 27. Proverbs 27:1 speaks of not boasting about tomorrow; perhaps it is implied here that the future is known only to God, although it is not specifically said.

In chapter 28, there are three Yahweh proverbs, in verses 5, 14 and 25, but arguably the operation of divine justice is implied throughout. Three verses refer to תורה (Torah) (verses 4, 7 and 9) and I see no reason to regard the references as being to different types of law.[19] In verse 1, the implied reason for the assurance of the righteous is that they trust in God's support of them. However, this is not said, and a simple contrast is drawn between righteous and wicked here. In verse 4, to keep the law is to strive against the wicked and this is associated in verse 5 with seeking the Lord. In verse 7, the law is associated with wisdom in that the one who keeps the law is wise (cf. the injunction to wise behaviour in Prov. 10:1; 27:11, but without a specific connection to keeping the law). In verse 9, law is again mentioned and the context is that those who neglect to obey it offer futile prayers; again 'to God' is implied (cf. Prov. 15:8). In verse 14, there is a reference to fearing the Lord. The antithesis is one who

---

[19] Whybray questions whether law in the Deuteronomic sense is meant, especially in verse 9, where divine law could, he argues, be intended.

hardens his heart (cf. Exod. 7:3; Ezek. 3:7). Verses 24–6 are thematically related, with verse 25 mentioning Yahweh and reiterating the
need for trust in God rather than reliance on oneself. In verse 25 the
greedy man who stirs up strife is compared to the one who trusts
God (cf. Prov. 16:20 and 29:25 on trusting God, and Hab. 2:5 on
greed).[20] Verse 27, on giving to the poor, can be compared to Proverbs 11:24, 25; 19:17; 22:9. One wonders who the curse is from; God
is a possibility (as in Prov. 3:33), or perhaps the poor themselves.

There are three references to Yahweh in chapter 29, in verses 13, 25
and 26; and they occur, as elsewhere, in close proximity to mention
of the king or rulers. The references to the king in 29:4, 14, are of
interest in connection with the discussion of social context; it is also
of note that they are critical of the king in the main, unlike more
submissive and admiring references elsewhere. The reference to
Yahweh in verse 13 is in the context of God's provision of light to
the eyes of both poor and oppressor; the focus here is away from just
judgement (found in verse 14 in reference to the king), but conveys
the message of God's provision of light for all despite their deeds.
In contrast, the reference in verse 26 stresses God's justice in
comparison to the favour one might try to seek out from a ruler
(with the inference that the ruler might be open to corruption),
and hence that trusting God is better, a continuation of the sentiment of verse 25 in which trust in Yahweh is recommended over all
things. The effect of the two verses that mention Yahweh at the end
of the chapter is to round off the thought of the chapter with
reference to the divine and hence to round off the section, too, in
that vein.

There is in this section a relative paucity of Yahweh sayings, but
the placement of them is significant. Again, it is difficult to know at
what stage in the evolution of the material these sayings were
present. They are most likely to have existed as separate sayings
and then to have been placed carefully at the writing-down stage. It
is significant that there is not a large number of Yahweh sayings in
these chapters, a factor which would militate against the idea of

---

[20] In Prov. 11:25 the 'liberal man' will be enriched, and in Prov. 13:4 the diligent person is the
referent. It looks as if these phrases are starting to be used interchangeably. In this verse
greed is the theme and so the greedy man becomes the main referent.

gradual Yahwehization of the material, given that these chapters are likely to be later than Proverbs 10:1—22:16.

Proverbs 30

The first three verses of chapter 30 have the character of a psalm of lament, a calling on God for help, but it then becomes clear that the lament is about not having gained wisdom or knowledge of 'the Holy One'[21] – the opposite of the usual subject matter of a psalm of lament. Verses 5–6 affirm the reliability of God's word, and his promises to those who trust his word, and there is no mention of Yahweh here, which is perhaps surprising. The speaker moves from doubt to faith in verses 7–9. These verses have a more religious character than most of Proverbs and resemble theological discussion, as in Job, on the nature of the relationship between God and man. Here the divine name Yahweh is found in parallelism with Elohim. It contains a plea to God to provide, otherwise the speaker threatens to deny God. It may be that this passage is later and reflects some concern about how wisdom is regarded in the canon (Moore, 1994) echoing the insufficiency of human knowledge of wisdom and stressing the God-given nature of real knowledge. Perhaps the reference to Yahweh suggests that the answer to the problem posed in earlier verses lies in recognition of Yahweh.

In Proverbs 30:15–33, in this section of numerical heightening, there is an implicit religious content in that these verses show that God is ultimately in control of ordering an apparently disorganized world. Taken at face value, they can be seen as simply observations about human character in relation to nature and animals, perhaps with a note of wonder at the implicit order behind completely unlike items. However, it is of interest that the religious dimension is not lacking in that implicitly the thread that holds these verses together is the idea of God's control of the order of creation. God is mentioned in verses 4–6 and 9.

---

[21] קדשים, lit 'holy ones'. This is the only example of the use of such an epithet for God in Proverbs.

Proverbs 31

In the first part of Proverbs 31 there is no reference to Yahweh, but in the second half there is. The capable wife in these verses helps the poor, she sews and sells her products and, perhaps most important of all, in verse 30 she 'fears the Lord'. Some scholars have seen verse 30 as a religious addition to an otherwise secular poem, but Whybray (1994c) argues that this reference to religion may well be the climax of the poem; it is a longer verse than others and concludes the catalogue of the wife's virtues summing them up in the expression 'fear of Yahweh'.

It is significant that God is by no means absent in these more fragmentary sections of Proverbs – he is certainly present in Proverbs 30:1–9 in a more developed religious section – and therefore that these pieces are not to be regarded as secular in origin. Reference to the divine is clearly integral to the expression of the wisdom worldview, even if occasionally God appears to take something of a back seat.

CONCLUSION

Yahweh appears in a large majority of chapters of the book of Proverbs. The mention of him forms an integral part of the structure of many of the genres and of chapters as we now have them. Yahweh sayings also, arguably, form a crucial role in the literary development of the proverbial material, but this is not the only important stage; the oral formation of proverbs may well have contained a crucial religious and even specifically Yahwistic element. In Proverbs 1–9 the references are more numerous and hence more integral, and may well belong to the earliest stage of the development of both instructions and poems, whether oral or written. This is arguably true also of 22:17—24:22, in which the references to Yahweh are integral to the chapters in which they are contained, and hard to separate out as later additions. Proverbs 30:1–14 is the most religious part of the final chapters and displays quite a developed theology that would fit in with the stance found in Proverbs

1–9, but arguably it post-dates it in its questioning tone.[22] In Proverbs 10:1—22:16 and chapters 25–9 there is perhaps more significance in the placement of the smaller number of Yahweh proverbs, but still they are important in their own right as showing the religious nature of many proverbs and of the proverbial worldview. The religious and the less religious existed side by side, in my view, in the earliest wisdom traditions. There was no conception of dividing life out in terms of religious and non-religious, as we would do today. There is no reason why the religious element and mention of Yahweh were not part of the original oral context. This original oral context is, however, lost in the mists of time. The mix of subject matter in the Proverbs simply represented the mix of life. There is a need to probe more deeply into the significance of this religious emphasis in the overall theological emphasis of Proverbs and of wisdom in general. So I have placed a more general debate on the theology of Proverbs in the next chapter, before moving on to my other major concern, that of echoes of other Old Testament texts in Proverbs, in the final chapter.

---

[22] Proverbs 31 is hard to classify under either of these categories, since its reference to Yahweh is so slight. Similarly, Prov. 24:23–34 contains no reference to Yahweh at all and is too short to classify.

CHAPTER 5

Theological context

Wisdom thinks resolutely within the framework of a theology of creation.

(Zimmerli, 1964: 146)

EMPHASIS ON THE ROLE OF YAHWEH

In the previous chapter I argued for a stronger Yahwistic presence in the material of Proverbs than is often acknowledged by scholars, and I suggested that such reference is integral to the material rather than simply a later editorial stage. In reference to Proverbs 1–9, the concept of the 'fear of Yahweh' could not be dismissed as a secondary redaction added to an existent text, but often formed an important climax to a passage. It was noted that religious elements sat easily alongside general ethical or educational concerns. Furthermore, Yahweh and Wisdom were often interchangeable concepts. The reference to Yahweh was therefore seen to be integral to the material and arguably at a formative stage. In relation to Proverbs 10:1—22:16, reference to Yahweh was seen to be integral to a number of individual proverbs which probably circulated separately, but within these chapters the Yahwistic proverbs seem to have an important shaping role, indicating their importance both at a primary oral stage and at a second written stage when these proverbs were being placed where they are now. It was also noted in Chapter 3 that Proverbs 22:17—24:22 showed signs of similar context to Proverbs 1–9, while chapters 25–9 often echoed 10:1—22:16, and this division was backed up by the findings in Chapter 4 in relation to the way references to Yahweh were spread. Proverbs 30:1–9, a more developed religious section, echoed later wisdom texts of a questioning nature. In fact, none of the material in these more

fragmentary sections was found to be entirely without divine reference. I will go on to explore the significance of the integration of the
Yahwistic elements later in the chapter. First, however, I wish to
look in more general terms at the way the debate about wisdom's
'theology' has evolved, at the discussion of its place in the characterization of Old Testament theology, and at the relative claims of
creation and order to be the keynote of wisdom. Then I shall
consider the significance of this integral Yahwistic element in relation to that debate before moving on, in Chapter 6, to the question
of the thematic integration of wisdom with other parts of the Old
Testament.

WISDOM'S SEPARATION

In the Introduction I argued that, as with the discussion of social
context(s) in relation to the book of Proverbs, similar issues of
separation and integration confront us when we turn to consider
the theological emphases of the book of Proverbs. This means
involvement in a wider scholarly debate concerning the question
of how to characterize wisdom theology as a whole. I mentioned
(also in the Introduction) how wisdom literature has been separated
from the rest of the Old Testament canon for theological as well as
contextual reasons, and how its place in Old Testament theologies
has been difficult to establish. Here I shall look at the main issues
and points of disagreement among scholars and at the state of the
debate.

A major reason for keeping wisdom separate – and this especially
focuses on the book of Proverbs – is that its subject matter is very
different from other Old Testament material and often seen as
'mundane'.[1] Perhaps this is why Proverbs suffered neglect in critical
circles in the early nineteenth century, with only the occasional
commentary appearing and very little interest in it from those
considering Old Testament theology as a whole (for example, only
two references to Proverbs in A. B. Davidson, 1904). Emphasis
tended to be placed on the human acquisition of wisdom and its

---

[1] Blenkinsopp, 1995b, treats it in this manner.

primarily utilitarian function, to the neglect of the religious aspect. Oesterley (1929) drew attention to the religious aspect of the book in that all wisdom comes from God, even though an interest in human behaviour and its consequences is, he said, the predominant theme of the book. However, with its close relationship to international wisdom, the question was raised whether this followed a more ancient Near Eastern doctrine of God as creator and world-orderer rather than a particularly Israelite one (Fichtner, 1933). More recently, Fox (1968) has rejected a utilitarian view of Proverbs, arguing that even the oldest material in the book is 'ethico-religious', its purpose being 'to get people to behave morally'. However, he maintains that its religion is not the normative religion of Israel and that its God has virtually none of the characteristics of that religion.

Wisdom literature, as found in Proverbs, is generally characterized as containing, in form, mainly pithy, proverbial sayings and, in content, reflections on the meaning of life and on the relationship of human beings to the divine in the context of retributive justice. Although relationship with the divine is featured, notably in wisdom's later developments in Job and Ecclesiastes, earlier wisdom is regarded as a quest that is human-centred, with its starting point in human questioning and experience.[2] It is sometimes regarded as a secular enterprise and hence as non-theological.[3] As Westermann wrote in 1982, 'Wisdom has no place within the basic framework of an OT theology since it originally and in reality does not have as its object an occurrence between God and man; in its earliest stages wisdom is overwhelmingly secular' (Westermann, 1982: 11). This matter is seriously open to question. How wisdom is to be characterized in terms of the human and divine is a matter of emphasis. While wisdom, at its roots, springs from an attempt to understand human experience of life, much of its concern is with relationship with the divine, and there are serious questions whether the word 'secular' is at all appropriate when referring to wisdom literature,

---

[2] Von Rad (1972) argued this particularly for Proverbs, in which the act–consequence relationship was seen as primary.

[3] McKane (1970) argued that the proverbs were largely secular in their concern and only later subjected to a thorough Yahwehization.

which is grounded in experience of God and the created world. Once the religious dimension is acknowledged, the links with other parts of the tradition come more strongly into view. For example, as R. Davidson writes in *Wisdom and Worship*:

Of course it is possible to define the concerns of the wise in language which does not seem to employ specifically theological concepts – the search for an understanding of order within nature and society, the striving for meaning and self-understanding, the attempt so to regulate daily life in the light of such order and meaning that people would know how to act, mid the choices and the perplexing circumstances of life, in such a way that success could be guaranteed and failure avoided. Yet, behind the search lay a fundamental religious premise. The order within nature and society was divinely given, part of the cosmos as it had been determined by the gods in the beginning; and that order which the wise sought to explore and comprehend was the same order which the community was concerned to acknowledge, to respond to and to maintain in its various cultic practices and religious festivals. (1990: 13)

Here Davidson makes an interesting link between the order that characterizes the wisdom quest and the order sought in the cultic sphere, against scholars such as Dentan (1968), in my view an important link in the understanding of the influence of wisdom on Old Testament theology (see discussion below).

The question of how wisdom's theology is to be evaluated and characterized has led to some profound scholarly disagreements. Wisdom's theological value has been questioned by many scholars. Different scholars have placed different degrees of emphasis on it, and an evaluation of the theological value of Proverbs largely hangs on this debate. Many analyses have stressed the human aspect of wisdom[4] because, in comparison with other parts of the Old Testament, it is a very human emphasis. It was regarded as profoundly anthropocentric (Zimmerli in his earlier work, 1964), or even as a secular enterprise and hence non-theological in its earliest stages (McKane, 1970). This is to link up with a continuing debate about the anthropocentricity or theocentricity of wisdom, well summarized by Perdue in *Wisdom in Revolt* (1991). Perdue argues that a balance between the two is what is ultimately required in order to

---

[4] E.g. Brueggemann, 1972.

understand the right emphasis of wisdom.[5] Wright (1969) had a problem with its emphasis on reason and experience and noted that, according to the fall, those were not the way to a full knowledge of God. There was not enough emphasis on divine actions that led to salvation and redemption. However, I would side with Perdue (1991), following von Rad (1972), that the anthropocentric and theocentric are in a crucial dialectical relationship, and I would add that this balance is ultimately reflected in the figure of Wisdom, who represents divine revelation on offer to human beings and bridges the gap between the human acquisition of wisdom and the divine ownership of ultimate wisdom (Dell, 2000). Wisdom as presented in Proverbs is a two-sided coin; there is the human side and there is the divine, and, in my view, the figure of Wisdom provides a bridge that links the two.[6]

Wisdom's authority, as compared to other parts of the Old Testament, has also been questioned. The sages are seen to have founded their own moral code on experience. Zimmerli (1964) in his early work claimed that the teaching of the wise was no more than advice based on experience rather than a revealed law which imposed duties and obligations. He saw the reward of 'life' as desires fulfilled and good fortune. He saw wisdom as propounding the need for human beings to tune into a world order that was divinely appointed, the fear of God being the soundest means to good fortune.

These claims are seriously open to question. The discussion of social context showed how diverse the 'function' of wisdom was and how different parts of Proverbs indicate different situations. In Chapter 4 it was clear how embedded the divine references are, particularly in Proverbs 1–9 and 22:17—24:22, making a secular characterization entirely inappropriate. I also reject the idea that it is a different Yahweh who appears in this material (contra Koch, 1983; and Preuss, 1972; 1987) (see discussion below). As for its authority, wisdom is arguably not fundamentally at variance with the moral values found elsewhere (see Chapter 6); it has its own emphasis, but to downgrade its contribution is simply the result of

---

[5] See discussion of this balance between anthropocentric and theocentric in Dell, 1997.
[6] See Dell, 1997; 2000.

prejudice. Gemser (1960) attacked Zimmerli's early ideas on the authority of wisdom and argued that the demands made on human beings in Proverbs were not divorced from divine obligation.

A further problem is that even if one has decided that the emphasis should be placed on finding a theology of wisdom, the next question is how to characterize that, and from the identification of this problem further questions arise. Is wisdom theology synonymous with creation theology? How unified is the theological viewpoint even just within Proverbs? Did it develop and mature over time? What emphasis should be placed on world order (seen as paralleled in the Ma'at concept from Egyptian literature)? Is the concept of order – both world order and social order – fundamental to the worldview of the Proverbs, and should one regard this type of 'natural theology' (if that is the right characterization) as the ground of wisdom theology? The questions continue! I will now turn to look at some answers to them as given by scholars who have been particularly influential in this field.

CHARACTERIZING WISDOM'S THEOLOGY

An Old Testament theology that does justice to the thought of Israel must relegate creation to the sidelines. (von Rad, [1962] 1975: 1, 27)

An inheritance from past scholarship is a lack of emphasis on creation theology that has led to a certain downplaying of the importance of creation in the Old Testament in general. This means that recognition of its place in wisdom literature has also been slow to emerge, and only from quite recent times is this being fully acknowledged. This in turn has led to a re-evaluation of the place of creation within Old Testament theology and has provided a bridge by which wisdom's theology has become more integrated.

The work of von Rad in the 1960s in outlining an Old Testament theology was very influential in the characterization of the development of creation faith in the Old Testament, and it was he who held that an integrated view of creation as salvation was a relatively late development in Israelite faith. It came to prominence, in his view, only at the time of the exile in that it was a concern reflected in the exilic prophet Deutero-Isaiah. At that time a more universal and monotheistic view of God was emerging within the thought of Israel, and there was considerable threat from the gods of Babylonia, which heightened the polemic. Deutero-Isaiah, von Rad argued, makes explicit the link between creation and the saving history, a link not found in the J creation material in Genesis 1:12—3:24. Once again, one can see that the saving history was regarded as a central point; once creation was brought into line with that, it became integral, but before that it was, as was wisdom, on the outside. Von Rad suggested that Israel viewed creation with suspicion because it was associated with fertility religion and natural revelation.

In *Wisdom in Israel* (1972), later than his Old Testament theology, von Rad changed his emphasis, notably on the issue of the subordination of creation to salvation history. He now made the suggestion that the wisdom materials, with their interest in order and creation, are neither derivative from nor in response to the historical traditions, but that they have their own starting point in 'the problem of a phenomenology of man . . . tied to an environment' (1970: 314). This gives to wisdom its own set of traditions as an alternative to the historical model, and I shall explore this idea as it has been taken up by other scholars (see below). It is significant, however, that von Rad's view about the development of creation ideas so dominated the scholarly field that a whole generation of scholars hardly looked at the issue.

As with all attempts to find one key to unlock a rich and varied worldview, the description by Zimmerli (quoted at the beginning of the chapter) can be said to limit the definition of wisdom. Wisdom's themes are clearly more far-reaching than just a concern with creation. However, this was an apparent attempt to reassert the primacy of the creation idea within wisdom and it has certainly been quoted many times as a landmark in the appreciation of the place of creation in wisdom literature. It becomes clear that what Zimmerli was really wanting to emphasize in his later work (1978) was the place of creation in the theological thought of Israel as a whole, and by doing that, he managed to bring the wisdom literature into more central focus. He makes an important link between creation and wisdom in the realm of related ideas, but does not really provide an analysis of the importance of creation in relation to other theological emphases as found in the wisdom literature. He writes:

When it entered the promised land, Israel entered a world in which high gods were praised as creators of the world and the glory of the creation was displayed . . . Israel entered this world with the polemic confession "Yahweh is his name". Using this confession, Israel in turn sang the praises of creation in the words borrowed from this world. Now, however, they were understood with reference to the One God Yahweh; there was no second realm with any second god to be praised. This process was more than formal and intellectual. What happened was that Israel opened the entire world of creation and entered it with its faith in Yahweh, by subordinating the realms it discovered there to Yahweh. This is the locus of wisdom lore, whose international character . . . was well known to Israel. (Zimmerli, 1978: 158)

It is clear that Zimmerli follows the suggestion that Israel 'borrowed' ideas from the ancient Near East in the area both of creation motifs and of wisdom. Once creation was adopted by the Yahwists – and wisdom observations with it – they could all be accommodated within the Israelite worldview. This is again, in my view, a subordination of wisdom to the saving-history model by a more subtle route! Zimmerli writes: 'Laziness brings poverty (Prov. 10:4); sudden wrath engenders strife (15:18); a foolish son is a disgrace to his parents (10:1). These observations, too, could be borrowed in the context of a created world now ascribed to the creative act of Yahweh' (1978: 158). However, he does at least move towards the integration of the creation motif with other parts of the Old Testament. He argues for the Yahweh-centredness of wisdom:

When the observations or instructions approach the boundary line where human considerations reach their limit and the hidden background of the 'order' that affects all things becomes visible, in every instance it is Yahweh who is mentioned . . . Everywhere he is clearly the One in whose presence all human intellectual activity takes place. In him it finds its absolute limit; but in him it also finds reward when it has followed his will. Thus even in the many observations that wisdom makes in the natural world, which have no direct bearing on the service of God in the narrow sense or on his commandments, wisdom is aware of operating within the realm of Yahweh's creation. Even though Israel and its unique history never make an appearance, so that knowledge, counsel and understanding operate in the realm of what is common to all people, the 'man' under consideration here is still the creature of Yahweh. (1978: 159)

Schmid (1968) saw the concept of order as the fundamental assumption of the wisdom enterprise, a concept that linked up with creation but was broader than it.[7] His emphasis, in truth, probably describes only one aspect of wisdom, but it is an important one. It is clear that, in its maxim-making, the wisdom quest is designed to bring order out of chaos, and this can be said to be so on the divine level as well. Schmid was following a wave of scholarship begun by Koch (1983 [Ger. 1955]), in which Koch used Proverbs to argue for an inner retributive principle in human lives: namely, consequences follow deeds without God's involvement. This provocative thesis was challenged from all sides, notably by Gese (1958), who took up the question of retribution in Proverbs. He agreed with Koch that the proverbs presuppose an inner relationship between deed and consequence, and he likened it to the world-order idea parallel with Ma'at, but he did not see this as divorced from the action of God, who was responsible for the fates of individuals.[8] Although God was in charge of the order, he was also independent of it and superior to it: 'A man's mind plans his way, but the Lord directs his steps' (Prov. 16:9). Von Rad (1972) here followed Gese in that he recognized belief in a world order in Proverbs and stressed Yahweh's involvement in both establishing it and maintaining it. Schmid (1966) focused on other wisdom traditions and argued for close links with the monotheism and deed–consequence processes found in Egyptian instructions. He argued, however, that in its interest in human character rather than in actions, the anthropology of Proverbs was personalized into a retribution dogma.

This notion of order within the wisdom worldview is an important one, but it is widely recognized nowadays to have been overstated by Schmid and others. Murphy (1975) is among those who have rejected Schmid's thesis, arguing against the world-order idea, particularly in Proverbs 10–29, where he saw an attempt to find patterns in human life but no awareness of a universal order set

---

[7] See also Schmid, 1974; 1984.

[8] The question of the relationship of the figure of Wisdom to the Egyptian ideal of Ma'at is closely related to this discussion. This link has been particularly stressed by Kayatz (1966), and has been taken further into goddess imagery by Lang (1986) (see discussion above).

down in advance. The concept of order is a close companion to that of creation and can be held together with that doctrine as long as the concept does not become too deterministic. The work of Jenks (1985) demonstrates this. He argued that three basic theological presuppositions or principles undergird even the oldest section of Proverbs 10–29: first, that this is an orderly world ruled by Yahweh, its wise Creator; second, that knowledge of this order is possible for the person who opens himself to wisdom; and third, that the wise man who aligns himself with God's order in this way will experience good things, while the fool will suffer for his folly. Jenks argues that Old Testament wisdom was originally theological, based on order, knowability and justice.

Zimmerli's contribution, then, was to put creation back on the agenda. Even so, it took time for creation ideas to infiltrate wisdom studies. A number of scholars, taking Zimmerli's lead, have gone on to look at the place of creation in wisdom thought, but again one finds a variety of views and emphases. In general, scholars saw creation either as the main element, following Zimmerli, or as just one element within the wisdom tradition;[9] or, while seeing creation as the overarching principle in wisdom, found other themes that derive from it (Perdue, 1994b).[10]

An example of the first category, Hermisson (1978), argued for creation as the overarching horizon of wisdom, arguing that this was inherent even in Proverbs 10–29 (e.g. 16:4). Doll (1985) particularly challenged Hermisson's argument that creation ideas were to be found in Proverbs 10–29, and argued for Proverbs 16:4 as a later redaction. He pointed out the danger of ranging Proverbs 10–29 and 1–9 together, arguing that 1–9 does speak of the creation of the world by Yahweh and that the two parts of the book spring from completely different traditions. Doll's assessment is closely bound up with social context; he sees a development from a political, agrarian context for wisdom to a royal stage, and on to a more theological stage, as reflected in the wisdom poems, which locates

---

[9] For example, Boström (1990) sees the creation motif as employed in Proverbs primarily for ethical purposes.

[10] Perdue (1994a) complained that a theology of creation in wisdom had yet to be written and then did so himself in 1994b – both books were published in the same year.

wisdom in temple schools, with close similarities to the Psalms. This raises again the important issue of the character of different parts of Proverbs which is essential to this discussion (as aired in Chapter 2), and shows how the areas of social context and theology are intertwined. Are creation elements in Proverbs 1–9 arguably different from the worldview expressed in Proverbs 10–29?

Murphy (1985; 2000) has consistently addressed the issue of the place of creation in wisdom thought. He rejects making wisdom or creation faith into outsiders for Israelite faith, arguing that Israel made such traditions, even if they did originate elsewhere, into her own so that they became a genuine expression of Israelite faith. He speaks of two types of creation tradition in wisdom: first, creation as 'beginnings', as expressed in the poems on Wisdom that make the wisdom tradition the means of understanding the nature of reality, as revealed in the created world, and secondly, creation as the arena of human existence, an arena which, in its emphasis on experience, included experience of God. This is a useful distinction that hints that there may be different types of creation concept within the one text.

Along similarly helpful lines, Westermann characterized the two major creation traditions of the Old Testament as 'the creation of humans' and 'the creation of the world'. This model was taken up by Doll (1985), who found evidence of the former category in Proverbs 10–29 in awareness of the creation of rich and poor and in the creation of organs of perception which enabled a person to become wise. Awareness of God's creation of the world is found by Doll in Proverbs 1–9 where Wisdom becomes a theological construct (Prov. 3:8), and through praise to God as creator. I will bear these possible models in mind as I take forward my discussion.

WISDOM'S PLACE IN OLD TESTAMENT THEOLOGY

One can define Yahwism in terms of election, covenant and salvation history exclusively only at the price of ignoring the wisdom literature of ancient Israel. (Hoppe, 1979: 197)

In recent times, there has been then, an increasingly vociferous attack on the emphasis on revelation through history that failed to integrate wisdom into Old Testament theology.[11] There has been a fresh emphasis on the 'doctrine' of creation. Schmid expressed it succinctly when he wrote: 'The belief that God has created and is sustaining the order of the world in all its complexities, is not a peripheral theme of biblical theology, but is plainly the fundamental theme' (Schmid, 1984: 111). Lindeskog (1953) stressed the centrality of creation as a biblical doctrine. The place of creation in Old Testament religion is, he argued, closely linked with Yahwism, an emphasis which distinguishes it sharply from other ancient Near Eastern religions. The specifically Yahwistic nature of wisdom as a distinguishing aspect and its integration with other parts of the Old Testament is an important point here.

Furthermore, the emphasis of wisdom on human experience, world order and creation thought has been increasingly seen to have an authoritative status of its own (Hayes and Prussner, 1985). Hayes and Prussner write: 'Creation thought, priestly thought (cult and ceremonial), and wisdom thought have one major feature which they share in common: they order reality into meaning forms or create universes of meaning within which life can be viewed and understood without much special appeal to or reliance on historical thought categories or *Heilsgeschichte*' (1985: 275). The knock-on effect of such emphases has been to give creation and wisdom a greater place in Old Testament theologies.

Hoppe (1979) gives three reasons for creation's subordination within scholarship: first, von Rad's emphasis on creation as a late and secondary doctrine; second, suspicion of 'natural theology', which might water down the distinctiveness of revelation; and third, the emphasis on redemption, which subsumes creation under the rubric of soteriology. He asks whether the 'God of history' model is more Yahwistic than an understanding of God as manifest in nature and human experience. The inference of his response is that actually it is not. He stresses that human response to nature, the realm of interpersonal relationships and the development of maturity and self-understanding are all concerns of wisdom and of the people of

---

[11] Notably von Rad in his *Old Testament Theology* (1962), who characterized wisdom as Israel's response to Yahweh's acts in history (see discussion above).

God, and so wishes to redress the imbalance that has held sway in scholarly circles. He emphasizes the antiquity of creation faith as demonstrated in Genesis, Psalms, Jeremiah and Deutero-Isaiah in particular. He argues that the sages assisted in the process of making creation more central: it legitimated their enterprise, but more than this it functioned as a theophany, a means whereby the divine was revealed to those who devoted themselves to discernment. He argues that belief in an all-embracing cosmic order was the basis of the proverb's validity – that is, dependence upon the regularity and dependability of observable phenomena. God stands at the beginning and end of that order, and yet there is also an uncontrollable element in the quest to master life.

So, for example, among recent Old Testament theologies, Brueggemann in his *Theology of the Old Testament* (1997) considers creation before he considers the great historical acts of redemption. He begins with 'the practice of testimony' – that is, praise of God – and then moves on to the expression of that testimony in verbal sentences, starting with creation. It is not God's nature as Creator that is the prime factor, but his acts or deeds in the creative act (e.g. Isa. 42:5–6a). Creation itself witnesses to the Creator. This is not a doctrine of creation but, as Brueggemann prefers to term it, 'one utterance at a time' (1997: 163–4).

There is increasing awareness that wisdom is part of a wider theme counter to that of deliverance in historical terms. The wider counter-theme includes psalmic material and the creation theme as found in other Old Testament material. Westermann (1978b), for example, distinguishes between the saving acts of God in history and blessing from God that is apart from the temporal realm.[12] While deliverance happens within time, blessing is represented by the cyclical processes of nature. He also speaks in terms of a horizontal and vertical dimension, in which the horizontal is the plane of history, and the vertical is the ahistorical, the cultic and the cosmic, which has the creator God at its centre. Brueggemann (1980) sees Westermann and others as offering a fresh paradigm for Old Testament theology in this insistence on an alternative tradition. This

---

[12] See also Westermann, 1971b; 1979.

posited alternative tradition is clearly broader than just the wisdom literature itself, or even just creation traditions themselves. It involves an emphasis on the cultic, too (B. W. Anderson, 1987), and hence draws together material in the Old Testament in a fresh and creative synthesis that avoids traditional categorization.

Finally, I want here to reflect briefly on wisdom's relationship to major themes of the Old Testament, such as monotheism and universalism. It is clear that in the wisdom literature there is not only an individualistic worldview, but one which is universal and monotheistic, almost by default. There appears to be in the wisdom literature a presupposition of monotheism in that no other gods are explicitly mentioned (even if there is an overtone of polytheistic practice in the figure of the foreign/loose woman), and in that there is seen to be one God behind everything, including the order of the world. There is an implicit universalism here and no mention of any group that has been singled out for special attention. It would be easy to explain this away by saying that the literature was all post-exilic – or, as has been discussed in previous chapters, at least the parts that mention Yahweh are, along with Proverbs 1–9 – and therefore to be regarded as part of the monotheistic developments of the post-exilic period. However, on examination, there are good arguments for thinking that the theological aspects are not all late, and for seeing the Yahweh references as integral to the material rather than thinking that there was any special later development of theological ideas. Further, parts of Proverbs 1–9 have a good claim to be earlier than the post-exilic period in their formative stages, even if the section received a final shaping at that time. There is a distinct possibility, in my view, that there was a stream in pre-exilic Israel that had an important place in individual family life, and also at the higher levels of court life and in circles of the educated, which focused on human beings and their relationships with God within the context of a rather simple framework of God as the orderer and creator of the world, with Wisdom as both the agent of that ordering and as the mediator between God and human beings. This had universal overtones that avoided the exclusivism of other parts of the Old Testament.

CREATION TEXTS IN PROVERBS

I have mentioned my view that the figure of Wisdom is a vital nexus linking the human and divine aspects of wisdom, and, when turning to the creation texts, first of all in Proverbs 1–9, that is my starting point. The main texts that treat creation in any cosmic sense in Proverbs are 3:19–20 and 8:22–31, which form part of longer passages about woman Wisdom. These point out the divine element of the wisdom enterprise and introduce the revelation of the divine through wisdom and through the acts of creation. However, one can argue, as Perdue does, that the wider texts on woman Wisdom of 3:13–20 and 8:1–36 link up with this creation emphasis, even if creation is not explicitly mentioned (cf. Perdue 1994b). It is therefore important to take the explicit references to creation here in the wider context of the passages as whole units. Perdue points out that woman Wisdom links instruction in the moral life with more theological issues of creation and providence. In this assumption he is showing how the human aspect of wisdom that desires the gifts that woman Wisdom has on offer is in essential interaction with divinely given Wisdom (the cosmological/anthropological axis that he describes). Perdue (1994b) describes different 'voices' in Proverbs 1–9: that of the teacher, that of Wisdom and that of God, each of increasing authority and theological depth. Hence, the role of wisdom as 'teacher' is intimately related to other facets of her character. He also stresses the importance of 'the fear of the Lord', which he takes to refer to religious piety characterized by faith in God as creator and sustainer of life (1:7, 9:10, 15:33, 31:31) (cf. Chapter 4, where I laid a similar emphasis on these concepts plus the references to Yahweh). Wisdom has its beginning, he argues, in faith in God that seeks understanding. Perdue notes that the overall pattern of these chapters is that in chapter 3, verses 13–14 describe the human gain from wisdom and then verses 15–18 describe what is on offer to humans, bridging the human and divine aspects. Verses 19–20 move on to the divine side of the picture – Wisdom as given by God at creation. In chapter 8, too, Wisdom is introduced as teacher and her call to learn takes up the first eleven verses. In verses 12–21 her benefits are listed, and then at the end, in a pattern similar to chapter 3, her role in creation is stressed. Only in the final verses (32–6) is her role as teacher stressed again in a move back to the starting point of the poem. I noted in Chapter 4 how the figure of Wisdom links up with an educational context but is not confined or even primarily characterized by it.

Perdue writes: 'The faith of the sages in Proverbs 1–9 is expressed in a theology of creation. Drawing on a rich variety of creation myths and their root metaphors, the sages depicted God and the creator of heaven and earth, who used wisdom to create and then to continue to sustain the world' (1994b: 79). This emphasis on both past creation and present sustaining of the world is an important one. In this material there is mention of the act of creation in the past, but this is not the limit of reference to creation – it is an ongoing reality. Perdue finds categories of creation by word, artistry, fertility and battle. In 8:29, for example, creation is by word: an edict is given by God to the primordial deep, keeping it from overwhelming the created order. Artistry is emphasized in 3:19–20; 8:26–9, in the way the design and construction of the cosmos are described. The fertility theme comes in with the image of Wisdom as God's child; she is described as the first of the divine acts of creation. The battle or struggle with chaos, so that it is fashioned into an orderly world, finds echoes in the texts describing the creation of the world, but is also particularly represented by woman Folly, who represents this chaos.[13]

I find the first two of these categories more helpful than the second two. The mention of words and deeds in reference to creation are clearly essential in describing its nature, as paralleled in Genesis 1. This refers to both past event (the word of creation that was spoken and the ordering that was done at that time) and present reality (God's continuing word) – and indeed to the communicative 'word' in which we all partake (as especially stressed by the wisdom writers, notably in Proverbs), as well as to God's continuing presence in maintaining the world in order and keeping human history going. The theme of fertility is, in my view, a by-product of the recalling of creation in the past and serves to describe aspects of

---

[13] Perdue sees woman Wisdom and woman Folly in terms of two cultic goddesses, a picture with which I would disagree.

wisdom in the present (e.g. as a life-giving tree), rather than being a major theme in itself. Similarly, the battle theme is there in the recalling of the way creation was achieved and is a sub-theme to the main creation motif. It may be that the figure of woman Folly keeps the theme of impending chaos alive, but I would not go as far as to see this as an ongoing 'battle' between competing goddesses. However, Perdue's work is a major step in the process of actually unpacking the character of the creation elements in these texts, and it is on these texts that I shall now focus my attention.

I turn now to the main creation elements in these texts, Proverbs 3:19–20 and 8:22–31. Proverbs 3:19–20 links the wisdom figure with God's act of the creation of the world, an anticipation of 8:22–31 perhaps, but the explicit link of Wisdom's role in creation is not made. In verse 19, God established/founded (יסד) the earth and secured/established (כון) the heavens. His skill in creation is emphasized here, linking up with wisdom's interest in the skills of humans. These verbs denoting 'establishing' and 'founding' belong to common cosmological ideas of the time and are reflected in other texts. So the earth was conceived of as a plane mass, resting on an ocean (Ps. 24:2; 136:6), as having foundations (Isa. 51:13; Ps. 104:5; Prov. 8:29) and as supported by pillars (Job 9:6; Ps. 75:3(4)); Sheol lay beneath the ocean (Amos 9:2, 3). Above the earth, the heaven or sky was thought of as a material expanse (Gen 1:2), fixed in its place by God (Isa. 40:22; Ps. 104:2) and supported by pillars (Job 26:11; Ps. 18:7(8) – mountains). 'Heavens' represents both the sky and the heavens (probably conceived of as on different planes), that is, the celestial abode of the deity above the sky. There is similar language of creation in other texts in the Old Testament. For example, we find יסד in Isaiah 24:18; 48:13; 51:13; Amos 9:6 and Zechariah 12:1, as well as in Proverbs 8:29; and כון in Job 28:25, 27 and Psalms 93:1; 119:90, as well as in Proverbs 24:3 (to describe building a house, see below) and 8:27.

In verse 20, he (God) divided (בקע) the primeval deep (or he continues to do so, if the verb is regarded as present tense) and goes on providing water for the world. בקע is also found in Genesis 1:2, 7:11; Job 38:16, 30; Proverbs 3:20a; 8:24, 27–8 (cf. Ps. 74:12–15, where Tiamat's body is said to be divided). Reference to life-sustaining moisture is also found in Job 28:25–6; 36:27–8; 38:28, 37; Psalm

78:23 and Genesis 2:6. It is fascinating that both the idea of water as
the enemy of creation (Gen. 1) and the idea that it is the agent of its
continuance (Gen. 2) are found in this text. Waters are seen to be
flowing from the ground, and dew from the clouds; and the primeval ocean continues above the sky (cf. Gen. 7:11, where בקע is
used of the breaking forth of the fountains of the deep). Water,
then, comes from above and from below to fertilize the land.[14]

Turning to Proverbs 8:22–31, a rather different language of creation (קנה) is used in verse 22, which has led to much discussion of
meaning. The usual meaning of קנה is 'to acquire', but this is not to
suggest that wisdom pre-existed creation and was then 'acquired' by
God, and so 'created' would seem the more natural translation. The
other main option denotes 'fathering' or 'forming' in relation to
birth, which would fit in with the language used in verses 23–5,
which continues the origins. However, to translate 'create' also fits
in with what follows. Fox points out that in this passage the divine
acquisition of wisdom is a prototype of human acquisition (cf. the
use of קנה in Prov. 4:7, 'get wisdom'). Wisdom is depicted in verse
22 as the first of God's deeds. 'First/beginning' (רֵאשִׁית) echoes
Genesis 1:1 (בְּרֵאשִׁית). Again this has been seen to refer to Wisdom
as the firstborn of the creative process, although it is the specific
point of time of Wisdom's creation that seems to be the focus here,
and it is related to God's other acts, which come second. רֵאשִׁית is
also found in Job 40:19 and Psalms 78:51; 105:36. In verse 23 we
find 'set up' (נסך) (cf. Ps. 139:13; Job 10:11), which again some have
related to birth by translating 'poured out' (i.e. of semen at birth)
and which others have translated 'installed' (with possible royal
overtones of installation as king). An alternative is to translate
'woven together' in the sense of God knitting sinews together as
part of the creative process. The meaning is quite unclear here.
Verses 24–6 describe creation out of chaos (not *ex nihilo*). The
physical world is described here by its various parts (as in Gen. 1);
waters, mountains and soil are all described. The creation of
Wisdom seems to precede God's division of the waters in verse 24;
he had not yet shaped the firmament or allowed controlled springs

---

[14] See Emerton, 1966: 125, for an explanation of Hebrew cosmology in relation to the waters of
the primeval deep.

of water to nourish the earth. He had not yet shaped the mountains that would hold up the earth from the sea (cf. Jon. 2:6).

Although this passage primarily describes Wisdom's antiquity before the rest of creation, it also, perhaps almost by default, describes the creation of water, mountains and earth. It fits in with the description of the world in Proverbs 3:19–20. Verses 27–9 describe the creation of the heavenly vault that restrains the waters of chaos (cf. Gen. 1:6–8). The waters are both above and below; they need to be restrained by the creation of heaven and earth. It is not clear whether the 'fountains of the deep' refers to the waters of chaos or simply to the deeps of ordinary seas. It is clear from verse 29 that the important message here is of limitation. God gives limits to the sea and establishes the earth. He is in control. He makes order out of chaos. The message is one of stability; God secures, restrains, arranges. Much discussion has focused on the meaning of אָמוֹן in verse 30; the main suggestions are 'master worker' or 'little child'.[15] Both meanings link up with aspects of the poem, 'master worker' with the portrayal of God as architect of the universe, and 'little child' with the emphasis on creating and begetting. The latter suggestion links up with the Egyptian idea of Ma'at and is preferable, in my view, on linguistic grounds also. This would then fit the pattern of the delight of the parent in the child and of the child in the created world. Wisdom, then, is Yahweh's companion in the creation of the world, his intimate friend and part of the very construction of the world. So the wisdom quest should be in human life. Creation is being used as a direct parallel to the place of wisdom in human life; it is part of the order of what is and should be.

These two texts, then, are grounded in the traditions about creation with which we are familiar from other parts of the Old Testament, as has been pointed out – particularly Genesis and certain psalms. It is significant that in relation to Genesis there are elements of J and P imagery; there is no particular emphasis that would differentiate the two pictures of the creative process. The emphasis on ordering of the creation is more marked here than in other texts because of the important link with human experience

---

[15] Whybray (1994c: 136) suggests 'Creator'.

and social order that is being made. This in turn provides a link with
the rest of Proverbs, where order seems to be primary and where
there is less overt interest in the creation theme, as I shall go on to
discuss.

Before leaving consideration of the creation elements in Proverbs
1–9, it is worth mentioning 22:17—24:22, the section parallel to
chapters 1–9. There are references here to human creation which
could be seen to parallel divine creation, as in 23:22, 'your father
who begot you', in reference to a human father; and in 23:24, 'he
who begets a wise son will be glad in him'. In verse 22 of the same
passage, the mother is mentioned, and her role in bearing her son is
mentioned in verse 25. In 24:3–4 wisdom is likened to a house,
which could be metaphorical, paralleling God's creation of the
world. Perdue suggests that building imagery is an integral part of
the picture of creation in Proverbs 3 and 8. The nineteenth century
Polish Jewish scholar Malbim, in *Musar Hahokmah* (1923) (cited by
Fox, 2000: 160), compared Proverbs 3:19–20 to 24:3–4, since both
passages describe two stages, first creation (3:19; 24:3) and then
provision (3:20; 24:4). Finally, in the reference to 'Lord and King'
in 24:22 an integral link is made between God and the representative
of the social order, the king, which also could be seen as reflecting
the order of the cosmos. There is less in this section on creation *per se*
and more on the link with human experience, and yet the divine
aspect is presupposed behind the scenes.

In Proverbs 10:1—22:16, God's creation is seen more as a presupposition of texts than an explicit matter for discussion. The worldview of Proverbs is to see God as creator, which includes the role of
orderer, according to knowable lines that can be learned through
experience. According to Perdue, different and particular emphases
on creation are to be found in 10:1—22:16: in 14:31 in the mention of
justice for all; in 16:4, which treats creation and theodicy; in 16:11 on
creation and economic justice; in 17:5 on creation and the integrity
of the poor; in 20:12, a description of organs of knowing and
perceiving; and in 22:2 in the emphasis on rich and poor. I find
these a strange collection of disparate texts which perhaps need a
little more attention and a different categorization. Proverbs 14:31
does not in fact mention justice for all; rather, God is seen to defend
the poor man against oppression and to honour those who are kind

to such a person. This can perhaps be ranged with 17:5, which takes up the same theme, and 22:2. Perdue sees the underlying issue as justice for all rather than the partiality of God for one group or another, largely based on the observation that the wisdom writers seem also to support the acquisition of wealth. In this example he argues that, since the right to life's necessities is grounded in creation and providence, God defends those too helpless to achieve such basics. He contends that there is no 'order' being defended here. However, I would argue that we are here being given an insight into a social order that is being defended. The issue is the oppression of someone weaker than oneself, which God condemns. This is a violation of the social order grounded in God's righteous ordering of the created world. Similarly, in 17:5, punishment is due for one who mocks another more helpless than himself, who falls into calamity. In 22:2 it is evident that God is not just on the side of the poor; he created rich and poor and both have their place in God's creative ordering of the world. This links up with some of Perdue's other examples. In 16:4 it is clear that God is in control of everything, including moral categories of righteous and wicked. Perdue is against seeing a predetermined order here. I would agree that 'predetermined' is not the right term to use, but there is certainly an order that is inherent both in society and in the world.[16] In 16:11, too, in the image of the balance in which everything is weighed, one has the impression of a social order being maintained in an active fashion by God. Perdue (1994b) makes the interesting point that the image of the just balance has its ground in creation theology here, rather than in the liberation theology of Leviticus 19:36, where the same imagery is used. In 20:12 the reference to the eye and ear is, too, in my view, a reference to God's ordering of everything in human life, which parallels his creative ordering in past and present.

---

[16] I would not want strictly to equate ideas of 'order' in wisdom with natural theology in opposition to revealed theology. Murphy (1978), in not wishing to separate the historical/ahistorical aspects of faith in Yahweh, opposed the use of 'order' in reference to wisdom, but I think that this is a useful term if kept separate from more doctrinal distinctions. See discussion below.

In Proverbs 25–9, Perdue (1994b) finds just one example of the mention of creation, in 29:13 – the poor and the oppressor. This is similar in theme to 14:31, although here no moral judgement is made, just the comment again that God has created both; both are part of his social order grounded in creation. This is a consistent picture with 10:1—22:16. Proverbs 30 is the other text in which there is interest in creation. Perdue characterizes the themes as creation and rebellion (verses 1b–4) and the world turned upside down (verses 21–3). He argues that the underlying message of verses 1b–4 is that God, not human beings, rules the cosmos. However, these verses have more traditionally been seen to refer to the limits to human knowledge, along the lines of the Yahweh speeches in the book of Job. Verses 21–3 emphasize the social order expressed in a numerical saying. This seems to me to have little to do with creation, except in the loose sense that the order of the world is intimately linked to the order of the universe as created by God.

These texts in Proverbs 10–31 are somewhat miscellaneous, but the important difference between them and those in chapters 1–9 is the link forged between the creative role of God and the order established by him in human life (along the lines that Schmid (1968) discussed). In Proverbs 1–9 itself the stress on creation as past and present event is much more marked. This suggests that the more basic and primitive view of God as creator in Proverbs is as orderer. Such a picture appears to have given way to more profound musing on God's creative role in the past and in a continuing sense. This has the effect of marrying the more human emphasis on social order as reflecting that of the divine order with the more cosmological starting point where God is seen as ultimate creator and orderer, with the figure of Wisdom as the mediator between the two.

LINKING THE YAHWISTIC EMPHASIS WITH THE WIDER THEOLOGICAL DEBATE

In the last chapter I established that mention of Yahweh or the fear of Yahweh is integral to the texts themselves. This now needs to be made sense of in relation to the wider theological discussion about the character of wisdom's theology. I have argued for various social contexts for wisdom within Israelite society, and suggested that the quest for ancient Near Eastern parallels, notably Egyptian, has distracted scholars from looking at the Israelite character of wisdom material. It is important to remember that in Proverbs we are in the heartland of Israelite wisdom and of Israelite interpretation of their experience in relation to God and the world. Another aspect of this is theological, in that the wisdom worldview can be seen as theologically integrated with other parts of the Old Testament. The suggestion that this was somehow a different 'God' that wisdom literature is conceiving seems to me to be patently absurd. And yet there seems to be a caution in using the expression 'Yahwism' to refer to wisdom literature. Crenshaw, in particular, does not believe that the ancient sages accepted the Yahwistic worldview. He writes: 'The sages offered an alternative mode of interpreting reality to the Yahwistic one in which God was actively involved in guiding history toward a worthy goal . . . In their view, revelation took place during the creative act, and when human capacity to discover this hidden mystery seemed inadequate, God continued to make known his will through personified wisdom' (1981b: 208–9).[17] That worldview is increasingly being seen to include creation and wisdom, albeit on a different axis from the historical.

Murphy has consistently maintained that Yahwism and wisdom are not incompatible. He famously wrote, 'Wisdom and Yahwism go together' (1975: 117), and comments that the 'problem' here is a false one in that 'ultimately the alleged incompatibility of wisdom and Yahwism is a logical creation (and Western logic, at that), and it is not real' (1975: 118). In a later article in which he returns to the topic, he writes: 'Is it legitimate to separate Yahwism and wisdom from each other and then discuss whether they are compatible? In other words, does the very discussion concede more centrality, more importance, to Yahwism (understood as the Exodus-Sinai revelation and all that this involved), making it the criterion by which everything else is to be judged?' (2000: 193). These comments indicate that scholars are still tied to the outmoded definition of Yahwism that restricts it to the saving history and its wider ramifications on a

---

[17] I used this quotation in my own summary of the nature of wisdom (Dell, 2000: 173), but I find myself in increasing disagreement with it.

historical level and devalues the more experiential angle of human experience as represented by wisdom. Zimmerli criticized this assumption when he argued that wisdom might be seen as deliberately formulating a different set of questions: 'By neglecting any reference to the historical memory of Israel's faith, wisdom puts a question to Old Testament theology, Must one always have a historical explanation, explicitly referred to and fully formed, as the centre (of theology)?' (1974: 50) Murphy points out that it was Yahwists who experienced the world and wrote down their experiences in Proverbs; it was just a different part of their worldview to react to the creator, his creation and to other human beings within that creation.

The passages that I have pointed to that feature Yahweh as an essential part of their structure indicate the embeddedness of this tradition. Murphy sees the separation between Yahwism and wisdom as being reflective of the distinction between revelation and natural theology, the latter being seen as the product of human reason alone and therefore not God-inspired. Barr (1993) has risen to the challenge of questioning such a distinction. Murphy then stresses the integration of worldview between the wisdom writers and other canonical literature; after all, the wisdom writings do form part of the 'revealed' canon of scripture. Murphy cites Plöger, who puts the issue succinctly: 'Would it not be astonishing if an Israel that meets us primarily as the people of its God, Yahweh, in the Old Testament, would have pursued questions about life-style with a conscious exclusion of Yahweh? Even in the old wisdom period Yahweh will have certainly been known to sapiential thought, to the consideration of the expert sages, even though they will not always have used the name so readily' (Plöger, 1984: 35; Murphy, 2000: 198). Murphy raises some tantalizing questions here, but does not really go far enough in establishing the Yahwistic nature of wisdom. He speaks of the Yahweh sayings and how they link the demands of wisdom for wise and righteous behaviour to the central demands of God. This needs to be spelt out more fully.

The issue of the mention of God in Proverbs has another dimension: the prevalence of the use of Yahweh and paucity of the use of 'Elohim'. During the course of my discussion of Proverbs, I have already noted where Yahweh is mentioned. It might be worth pausing here to repeat my observation made in passing in previous chapters, that in Proverbs 1–9 there are only three uses of 'Elohim'. The first is in 2:5, where 'the fear of the Lord' is balanced with 'the knowledge of God' in an example of poetic variation in two lines. In 2:17 'the covenant of her God' refers to the god of a foreigner, which one would expect to be defined by, 'Elohim'. In 3:4, 'in the sight of God and man' is a pair of words indicating everything that can be seen and hence is a general phrase rather than a specific mention of a particular god. 'Elohim' tends to be used when speaking of God in more general terms. In Proverbs 10:1—22:16 there is only one possible reference to Elohim in a verse that is difficult to translate (14:9), but which appears to refer to those who are 'upright' being the receivers of God's favour; in fact, an emendation to 'Elohim' needs to take place here. Otherwise, it is striking that only 'Yahweh' is used in this whole section – not forgetting, of course, that many proverbs do not mention God at all. In 22:17–24:22 'Yahweh' is used once, in 22:23, and 'Elohim' is not used. In 24:23–34 there is no mention of the divine at all. In chapters 25–9 we read, in 25:2, that 'it is the glory of God (Elohim) to conceal things', and again a contrast is being made between God/gods and kings. Apart from that, the name Yahweh is predominantly used, but the number of Yahweh proverbs is small. In Proverbs 30, קְדֹשִׁים (Holy One) is found in verse 3; God (אֱלוֹהַּ) in verse 5, and 'the Lord and 'God' in parallel in verse 9. This section of chapter 30 does seems to have a different character from the rest, which may explain the usage of different divine names. Finally, in Proverbs 31, there is just one reference to 'the fear of the Lord' (verse 30), a phrase that is commonly found throughout Proverbs.

Rejecting the later-redaction argument, how else can one account for the predominance of Yahweh here? It is quite clearly the same God who is being spoken of here as is spoken of throughout the Old Testament, and the fact that he has different characteristics here or is considered from a different angle does not make him a different God. However, one is dealing with a portrait gallery of understandings of God and of encounters with truth, and in that sense no one understanding of God was identical to any other. Although consensuses emerged regarding how God was seen, there was room for continual change and the emergence of ever new symbols and meanings.

One concern is whether the portrayal of God in wisdom literature is theologically consistent with his portrayal elsewhere, but the problem here is how one defines Yahwism in the first place. It is likely, in my view, that the fairly simple wisdom view of Yahweh as creator was an early conception of God and that its influence on other material was fairly primary (see Dell, forthcoming, 2006). In that case, an essential part of the definition of Yahwism would be the wisdom/creation axis.

The daily experience of human beings may not be the most profound theological starting point for an Old Testament theology, but it is a fact of life that unites all our kind. Our response to each other, to God and the world; our growth in knowledge and self-understanding through experience (not just our own but that of others) – this is all basic to human life, covered to some extent by legal stipulation such as the ten commandments, but going well beyond that, to the formation of character. Guidance in ethical decision-making is at the heart of the wisdom enterprise and this is where a link with an educational context is formed. The perception of God informs the ethics in that he is the source of all right and wrong and judges along those lines. Yet, ultimately, fear of Yahweh will lead the wise person along an ethical path, quite apart from human experience and opinion. And that same Yahweh was viewed by these writers primarily as creator and orderer of the universe. This perception is found also in the Psalms (e.g. Pss. 19:2; 8:5) and in the realm of the sacred, so it does not exclude wisdom literature from that sphere; it is also found in legal material and in the prophets. So it is to the issue of mutual influence that I shall turn in the next chapter, hoping to bring together this discussion of social context and theology under the one umbrella of the integration of concepts rather than their dispersion. The arguments that I have presented for closer integration of wisdom with other texts come in here to challenge the chasm that scholars have opened up between wisdom literature and other genres, as I shall go on to discuss below. Furthermore, by showing the mutual influence of texts in the next chapter I hope to show that, not only in terms of theology, but also in terms of social context, the wisdom writers were aware of the broader Israelite heritage, and that it in turn was aware of them.

WISDOM'S THEOLOGICAL INTEGRATION

I have argued that uncertainty over social context led to more separation of wisdom than is necessary. More integration with social context might improve the situation. Putting more emphasis on the theological aspect of wisdom might mean positing a more overtly religious social context, not just as a final stage of the redaction of the material, but as a more primary stage. More theological integration has also become a real possibility with the renewed emphasis on creation as a doctrine within the Old Testament as a whole and within wisdom literature. This has led to wisdom having more chance of integration in Old Testament theologies in recent times. Fontaine argues, for example, that creation theology, reflection on human experience and the belief that actions produce their own consequences are notions found elsewhere in the Old Testament; and the belief expressed in Proverbs that 'all causation is negated when Israel's God wills it so' (1993: 112) is fully in line with Israelite beliefs. This is a flexible order, not a static one. Fontaine writes: 'Hebrew *hokma* is not Egyptian *ma'at*, for all that they share important characteristics' (ibid.). I would add that it also provides the essential bridge with God as creator. She argues that the figure of woman Wisdom provides the summation of the concept of wisdom in the book of Proverbs. She is 'the most unique and expressive answer to the question of the meaning of wisdom in the Book of Proverbs' (1993: 114), described by Fontaine as 'a sort of cosmic will-to-harmony' (ibid.).

As seen when noting the shift that is occurring in the evaluation of wisdom in relation to the writing of Old Testament theologies, in recent times there has been more interest in showing wisdom's place within the rest of the Old Testament, as Fontaine makes clear: 'The worldview of wisdom in Proverbs does not represent a sharp break with the rest of ancient Israel's society, but only reflects a difference in emphases and interests' (1993: 111). She argues that there is no incompatibility between Proverbs and the central Israelite traditions. Theological integration has, therefore, also come as a result of a realization of wisdom's thematic links with other parts of the Old Testament. Childs, when discussing the nature of the wisdom quest in Proverbs, argues that Proverbs 10ff. is more of an intellectual process seeking to discern patterns of truth from the context of experience, while Proverbs 1–9 increasingly saw wisdom as a gift of God. He sees this as an important dialectic between actively pursued acquisition and divine gift. It is broader than just ethics; wisdom is not just about moral decisions, but is an encompassing of the whole of experience. Childs notes an overlap with law and covenant prescriptions in that both are a common expression of the good and faithful life: 'In spite of the striking variety in theological stance, the canon has correctly recognized the profound unity between these biblical witnesses and used them both without the need for serious adjustment in order to instruct and guide God's people in the way of right response' (Childs, 1985: 212). Toombs (1955) also stresses the links of wisdom with the common, humanistic law, as in Proverbs 2. He therefore sees wisdom as a basic idea of the Old Testament, alongside covenantal faith.

Hubbard (1966) stresses connections between wisdom and prophecy, wisdom and the cult, and the covenantal aspects of Israel's faith.[18] He stresses the close relationship of kingship and covenant and the close mutual influence of prophets and wise men – Amos, Isaiah and Jeremiah in the area of individual retribution, for example. The prophetic appeal to ethics was, he argues, harking back to the order of society of the wisdom literature. He also looks at the influence of wisdom on Deuteronomy. He argues that the use of the name Yahweh in proverbs is a reference to the same Yahweh as elsewhere in the Old Testament. He also stresses the link between wisdom and cult. Hence his emphasis is on the overlap in subject matter between wisdom and other 'genres' of Old Testament material. He also plays down the idea of separate offices of priest, prophet and wise man. He argues for the early influence of wisdom on other parts of the Old Testament, although he is against strict lines of development. This work links up with a broader social context for wisdom.

Høgenhaven (1987) takes a similar integrative line. He writes: 'We have little reason to doubt . . . that the roots of the Old Testament

---

[18] He in turn was influenced by Eichrodt, 1961–7.

wisdom literature are to be sought in an early stage of Israelite history' (1987: 99). He continues:

As a way of thinking, wisdom is rooted in the immediate experience of daily life. In Wisdom – in Israel as in the whole of the ancient Near East – people are engaged in a continuous struggle to understand, to interpret and to relate actively to reality, as they encounter it in its variety of phenomena and situations. The results of these endeavours are seen in the rules and sentences of wisdom literature. At a more advanced level, however, wisdom involves the conception of a comprehensive world view in which cosmology and ethical laws and regularities are ascertained. It would seem in many respects justified to argue that this understanding of reality, which may be called the theme of Old Testament wisdom literature, forms an important part of the background for most of the literature in the Old Testament. So Schmid (1968, 1974, 1984) has convincingly shown that even large parts of the historical and narrative literature in the Old Testament are structured according to motifs known from wisdom literature. The Deuteronomists depict Israelite history as a sequence of sins against Yahweh, sins which are then inevitably punished, and meritious deeds, which are always appropriately rewarded, clearly reflecting the scheme of just retribution familiar from wisdom literature. Likewise the presence of motifs known from wisdom literature in the prophetic writings and in the legal literature of the Old Testament has been pointed at by many scholars. All this may serve to illustrate how wisdom, understood as a pattern of thought, is a very broad phenomenon, the basic characteristics of which are reflected with particular clarity in the books we term 'wisdom literature', although the same ideas would seem to have left their mark on considerable portions of the Old Testament. (Høgenhaven, 1987: 99–100)

I find myself in agreement with this fine summary of the state of the question. The problem has generally been that wisdom literature has been seen as the antithesis of other canonical literature – and yet the link is perhaps to be found in the emphasis on creation and the universal orientation of the wisdom approach. 'Israel's sages utilized creation theology to speak to the happy and productive life in such a manner as to be complementary rather than antithetical to Israel's covenantal affirmation' (Eakin, 1977: 220). A broader definition of creation theology is perhaps required, for which Eakin calls – one which indicates a faith awareness that God is creator, that Wisdom is dependent upon him and that his role as creator is the basis for demanding ethical propriety in interpersonal relationships. In this sense creation characterizes even the earliest wisdom literature (e.g.

Prov. 14:31; 16:4; 17:5; 20:12; 22:2), but more in terms of order, as argued above. Clearly, this comes to fuller expression in Proverbs 3:19–20 and chapter 8, where creation acts in the past are recalled and their meaning for the present is indicated. For Eakin, creation faith is affirmed by the ethical response of the learners, so forging a link with covenantal responsibility, especially as proclaimed by the universal Noachic covenant tradition. Eakin (1977) argues that ultimate dependence upon God unites the different traditions, despite their different emphases and starting points.[19]

These points about integration of wisdom's theology with other parts of the Old Testament needs exploring in more detail. My purpose in the next chapter is to look at echoes of texts from elsewhere within Proverbs to see if any 'internal' relationship can be found, as well as the many 'external' influences of wisdom upon other literature. This will in turn affect my conclusions about integration. I have noted the moves towards theological integration in this chapter and I now go on to consider an area which has the effect of linking wisdom, not only theologically, but also possibly in terms of social context, bringing the two discussions together.

[19] See Dell, 2003.

CHAPTER 6

Echoes of other Old Testament texts and contexts in Proverbs

> I have called and you refused, have stretched out my hand and no one heeded.
>
> (Prov. 1:23)
>
> Bind them [loyalty and faithfulness] around your neck, write them on the tablet of your heart.
>
> (Prov. 3:3)
>
> The sacrifice of the wicked is an abomination to the LORD, but the prayer of the upright is his delight.
>
> (Prov. 15:8)

In this chapter I wish to look at possible areas of influence from other areas of Old Testament life on Proverbs. The aim is to see how grounded Proverbs is within Israelite tradition. The wisdom literature is often said to be without reference to wider Israelite tradition and to stand alone. I believe that this assumption is highly questionable in relation to wisdom's influence outwards on other texts, but is it also true of influence inwards on texts such as Proverbs 1–9? Wisdom's wider influence on Old Testament literature is fairly well discussed (see Morgan, 1981), but what about influence coming into the wisdom material?

LINKS WITH WIDER OLD TESTAMENT TEXTS, TRADITIONS AND GENRES

There is a small group of scholars who have stressed links between Proverbs 1–9 and home-grown Israelite traditions. Early scholars drew parallels, and generally Proverbs was regarded as late and hence beholden to other traditions for the presence of such influences. For example, Robert (1934–5) suggested that Proverbs 1–9 reflects reutilizations of material in the book of Deuteronomy. This is reflective of a period in scholarship when this discussion was marginalized in the light of the stress on Egyptian and other ancient Near Eastern wisdom and its influence on Proverbs 1–9, which led scholarship off in a different direction. So Whybray argued (in 1965) that, while attempts had been made to demonstrate that the author of the instruction texts derived his terminology from biblical sources, especially Deuteronomy, Isaiah and Jeremiah, the parallels with *Amenemope* and other instructions are closer. He writes: 'It is true that such phrases as "teach" (*hora*), "teaching" (*tora*), "do not forget", "attend" etc., occur also in Deuteronomy, but these are merely the common vocabulary of education in Hebrew and do not prove anything' (1965: 37). I suppose one could equally argue that coincidence of language between instruction texts from Egypt and Israelite versions were equally 'common vocabulary'. In relation to the Old Testament, it is true that the context is different, in that Israel is not being addressed as a unity or as a covenant nation in Proverbs (as in Deuteronomy), but does this mean that one needs to divorce it from other Old Testament tradition? Whybray again sees the influence as a general one and writes of the material in these core instructions: 'The subjects with which these ten discourses deal – avoidance of evil company, avoidance of entanglement with immoral women, duties towards God and neighbour, prudence and self-control – are subjects which one might find in any book of ethical teaching addressed to young men, and general parallels can be found for almost all of them in the Old Testament (not only in the wisdom books but in the prophets and the laws) and in Egyptian and Mesopotamian wisdom books' (1965: 51). However, he argues against direct literary dependence on any text, biblical or non-biblical. This sounds to me a little like a case of special pleading.

Steiert (1990), on the other hand, builds on Robert's insights, noting examples of intentional theological influence and background. She stresses the didactic tendency common to Proverbs 1–9 and Deuteronomy and the link between moral instruction and law, which came increasingly to be identified as canonical scripture developed. Steiert stresses also the dependence of Proverbs 1–9 on texts from Deuteronomy and Jeremiah, and S. L. Harris (1996) indicates such echoes in Proverbs 1:20–33. Gilbert (1991) supports the idea of prophetic influence on the portrayal of Wisdom in 1:20–33, in which he sees Wisdom as adopting the condemnatory tone of many an Old Testament prophet. Fox (2000), following Harris (1996), stresses the strength of the Jeremiah parallel in particular (Prov. 1:20–33; cf. Jer. 7; 20). Harris identifies similarities in diction, phrasing and structure between these passages as well as the more significant thematic parallel, namely God's complaint that, although he spoke, the people did not listen, and although he called, they did not answer. In Jeremiah this stubbornness on the part of the people leads to the fall of Jerusalem. Harris calls Proverbs 1:20–33 a 're-contextualization' of Jeremiah's words, while Fox is happier to see the link as an acquaintance with prophecy in general rather than as a specific allusion, given wisdom's preference for individualism rather than for national concerns. Fishbane (1985) went a step further and argued that, while similarity in terminology exists, borrowing, adaptation or dependence is unlikely. It is significant that the passages in Jeremiah that find an echo in Proverbs 1:20–33 are generally regarded as Deuteronomic. Harris makes a further link with Deuteronomic language in Isaiah 65:12 and 66:14, and argues that it is therefore the Deuteronomic additions to Isaiah and Jeremiah that show links to the Wisdom poem in Proverbs 1:20–33. These additions in the prophets (e.g. Jer. 7:24–8) are in the context of the recalcitrance of the people from the exodus to the present in terms of cultic practice. This is interesting in the light of the work of Perdue (1977), who has drawn attention to the mention of the cult in Proverbs 3:9–10 as part of a wider discussion of the relationship between wisdom and cult (see below).

Perhaps the most vociferous opponent of the attempt to link up with other parts of the Old Testament is Crenshaw (1992), who argues against Gerstenberger (1965a; 1965b) and Blenkinsopp (1995a) for a link-up with the Deuteronomic law. He also mentions Wolff (1974; 1977; 1981) in a footnote, in connection with the debate about the prophecy-and-wisdom link-up. He argues overall that, although similar expressions can be found, this does not mean that they belong in the same group. However, it does show at least, in my view, that interaction with a broader thought-world is being considered.

What is treated in this chapter, then, is not 'wisdom influence' on other texts where scholarly interest has tended to focus, but influence from other thought-worlds of Israelite life on Proverbs 1–9. This is linked up to issues of date and priority, for if Proverbs 1–9 is later material within the book, one might perhaps expect that there would be more link-up with other parts of the Old Testament, the presupposition being that this process developed over time (presumed by S. L. Harris, 1996), and that later, there would be more influence coming in from exilic and post-exilic texts.[1] The question of direction of dependence is consequently raised: if the section is earlier, at least in parts, than some suppose, this could indicate more primary influence of other texts upon Proverbs 1–9 with early cross-fertilization of ideas. Kayatz (1966) argued along these lines that there were striking similarities between Deutero-Isaiah, Trito-Isaiah, the Deuteronomic portions of Jeremiah, and Proverbs 1:20–33, but that the wisdom material embodies an earlier form of speech which appears later in the exilic prophets, especially in Jeremiah.[2] She sees the direction of dependence as being this way round because she is concerned to stress that Proverbs has a date at the Solomonic enlightenment. She argues that the intimacy between Yahweh and pre-existent Wisdom results in speech patterns that are noticeably similar to later prophetic forms. This, however, is not the majority view, which regards the direction of dependence (if indeed it is that) as the other way round.

One of the main reasons for Whybray's (1965) developmental model of the gradual emphasis first on Wisdom and then on Yahweh in Proverbs 1–9 was the relationship of 'the wise' and the prophets. He noted the polemic against 'the wise' in Isaiah and Jeremiah in particular, and so concluded that there must have been

---

[1] A point made by Perdue (1997) who argues for its placement in the Persian period; cf. Whybray, 1974.

[2] In reference to Proverbs 1: 20–33, Kayatz (1966) noted the use of 'how long' in verse 22 (cf. Jer. 4:14; 31:22; Hos. 8:5); 'turn back' (שׁוּב) in verse 23 (Jer. 15:19; 18:11; 25:5), the accusation of not listening introduced with יַעַן, 'but since', in verses 24–5 (cf. Isa. 65:12; Jer. 7:24ff.; 11:8; 17:23; 25:7; 32:33; 24:17; 35:14, 17); sentences of coming destruction introduced by אָז, 'then' (verse 28) and תַּחַת, 'because', in verse 29 (cf. Jer. 4:18; 21:14; 35:17; 48:16; 49:8); sentences of sinners' calling in vain, in verse 28 (cf. Isa. 1:15; Jer. 11:1, 14; Ezek. 8:18; Hos. 5:6; Mic. 3:4, Zech. 7:13), and condemnation for faithlessness in verse 32 (cf. Jer. 2:19; 3:6, 11–12; 8:12; 14:7; Hos. 11:7; 14:5).

awareness of the wise and interaction with them. He noted that the divine quality of wisdom was already to be found in the prophets, for example in Isaiah 28:29; 31:2, in the emphasis on the character of God as wise; and in Jeremiah 10:12 (cf. Jer. 51:15) in its echo of Proverbs 8 – and that the Israelite concept of Yahweh was already at that stage influenced by wisdom. However, he also held that it was in encounter with other areas of Israelite thought that the Wisdom idea itself developed. 'Wisdom' as a figure was added, he maintained, to bring wisdom ideas more into line with Israelite thought (although one might point out that it was hardly mainstream, even after these additions!). Wisdom was being set over the 'word of Yahweh' and needed to be reconciled with that. He finds conflict in Isaiah 29:13–16 between wisdom matters and religious matters, leading to attempts to bridge the gap between wisdom and Yahwism as early as the time of Isaiah. This takes us back to the eighth century BC, arguably at the time of the formulation of much of this material, so is it necessary to see the material as having developed in these complex redactional stages? Is it not plausible that wisdom material was shaped with these theological ideas from elsewhere in view? The influence of wisdom upon Isaiah is often posited, which would perhaps indicate that the prophet was already aware of wisdom ideas in theological form, so why not vice versa?

In relation to Proverbs 10:1—22:16, I have already mentioned in Chapter 2 the scholars who considered that there was some link-up of the proverbs in the main section of Proverbs with the law: a common origin was suggested, which then diverged into two channels, one law and the other wisdom. This arose out of a discussion of the nature and context of the popular saying. This possibility has been recently given new impetus by Lohfink (1991) in an examination of poverty in the laws of the Bible and ancient Near East, in which he claims that there is an integral relationship between law and wisdom on this subject, and draws particular attention to Egyptian wisdom parallels. The links with law and prophecy are of interest in the light of scholarly suggestions of a relationship between Proverbs and Deuteronomy (Weinfeld, 1977; see discussion below).[3] Perhaps even

---

[3] These suggestions also have their opponents. Crenshaw (1992) argued against such links with the law and found a distinctive style and content for wisdom prohibitions. Hermisson

more significant, however, in relation to this part of Proverbs is the suggestion by Perdue (1977) that there are echoes of the cultic situation in a number of proverbs which may indicate a closer relationship with the cult than previously thought. His views have not particularly been taken up by wisdom scholars, and I think that they have more mileage in this discussion than they have been given credit for. I will go on to explore this below, and I will also discuss any links of Proverbs 22:17ff. with other areas of Israelite life.

INFLUENCE ON PROVERBS FROM OTHER AREAS OF ISRAELITE LIFE

Prophetic links

The influence of wisdom was pointed out, in particular in the prophets and more especially in Amos (Wolff, 1977) and Isaiah (Fichtner, 1976). In fact, such was the extent of wisdom influence in Isaiah that it seemed that evidence existed for a prophet trained in the royal court wisdom school.[4] These claims were sometimes far-reaching, maybe too much so; but it is interesting that some mileage was made.[5] Little attention has been focused, however, on possible links the other way. When looking at texts earlier I noted the occasional echo of a prophetic idea or term, but is this enough to have a worthwhile discussion about links between wisdom and prophecy? Here we are in the area of influence *out* from wisdom to prophecy, but not of influence *in* of any substantial quantity. It is in the eighth-century prophets that perhaps the strongest echoes of wisdom can be found, suggesting that the wisdom worldview influenced the formulation of prophetic messages at that time. It has often been noted, however, that the wisdom worldview is very different from the prophetic. The prophets not only stress the covenant with Yahweh in a particular historical context, but they

---

(1968) strongly challenged the links of proverbs not only with law but also with narrative and prophetic material, arguing that the proverbs in Prov. 10:1—22:16 are sufficiently distinct to make this an unlikely area of cross-fertilization.

[4] Whedbee (1971) claimed, for example, that Isaiah was probably trained as a scribe in a royal court wisdom school.

[5] Morgan (1981) finds wisdom influence in a wide range of biblical books.

champion the cause of the poor or of the underdog in a way that is inimical to wisdom, with its acceptance of rich and poor in an overall scheme. Wisdom influence on prophetic texts tends to be less of ideology than the occasional proverb or expression that echoes the wisdom stance (Dell, 2000). When speaking of wisdom influence on the prophets, we may be more in the realm of wisdom as a part of everyday life and so, hardly surprisingly, entering the consciousness of the prophets, rather than in that of a more profound and far-reaching influence (despite Whedbee's protestations about a court context). If this is the case, one might perhaps expect there to be some reciprocity between prophecy and wisdom in matters of echoes of terminology. Although they are few and far between in Proverbs, I would argue that such echoes can indeed be found. There is one area in which more extensive prophetic portrayal can be argued for, and that is in the realm of the portrayal of woman Wisdom. The speech in 1:20–33, in particular, has been seen to contain prophetic overtones (see below). It will be worth pausing to look at the case for such links in this particular instance.

In Proverbs 10:1—22:16 there is little awareness of the prophetic world. The mention of false weights in 11:1 as 'an abomination to the Lord' recalls both law and prophecy (cf. Ezek. 45:10; Hos. 12:7; Amos 8:5; Mic. 6:10–11; see also the phrases 'abomination to the Lord' and 'his delight' in Prov. 12:22). One could also see this sentiment in ritual terms (cf. Deut. 7:25). Therefore the different traditions are intermingled. The mention of Yahweh here is unusual in its linking of the divine with the commercial world (and has led some to regard the verse as later addition), showing Yahweh's involvement in all areas of human life. Verse 4 also links up with the prophetic theme of the day of wrath (cf. mention of riches and the day of wrath in Ezek. 7:19, and of the day of wrath in Zeph. 1:15). Verse 18 echoes prophetic sentiments about sowing righteousness (e.g. Hos. 10:12). The 'straight path' in Proverbs 11:5 is an important theme in the book and likewise echoes Isaiah 40:3; 45:2. Proverbs 12:7, in its mention of 'overthrowing the wicked', recalls Amos 4:11. In Proverbs 14:22, loyalty and faithfulness are mentioned (an important prophetic motif), which in Proverbs 16:6 are equated with the fear of Yahweh. In Proverbs 16:8, righteousness and justice (in terms of injustice) are mentioned rather than the fear of the Lord, although they can be seen as an illustration of pleasing the Lord, as in Proverbs 16:7. The point here, then, is that when an echo of the prophetic is found it is often in the more Yahwistic passages, which seem to link the proverbial material with the more specific Israelite situation.

In Proverbs 22:17—24:22 the only possible connection with the prophets that I can find is the mention of Yahweh's protection of the poor in 22:22–3, in which an admonition is given a context in verse 23 with the reference to Yahweh's protection of the poor. He will argue their case and see that justice is done. The 'gate' in verse 22 indicates the city gate, as in Amos 5:12, where afflicting the righteous and pushing the needy aside are condemned. Again there is a link with Yahweh's specific brand of justice (cf. also Prov. 24:24; Ezek. 18:9). In Proverbs 25–9 there are a few echoes of prophetic texts in isolated verses. For example, Proverbs 26:6, in its reference to 'drinking down violence', recalls Ezekiel 23:32, although the context in Proverbs is a more ethical than metaphorical one; other references are little more than overlaps in the use of imagery or language; for instance, Proverbs 27:8 possibly recalls Isaiah 16:2 in its use of bird imagery.[6] In Proverbs 29:18, prophecy and law are mentioned in the context of the restraining aspect of prophecy and the importance of keeping the law.

In Proverbs 1–9, slightly more extensive links are to be found, which may indicate a later text in which the possibility of infiltration of more specifically Israelite ideas is higher. However, again, it is only echoes; for instance, in Proverbs 1:3b, 7, there is emphasis on the ethical and religious; 'righteousness' and 'justice' are key terms in the prophetic corpus, used to sum up the nature of the ideal moral order of society.[7] These concepts also link up with legal teaching in Deuteronomy and the Holiness Code in Leviticus 19–26 (see below). The mention of 'righteousness, justice and equity' here in verse 3 is not intimately linked to the Yahwistic context in the verse itself, but is part of a section that has its climax

---

[6] For one-word echoes, see Prov. 26:8, 'stone' (cf. Zech. 3:9; Isa. 8:14) and Prov. 26:18–19, 'shooting arrows' (cf. Jer. 4:29).

[7] Such that McKane saw the use of these words as evidence of a prophetic 'reinterpretation of the vocabulary of old wisdom' (1970: 21), a thesis he explores throughout his commentary.

in the fear of the Lord and so arguably acquires a religious context. The introduction to the book of Proverbs therefore has both an ethical focus that naturally links up with familiar phrases from other parts of the Old Testament, and a religious focus in the climactic verse 7.

I wish to look first, within Proverbs 1–9, at a sample of the instruction texts, notably at the first three instructions, in which there are some allusions to prophetic texts.[8] In Proverbs 1:8–19, the first instruction, there is a quite specific allusion to a prophetic text in verse 16: 'for their feet run to evil, and they make haste to shed blood'; compare Isaiah 59:7 (the only difference being that in Isaiah the blood is 'innocent'). The verse has been omitted in some commentaries (because of its absence from certain Septuagint manuscripts), and it has been widely regarded as a gloss from the Isaiah text by an editor who did not fully understand the passage that immediately follows about the bird in the snare. However, another possibility is that both texts are quoting a common proverb, which is also incorporated in verse 18 within the section of Proverbs 6:16–19. Isaiah 59:1–8 has strong links with wisdom anyway, in its imagery of paths, so one is led to ask: what is the direction of dependence here, if indeed there is any? Much is made of the parallel by S. L. Harris (1996), who sees this 'gloss' from Isaiah as an example of deliberate inner-biblical exegesis.[9] There are lexical overtones between the two passages as placed alongside, but one wonders whether such links are enough on which to build any theory of deliberate overtones or dependence. The Isaiah link is perhaps the more significant, and suggests interaction with the thought of that prophet on some level, whether that be redactional or not.

---

[8] I have found very little allusion to prophetic texts beyond these three instructions except in Prov. 5:18, 'wife of your youth' (cf. Mal. 2:14ff. for the phrase); Prov. 6:24, 'smooth words' (cf. Isa. 30:10); Prov. 6:26, 'very life' (cf. Ezek. 13:17–23); Prov. 6:34, 'day of vengeance' (cf. Isa. 59:17; Zeph. 1:18; cf. Prov 11:4). These are, though, little more than parallels of a single word or phrase. However, this study, while thorough, does not claim to be exhaustive, and there may well be more echoes than I have mentioned here.

[9] With the evidence of the summary appraisal form in 1:19, also a keynote of Isaiah editors, S. L. Harris (1996) posits a close link between editors of the two works. He goes on to draw a close parallel between words used in this passage and in Gen. 37:12–36, the account of Joseph's search for his brothers and their attempt to get rid of Joseph by selling him to the Midianites.

In the second instruction, in 2:1–22, the phrase 'knowledge of God' is found in verse 5 in combination with 'the fear of the Lord', a phrase familiar from the prophets (cf. Hos. 4:1; 6:6). Fox writes of this concept: 'Its incorporation in Wisdom literature and identification with wisdom are among the earmarks, and probably the innovations, of Prov. 1–9' (2000: 112). Fox argues that in the climactic verse 5 one can understand, and not just feel, the fear of God, because it has 'cognitive content' (2000: 110), and he draws a parallel with Psalm 34:11(12) in which the fear of God can be taught and from which certain moral principles can be derived. In Proverbs 2:9, echoes of Proverbs 1:3 resound in the mention of righteousness, justice and equity; in 2:17, 'the partner of her youth', in reference to the loose woman, is abandoned along with 'her sacred covenant'; compare Jeremiah 3:4, where the people address God as 'friend of my youth' (cf. Jer. 2:2).

Within the third instruction, Proverbs 3:3 (cf. 7:3) recalls Jeremiah 31:33 (and Deuteronomy, see below). Proverbs 3:5, 'with all your heart', recalls Jeremiah 29:13 (also Deuteronomy), Zephaniah 3:14 and Joel 2:12; and not relying on one's own insight echoes the stubbornness of 'following their own hearts' in Jeremiah 9:13. Proverbs 3:7–8 opposes self-sufficiency and favours trust in Yahweh (following on from verses 5–6; cf. Prov. 12:15; 26:5, 12; 28:11). Comparisons have been made with Isaiah 5:21 (and with an important theme in Isaiah generally) and Jeremiah 9:23–4, von Rad (1972) having argued for the influence of wisdom on Jeremiah; McKane (1970), however, argued for a prophetic attack on old wisdom that led to this reformulation. There are a few echoes of prophetic texts in these instructions, but, as I will show below, they are not as extensive as in the poetry.

Among the poetic texts, I wish to turn first to prophetic overtones in the picture of woman Wisdom in Proverbs 1:20–33. In the first speech of Wisdom in 1:20–33, Wisdom is aligned with God, and, as Oesterley commented, 'the general tone of this section recalls the utterances of the prophets; like the prophets of old, Wisdom goes out into the broad places of the city with denunciation and the prophecy of doom' (1929: 10). The opening context of calling in the street, in verses 20–1, is being noted here, but more significantly the admonitions of verses 24–31 are reminiscent of denunciations of

pre-exilic and exilic prophets, with accusation followed by announcement of inescapable judgement (cf. Isa. 6:9–13 and Ezek.
3:7 on listening without understanding). Verses 24–7 use the first
person and then the speech shifts unexpectedly to the third person
in verses 28–31. This has led to the suggestion that verses 24–7 are a
quotation (S. L. Harris, 1996). Verses 24 and 28 are both reminiscent
of Isaiah 65:1–2, the beginning of a judgement speech by Yahweh.
The emphasis on calling and not receiving an answer from Yahweh
in verse 28 recalls Isaiah 50:2; 66:4; Jeremiah 7:13, 24–7; 35:17; Psalm
22:2; and Zechariah 7:13; and the mention of seeking and finding
recalls Deuteronomy 4:29 and Jeremiah 29:13 as well as, in its
negative formulation, Hosea 5:6. The main question that is raised
by these prophetic images and overtones is whether this speech is in
any way modelled on such or whether there is any dependence on
particular passages. There are parallel motifs, such as the expression
'How long?' (verse 22), found in Jeremiah with some frequency
(4:14, 21; 12:4; 13:27; 23:26; 31:22; 47:5) and in the Psalms (6:3;
74:10; 80:4; 82:2; 90:13; 94:3). 'Pouring out' thoughts in verse 23
has been likened to the prophetic promise of pouring out the spirit,
as in Isaiah 44:3; 'stretched out my hand' (verse 24) is a prophetic
gesture (cf. Isa. 65:2). Divine laughter is reminiscent of Psalm 2:4,
and verse 27 arguably echoes the language of terror used in prophetic and apocalyptic literature to describe a coming doom. The
reproof and threat elements of the passage and the appeal to the
authority of Yahweh sound very prophetic.

   S. L. Harris (1996) goes to extensive lengths to argue for dependence between this passage – notably Proverbs 1:25 – and both
Jeremiah 7 and 20 and Zechariah 7. He sees Proverbs 1:20–33 as a
recontextualization of Jeremiah's words: 'a verbal montage of prophetic direct discourse' (1996: 85). However, as has just been seen, the
passage may have been influenced by wider prophetic influences, or
indeed may itself have shed its influence on prophetic texts. Robert
(1934–5) argued that portions of Jeremiah 7 and Isaiah 65 and 66
stand out in Proverbs 1:24–33, and saw the most notable parallel as
Jeremiah 7.[10] Harris argues that not just vocabulary, but prophetic

---

[10] The Jer. 7 passage is, of course, generally regarded as Deuteronomistic, and so the
   relationship may be as much with Deuteronomic language as with prophetic. The Jeremiah

speech forms and compositional devices, were used by sages, not just because they were authoritative, but because they were specific historical and theological references providing a common biblical explanation of the exile. However, specific references are not a keynote of wisdom style. Harris provides a chart of shared vocabulary and phraseology between Jeremiah 7 and Proverbs 1:20–33 (1996: 93–4), as well as pointing out thematic similarities (see discussion above). He then aligns these passages with Zechariah 7, which he sees as reutilizing Jeremianic traditions. Therefore the thrust of Harris's argument in relation to Proverbs 1:8–19 and 20–33 is that 'traditions from the Torah and the Prophets are freely played upon in order to form new discourse units in a sapiential context' (1996: 108). Harris is regarded by some as having overstated the case,[11] but his arguments for prophetic/Deuteronomic links seem to me to be quite strong.

In the second poem on Wisdom, in Proverbs 3:19, a link is drawn between wisdom and the structure of the created world. Creation is associated with divine power and wisdom also in Jeremiah 10:12; 51:5 (cf. Pss. 65:7; 104:24; Job 28:27). McKane (1970) points out a link between verse 19 and Deutero-Isaiah in Isaiah 40:12–17; 28–31, and argues that this demonstrates the later integration of wisdom with Yahwism in that the vocabulary of wisdom is used in Deutero-Isaiah.

In Proverbs 8, the main wisdom poem in Proverbs 1–9, Wisdom speaks in praise of herself, a genre not unknown in the Old Testament, in which Yahweh sometimes speaks in praise of himself (cf. Isa. 42:8–9; 44:24–8; 45:5–7). As already seen, in Proverbs 8:12–16, Wisdom is associated with kings and governing. It should also be noted that such words recall Isaiah 11:2 (which speaks of an ideal future Israelite king) and Job 12:13 (in a listing of God's attributes). Robert (1934–5) wondered whether Proverbs 8:14 is dependent on Isaiah 11:2, but even he pointed out that the chronological priority of

---

passage relates to forbidden cultic practices that continue to be perpetuated, and in that context the long-standing recalcitrance of the people is recounted. Speaking and not listening is at the heart of the problem for Jeremiah (cf. Jer. 35:17, another Deuteronomistic passage).

[11] This is certainly the case, in my view, in relation to S. L. Harris's claims about links of Prov. 6 with Gen. 37; see below.

Isaiah 11 is not certain. McKane (1970) argues that the two passages are theologically very different: Isaiah 11:2 speaks of the spirit of wisdom, a phrase that has a totally different resonance from the personal assertiveness of Wisdom in Proverbs 8:14–15. If they were borrowed from a similar tradition, the borrowing may have been independent, the Proverbs' use being of traditional terminology to claim for Wisdom qualities otherwise attributed to God.

In the final poetic section in Proverbs 9, the title 'Holy One' for God in verse 10[12] recalls Hosea 12:1 (cf. Prov. 30:3), and 'knowledge' has the sense of obedience found in Hosea 4:1; 6:6; Prov. 2:5). In verse 11, 'days and years' is a common biblical phrase (Deut. 32:7; Job 10:5).

There are, then, clearly more prophetic overtones in Proverbs 1–9 than in other sections, notably in 1:20–33. Proverbs 1–9 can be seen to have received some influences from outside texts. This might indicate a slightly later text, drawing on other influences, and it certainly indicates a more integrated thought-world for the sages who compiled it. Significantly, within Proverbs 1–9 there are more links with prophetic texts in poetic sections than in instruction texts, notably in the portrayal of the figure of Wisdom, particularly in the first Wisdom poem. This might indicate that prophetic ideas helped to shape this portrayal.

While some scholars formulate the issue in terms of dependence of one text on another, the more modest suggestion here is that one should rather speak of 'echoes', 'overtones' or 'reminiscences' of other texts in relation to this text in Proverbs. What is fascinating is that such links from within Old Testament tradition can be found, and that they have the effect of grounding Proverbs 1:20–33 within a wider thought-world than in Israelite wisdom alone or even in the ancient Near East. I will explore next the Deuteronomic link in this material.

DEUTERONOMIC INFLUENCE

It would seem natural that wisdom, with its emphasis on individual ethics, would have a relationship with Israelite law. And yet, the

---

[12] קדשׁים could arguably indicate 'holy ones' or 'heavenly beings', but is often taken as a title for God.

actual reference to law is of the nature of echoes of other texts rather than anything more extensive. The book of law with which Proverbs has most in common is Deuteronomy, which has often been regarded as broader than a law book, itself including some more 'wisdom-like' motifs (Weinfeld, 1977), a curious contrast to its very nationalistic tone in places (e.g. Deut. 7). There is a mixture of the universal and the nationalistic in Deuteronomy. Deuteronomy contains a broader ethic than simply a legal framework would seem to imply; good treatment of slaves and widows is advocated, for example, along the lines that the wise would normally advocate. There is also a stress on humanism in Deuteronomy, and a didactic tone that resembles the instructions of father to son in Proverbs 1–9. There is a similar note of just reward in Deuteronomy, often seen in more nationalistic terms of covenant or land. And, indeed, wisdom is equated with observance of commandments (Deut. 4:6) in a way not found in Proverbs, but apparent in later wisdom in Ecclesiasticus.

Weinfeld (1977) has studied Deuteronomy for signs of wisdom influence, and notes the use of parallel phrases. He sees Deuteronomy 27:15–26 as having many similarities to wisdom literature in subject matter, such as dishonouring parents and unjust treatment of aliens. It is hard to know where the direction of dependence lies, if indeed there is any. It is arguable that more general proverbs are reformulated as laws, such as Proverbs 20:10 on diverse weights and measures, and Deuteronomy 25:13–16. Weinfeld notes that there are some laws in Deuteronomy that lack parallels in other lawcodes but which are parallelled in wisdom literature, such as injunctions about removal of boundaries and falsification of weights, which have verbal parallels in Proverbs 22:28 and 23:10, and Proverbs 11:1 and 20:10, 23. Weinfeld is concerned with questions of social context and with the issue of whether Deuteronomy was composed by scribes at the time of Hezekiah (Prov. 25:1), in a kind of enlightenment resembling the Solomonic and, in turn, influencing the development of wisdom in a fresh direction.

Proverbs 1–9, in particular, has been seen to have a relationship with Deuteronomy, and many have argued that allusions to Deuteronomy prove that Proverbs 1–9 is a later text. It is quite hard, in my view, however, to know which way dependence lies, if at all. Maybe the most that the echoes of other legal texts show is that wisdom is part of a wider thought-world and that, despite its famous separate concerns, it was not totally immune from the language and ideas of other parts of Israelite life. There is also, as noted above, an overlap between prophecy and Deuteronomic language; for instance, 'justice and righteousness' is a prophetic expression, but it also links up with legal teaching in general in Deuteronomy, and in the Holiness Code, of which it is a keynote. This suggests that it is hard to characterize the nature of an influence which may well span more than one genre of Old Testament material. The concept of Sheol is an example of this; it is found first in Proverbs 1:12 and is generally used to characterize the result of following the path of the foreign woman. Images of Sheol are found throughout the corpus (e.g. Num. 16:30; Isa. 5:14; 38:18; Hab. 2:5), and Job is particularly full of references, as are many psalms (e.g. 28:1; 55:15; 88:5; 143:7). Little can be built on such parallels except to say that it is a common Old Testament belief and that the language about it tends to be similar in many texts.

The instruction texts in Proverbs 1–9 are the first place to look for echoes of Deuteronomic ideas. The parallels tend to be in the instruction sections rather than in the poems, a point which is significant in itself, so it is on those sections that I will focus. The first instruction (1:8–19) does not appear to contain anything that can be called Deuteronomic, so I will begin in the second instruction, in Proverbs 2:1–22.

In Proverbs 2:1–4, the intensity of the teacher's appeal is reminiscent of the intensity of Moses' speeches in Deuteronomy (e.g. Deut. 4:6), although מצות here refers to the teacher's authoritative commands, rather than to the ten commandments as in Deuteronomy. Overtones, however, may have been present for those familiar with the two texts. In Proverbs 2:12, the word תהפכות, 'perversity', used widely in Proverbs, is found elsewhere in the Old Testament only in Deuteronomy 32:20, in reference to a perverse generation. In Proverbs 2:16, knowledge and understanding are said to come from God's mouth; compare Deuteronomy 8:3, in which man's dependence on what comes from God's mouth is stressed. In 2:21–2, the reference to 'the land' has led many scholars (e.g. Gemser, 1938) to draw a close parallel with the promise of the land of Canaan in

Deuteronomy (e.g. Deut. 28:1–14).[13] It is questionable whether it is the land of Canaan that is being explicitly referred to here. It is more likely that 'the land' is being used more generally as a metaphor. Those who are righteous will go on living in the land and have long, fruitful lives, but those who are wicked will be uprooted from it. However, it is possible that echoes of a well-known biblical theme, that of the land of Canaan, may have resonated in the ears of readers or listeners.

In the third instruction, notably in Proverbs 3:1–4 (cf. 6:21–2; 7:1–3), vocabulary characteristic of Deuteronomy concerning 'teaching', 'commandments' and 'affixing teaching to one's body' (Deut. 6:8) has led many to compare the two texts and to look for literary influence between them, either one way or the other (see Whybray, 1994c: 59). The main point of comparison is Deuteronomy 6:5–9, which led Robert (1934–5) to find Proverbs 1–9 dependent upon it, but Whybray to posit dependence the other way around. The question is raised whether Proverbs is alluding specifically to the Deuteronomic law, or whether this is a common tradition of exhortation, or whether indeed Deuteronomy is employing wisdom techniques. To what extent does the common vocabulary of education appear in the two texts? Given that there are similar expressions in other instructions, it does not look as though this text should be singled out. However, the parallels here are quite striking. Whybray argues that 'the author of the homiletic introductory chapters of Deuteronomy may have used the already existent language of family education in order to emphasize the mandatory nature of the law of Yahweh, the rewards of obedience to it and the dire consequences of disobedience' (1994c: 60). There are also overtones of other texts in the use of the two words חסד (kindness) and אמת (fidelity/truth), which refer elsewhere to divine qualities (Exod. 34:6) as well as to human ones (Ps. 25:10). In Proverbs 16:6, the phrase is parallel to fearing God. In the injunction to write such qualities on the tablet of one's heart there are echoes of Proverbs 7:3 and Deuteronomy 6:8; 11:18, 30:14; and also Jeremiah 17:1; 31:33. In 3:5, 'with all your

---

[13] Another parallel is with Ps. 37, often considered a wisdom psalm, in which the land as an image of bounty is found (in an unspecific sense) in verses 3, 9, 11, 22, 28b, 29, 34 and 38 (cf. Prov. 10:30).

heart' is an expression found in Deuteronomy (e.g. Deut. 4:29; 6:5; 10:12; 11:13; 13:3; 26:16; 30:2, 6, 10).

Still in the third instruction, in Proverbs 3:9–10 there is the liturgical mention of making sacrifices. This links up with the giving of the first fruits of one's crops and a portion of one's wealth to God, in the legal material of the Old Testament (Exod. 23:19; 34:26; Lev. 23:10–14 Deut. 26:1–11;). אסם, 'storerooms', is found only in Proverbs 3:10 and in Deut. 28:8. In 3:11–12, there are overtones again of Deuteronomy, this time of Deuteronomy 8:5, in which discipline from God was represented by the harsh experiences of Israel during the period in the wilderness. There is also an image here of God as a parent disciplining a child (cf. God as father in Deut. 32:6). Again, whether there is any dependence, and the direction of it, are disputed. Fox (2000) concedes that God's discipline as likened to that of a parent could be a quoted maxim or well-known turn of phrase. There are also overtones of the problem of suffering as found in Job, notably similarities of wording with Job 5:17–18 (cf. Ps. 119:71, 75). These verses argue against those who find a mechanistic system of reward and retribution in Proverbs in their inculcating of the right attitude to suffering.

Proverbs 3:24, part of the fourth instruction, recalls Deuteronomy 6:7 and 11:19 in its reference to sitting and lying down, as well as Psalm 91:12 in referring to walking without mishap and sleeping without fear. One can cross-refer to the Psalter to find the sentiment of the Lord's protection of his followers when they are sleeping (e.g. Ps. 3:6; 4:9), safe from the terrors of the night (Ps. 91:5). Proverbs 3:27 speaks of another person's claim upon us in reference to his own rights (cf. Deut. 15:9; cf. Ecclus. 4:1–6).[14] Proverbs 3:28 also stresses sensitivity to the needs of another in returning something promptly, and one might recall Exodus 22:25–6, which speaks of the urgency of restoration of a pledged garment by sunset. Verse 32 recalls wisdom psalms on the topic of the envy of the wicked (e.g. Pss. 37:1; 73:3). It uses the phrase 'abomination to Yahweh', found only in Proverbs and Deuteronomy. It has been suggested

---

[14] Fox (2000) illustrates this point with an example from Exod. 23:4, the obligation to raise up someone's fallen ass, even if that someone is your enemy.

that 'abomination to the Lord' has cultic associations.[15] McKane (1970) held that the question of the relationship of Proverbs and Deuteronomy is again raised in this context, and concluded that if there is a relationship the dependence is more likely to be of Deuteronomy on Proverbs, since many of the proverbial examples are in Proverbs 10:1—22:16. Deuteronomy could, he maintained, have given a broader concept a more cultic and exclusive meaning. He argues, however, that the usage of 'abomination to the Lord' in the two books is different; in Proverbs it is associated with moral and intellectual flaws, a usage paralleled in the Egyptian *Instruction of Amenemope*. More recently, Fox (2000) has proposed that this concept is not necessarily or originally a cultic one. Verses 33–5 have the character of originally separate proverbs, as Fox has shown. God's curse in verse 33 recalls Deuteronomy 28:20 and Malachi 2:2.

In the sixth instruction, there is an emphasis on the benefits of following the way of wisdom. One of those benefits is long life (Proverbs 4:10, 13), which is an emphasis of Deuteronomic theology as well (cf. Deut. 30:16, 19). In Proverbs 4:27, at the end of the seventh instruction, the injunction to avoid 'swerving to right and left' is a phrase known from elsewhere in the Old Testament, notably Num. 20:17; Deuteronomy 2:27; 5:29, 32–3; 28:14; Joshua 1:7. Is there reason, with Robert (1934–5), to suspect Deuteronomic influence? Within the eighth instruction in 5:9–13, a section mentioning the dangers of adultery which culminates in death and destruction (verses 11–13) echoes legal texts. In fact, death is the prescribed punishment for adulterers and adulteresses in Leviticus 20:10 and Deuteronomy 22:22.

The question has been raised whether 6:21–2, part of the ninth instruction (as previously Prov. 3:1–3 and 7:1–3), is based on Deuteronomy 6:6–8. There are some striking similarities. Interestingly in the light of a discussion of the correspondence between introductions, Murphy writes: 'The agreement among these three introductions is significant. One may even draw the conclusion that sapiential and "Yahwistic" teaching do not differ, one from another'

---

[15] Cf. Prov. 11:20; 15:8, 9, 26, and Deuteronomy, the only two biblical books in which this phrase appears.

(1998: 38–9). As regards the Deuteronomy comparison, the imagery of enjoining attention and obedience to the teaching just given, or about to be given, is similar. In the case of Proverbs, parental teaching is the subject, while in Deuteronomy the content of the teaching is the law of Moses. Both employ the language of the 'heart' as the inner self and as the place where the teaching is inwardly digested, and they all use the expression 'bind' as a metaphor; Proverbs talks of binding on the heart and Deuteronomy of binding on the hand (cf. Exod. 28:29; Song 8:6). They both stress that such is the importance of the teaching that it must be in one's mind all the time, when walking or lying down or when one is awake. Whybray writes of this correspondence: 'It is generally admitted that there is some connection between them; but there is no agreement about the direction of influence, nor, supposing it to be a direct one, on its direction' (1994c: 103). McKane (1970) saw Proverbs as a free adaptation of the Deuteronomy texts, while Weinfeld (1972) saw the direction of influence as being the other way round. Whybray prefers to speak of convergence rather than of dependence. In 6:31, the expression 'seven-fold' is unusual, because penalties for theft in the Old Testament law are usually two-, four- or five-fold (Exod. 21:37; 22:1–4, 8). Verses 31, 33 and 35 refer to customs more lenient than lawcodes prescribe, and so might suggest a non-legal tradition as their origin.

Turning to Proverbs 7:1–3, the introduction to the tenth instruction, there are, as already noted, overtones of Deuteronomy in the use of 'apple of your eye' (verse 2; cf. Deut. 32:10) and the idea of 'binding' the teachings (verse 3; cf. Deut. 6:8; 11:18); the latter could refer to finger ornaments. Murphy (1998) regards the tie-in between these introductory verses and Deuteronomy 6 and 11 as significant because of the way parental teaching becomes analogous to Yahwistic doctrine as expressed in Deuteronomy.

Therefore, in virtually every instruction text (except 1 and 5) there are some echoes of Deuteronomic texts. This is a sufficient proportion of the instruction texts to have some significance. Consideration of the wider significance of particular words or phrases found in both texts is also required.

Certain words and phrases appear in both Proverbs 1–9 and Deuteronomy (and elsewhere), leading to a debate about whether one can judge such words and phrases to have the same meaning in different genre contexts. The word תורה, for example, is used in Proverbs (e.g. 1:8; 3:1), and there is a debate concerning the specific sense of that usage. Is this a different 'wisdom' usage, or are there overtones here of other Old Testament passages? Baumann (1996) observes that, outside Proverbs, תורה (and מצוה, 'precept', as found in Prov. 2:1; 3:1; 4:4; 7:1–2) with the possessive suffix, is almost always divine and so concludes that the suffixed forms in Proverbs 'transgress or blur the border between human and divine command-ments' (1996: 295).[16] Fox sees the use of torah as referring not to law, but to authoritative injunctions, תורה and מצוה being virtually interchangeable terms in his view. There is no reason, in my view, why תורה should not have the same sense in Proverbs as elsewhere in the Old Testament, with the proviso that it has not yet developed into a formal description of the Pentateuch or even into the formal lawcodes within that corpus.

In the context of this debate, an example of a significant phrase is the 'fear of Yahweh' in Proverbs (1:7, 29; 2:5; 3:7; 8:13; 9:10; 10:27; 16:6). In Chapter 4 it was noted that this is an important phrase when evaluating the Yahwistic content of Proverbs. It is, perhaps not surprisingly, pointed to as being at one remove from the use of the phrase elsewhere in the Old Testament, although Becker (1965) argues that its ethical emphasis means that it is home-grown. Some have found differences between the use of the phrase in Proverbs 1–9 and its use in chapters 10ff., and have seen the phrase as a later addition in both contexts. Others (e.g. A. Meinhold, 1991) have argued that the concept is not added on, but belongs essentially to the structure of the proverbs collections as they were systematized into written form. Once again, a false separation is being made, in my view, between its use here and its use elsewhere.

'The fear of the Lord' occurs frequently, especially in the Pentateuch (notably in Deut. 5:29; 6:2, 24; 10:12; 13:4; 28:58), Isaiah,

---

[16] Baumann (1966) finds some further parallels between wisdom and law in Deuteronomy in the call to obey both Yahweh's and the teacher's instructions, and he likens Deuteronomy's stress on love of Yahweh paralleling obedience to Torah and Proverbs' alignment of Wisdom with Yahweh. There are also links with Deuteronomy in the motif of father as teacher; cf. Deut. 6:6–7, in which teaching one's children about God's commandments is a duty.

Jeremiah and the Psalms (for instance, it is found in the Deuteronomistic history in 1 Sam. 12:14 and 2 Kings 17:28, 34; in psalms
such as 55:19 and 112:1; and in Eccles. 12:13). Its range of meaning is
quite wide, and different senses lead to a grey area in their overlap; it
ranges from terror (e.g. Moses and the burning bush in Exod. 3:16;
Pss. 2:11; 119:120) to more positive human reactions to God's power,
such as obedience and loyalty (e.g. Abraham's loyalty that drives
him to near sacrifice of his son in Gen. 22:12; Ps. 25:12). Murphy
(1998) emphasizes the first of these when he writes: 'It seems
undeniable that fear of God is rooted in a basic attitude of mortal
beings before the Numen' (1998: 255). He cites the reaction of fear
by the people in the Sinai revelation in Exodus 19:16; 20:15–18. One
might also cite Psalm 111:10, where the fear of the Lord is mentioned
in a worshipful context, but also in the context of wisdom and its
practical outworking, in a psalm that is often, at least in part,
classified as a wisdom psalm. The fear of God (in a non-Yahwistic
sense) can also have a purely moral content (as when Abraham
expected to find the practice of the fear of God as a universal moral
norm, Gen. 20:11).[17] In Deuteronomy, the fear of the Lord denotes
cultic loyalty to the exclusive worship of Yahweh (Deut. 10:12). It is
also linked with religious instruction, which has to be both taught
and learned (e.g. Deut. 17:18–20), and the content of fearing God is
often adherance to the words of the law (Deut. 4:10; 14:23; 17:19;
31:12).

While different contexts may indicate nuances of meaning, the
question is raised whether one needs to posit a whole different set of
meanings for the use of such terms in wisdom literature, or whether
in fact one should bring to the wisdom context the wider overtones
of meaning contained in the concepts as used elsewhere. I propose
the latter path, and suggest that those who try to find an alternative
sense for these terms are simply promulgating the 'separateness' of
wisdom that I have mentioned. The integration of religion and
education in instruction in Deuteronomy could give a lead for
suggesting that, although Proverbs 1–9 had an educational purpose
from the start, religious concerns were never far away and were in

---

[17] There is some discussion whether the concept of the fear of the gods was common to other
Near Eastern religions; it expressed both terror and devotion.

fact very important in the overall formation of character. This could have some bearing on wider issues of social context; Clifford, for example, argues that 'the exhortatory rhetoric of Deuteronomy and Proverbs had a common origin in the scribal class of Jerusalem responsible for their writing' (1999: 51).

In conclusion in relation to Proverbs 1–9, links with Deuteronomic ideas have been found in the instruction texts. The context of instruction to young men in itself provides quite a few of the parallels, notably in the repeated injunctions of 3:1–3; 6:20–2 and 7:1–3, at home in educational or legal contexts. The concepts of law and the fear of the Lord straddle educational, legal and cultic boundaries and have essentially the same meaning as elsewhere in the Old Testament.

There are few links in the rest of Proverbs with the Deuteronomic literature. As with prophecy, these usually amount to little more than a usage of words or a turn of phrase. For example, in Proverbs 10:1—22:16, the idea that good words benefit the whole community (11:11) is echoed in Genesis 27:49 and Deuteronomy 32. Proverbs 12:22, in its use of 'abomination', recalls the legal, prophetic and ritual overtones of the word. Verse 10, on the treatment of animals, recalls Exodus 23:12 and Deuteronomy 25:4. Furthermore, verse 17, in the stress on honest evidence or justice, recalls the principle of justice that is the basis of Israel's claim to the land in Deuteronomy 16:20. The statement about diverse weights and measures in Proverbs 20:10 recalls Deuteronomy 25:13–16. This does not appear to stand in close relationship with the nearby verses, despite Whybray's attempt to link it all together. In verse 16, the image of a garment used as a pledge recalls Proverbs 6:1; 11:15; 17:18; 22:26–7; 27:13 and Deuteronomy 24:10–14, 17. Verse 20 is again recalling the decalogue (Exod. 20:12; Deut. 5:16) regarding respect for parents. In verse 22, Yahweh avenges crimes (cf. Deut. 32:35–6), while in verse 25 there is a warning against making hasty vows, and it is understood that vows to God are meant (cf. Deut. 23:22; Lev. 27:28).

In Proverbs 22:22–3, the admonition is given a motive clause in verse 23 with the reference to Yahweh's protection of the poor. He will argue their case and see that justice is done. One might recall laws in Exodus 22:21–3; 23:6 and Deuteronomy 24:14–15 (cf. Pss. 68:5 and 146:9). 'The gate' in verse 22 indicates the city gate, which was the site of legal trials (Deut. 21:19). The death penalty is indicated in verse 23. Verses 26–7 are about the giving of surety, a sentiment grounded in Proverbs itself, although in biblical law there were strict guidelines regarding the behaviour of debtors (cf. Exod. 22:25–6; Deut. 24:12–13). Verse 28 is also a close variant of Deuteronomy 19:14, where it is a law of Moses. In Deuteronomy 27:17, those guilty of this offence will be accursed. In Proverbs 23:12, references to 'ear' and 'mind' parallel Deuteronomy 29:3. Proverbs 23:20 recalls Deuteronomy 21:18–21, the law concerning the rebellious son. Is there a deliberate allusion to this here? The verbs 'build', 'establish' and 'fill' are used of houses in Proverbs 24:3–4 and in 2 Samuel 7:15 and Deuteronomy 6:11.

In 24:23–34, verses 23–5 concern judges and the question of partiality. Verse 23 recalls Deuteronomy 1:17; 16:19, as well as Proverbs 28:21. Verse 24 recalls a verse from prophecy (Ezek. 18:9); and the communal curse of the nations is mentioned in Proverbs, while the Ezekiel reference is to an individual retribution. This represents a strange reversal of the usual individual emphasis in Proverbs, and a fresh emphasis on the individual in Ezekiel, which arguably sets him apart from his prophetic predecessors. The need to judge justly is stressed in both cases, however. Verse 28 matches verses 23–5 in warning against being a false witness (cf. Prov. 20:16, and commandment nine of the ten commandments in Exod. 20:16; Deut. 5:20).

In Proverbs 25–9, 25:7c–8 recalls Deuteronomy 21:7; 18; 5:20 (also Jer. 5:31; Isa. 10:3; Hos. 9:5). Proverbs 28:7 associates law and wisdom, saying that the one who keeps the law is wise (cf. Deut. 21:18–21). In verse 8, lending at interest to fellow Israelites is forbidden, in line with legal texts (e.g. Exod. 22:25; Lev. 25:36; Deut. 23:19–20). In verse 9, the law is mentioned in relation to those who do not obey it. In Proverbs 30:1–14, there are a few echoes of other parts of Israelite life, and not just the Deuteronomic. For example, the first three verses have the character of a psalm of lament, calling on God for help, but it then becomes clear that the lament is about *not* having gained wisdom or knowledge of God – the opposite of the usual subject matter of a psalm of lament, using parodic style. Verse 5 reads, 'Every word of God (Eloah) proves true; he is a shield to those who take refuge in him', which is a direct parallel to Psalm

18:30 and is closely paralleled in 2 Samuel 22:31. Verse 6 recalls Deuteronomy 4:2 and 12:32 about not adding or taking away from God's commandments, although, as noted in Chapter 4, Yahweh is not explicitly mentioned here. Other texts from Amos and Jeremiah in praise of God as creator are possibly alluded to here. These reminiscences of other texts help to lead the speaker from doubt to faith and to the prayer expressed in verses 7–9.

The links with Deuteronomy are clearly less extensive in the rest of Proverbs. Perhaps the most significant echoes are in Proverbs 22:17—24:22. There are very few links in 10:1—22:16; 24:23–31; 25–9; and 30–1. Where connections can be found, they tend to be where God is mentioned (although not exclusively). When it comes down to usage of words, it is hard to know whether a similarity is an echo or simply down to a choice of vocabulary. Overall, there are many more echoes of Deuteronomic texts in Proverbs 1–9, to such an extent that it might indicate some cross-awareness of ideas. I will assess these findings at the end of the chapter.

CULTIC AND PSALMIC INFLUENCE

When we turn to the question of cultic and psalmic influence on Proverbs, there are two areas to consider. The first is whether there is any link-up of wisdom with cultic piety as expressed elsewhere in the Old Testament, and hence any mileage in a cultic context for any of this material; and the second, whether there is any influence on Proverbs from ideas expressed in any psalms. There is evidence of wisdom influence on the Psalter in the form of wisdom psalms; did this work both ways?

Perdue, in his book *Wisdom and Cult* (1977), is concerned to find links between wisdom literature and the cultic situation. He finds evidence of sacrifice and prayer in Proverbs 15:8: 'The sacrifice of the wicked is an abomination to the Lord, but the prayer of the upright is his delight.' Here mention of Yahweh accompanies reference to sacrifice and prayer. The emphasis is on the character of those who offer the sacrifice and prayer – just as most of Proverbs is about character formation – and not on more priestly matters such as one might find in legal stipulations regarding whether the sacrifice or prayer was ritually acceptable to Yahweh. The emphasis, more like that of prophetic texts, is on the moral integrity of the worshippers. Perdue cites parallels in Leviticus 19 and Psalms 15 and 24. Perdue's second example is Proverbs 15:29: 'The Lord is far from the wicked, but he hears the prayer of the righteous.' Access to Yahweh is through the prayers of righteous people, again through a cultic act, and this is, in usual proverbial style, contrasted with the lot of the wicked. Once again, moral integrity is being stressed over more ritual requirements, but it is interesting that it is phrased in terms of the cultic act of prayer.

In Proverbs 17:1 we read: 'Better is a dry morsel with quiet than a house full of feasting with strife.' The 'feasting' may refer to a sacrificial situation and show awareness of such, but the reference is not as clear-cut as in 15:8. The message here is that quiet is better than strife – an observation based on truth, using the 'house of feasting' as an illustration. The reference could be to any celebration; one thinks of Job's sons and daughters feasting, probably on their birthdays. In 21:3 we read: 'To do righteousness and justice is more acceptable to the Lord than sacrifice.' Here there appears to be a polemic against sacrifice, but maybe all that is being stressed is that moral integrity is the essential quality needed before any cultic participation is undertaken. This reminds one of Amos' stress on purity of heart and mind rather than empty sacrificial worship. Proverbs 21:27 says: 'The sacrifice of the wicked is an abomination; how much more when he brings it with evil intent.' Cultic language is used here; sacrifices from the wrong kind of people are an abomination, but the stress is on the morality of the one bringing the sacrifice – the sacrifice is even more abhorrent when brought with evil intention. Finally, Proverbs 28:9 states: 'If one turns away his ear from hearing the law, even his prayer is an abomination.' Here there is an unusual reference to the law; this could refer to sapiential instruction or to priestly law. If the latter, there is a fascinating link-up with priestly emphasis on the emptiness of worship that is not guided by obedience to the law. If the former, this would suggest a close relationship between obedience to wisdom's 'law' and prayer in a cultic setting. 'Hearing' is a wisdom motif; one who cannot hear cannot act wisely or pray properly. One might cross-refer to Proverbs 29:18, where law is mentioned in conjunction with prophecy, and the one who keeps the law is blessed. This might suggest awareness of Israel's legal tradition and that the latter option is the preferred one in the interpretation of Proverbs 28:9.

Perdue also looks at examples of vows in Proverbs 20:25: 'It is a snare for a man to say rashly, "It is holy", and to reflect only after making his vows.' This is a warning against haste before careful thought, but it is significant that the example of making a sacred vow, as one might in a cultic situation, is used. The message here is that before making a vow in haste one should reflect on one's capability for fulfilling it (Perdue cross-refers to Pss. 56:12–13 and 66:13–15; cf. Num. 30:21 and Deut. 23:21–3). Another example is Proverbs 31:2b: 'What, son of my vows?' This refers to the cultic practice of a woman making a vow or promise to a deity to fulfil certain requirements if the deity grant her a son. It recalls Hannah's vow in 1 Samuel 1:11 and Samson's mother's vow in Judges 14 to bring him up as a Nazirite dedicated to the Lord.

Perdue also points to an example of sacred lots being used as an illustration in Proverbs 16:33: 'The lot is cast into the lap, but the decision is wholly from the Lord.' Here the power of Yahweh to effect decisions is being stressed over that of lots that are cast at random and have no power. In Proverbs 16:6 there is mention of atonement, the inference being that moral qualities such as loyalty and faithfulness are more powerful to effect atonement than cultic activity. This again reminds one of the prophetic emphasis on moral qualities rather than empty cultic offerings. The language of atonement is used here, suggesting that the phrase has a polemical edge.

These examples may ultimately be purely a matter of illustration: the wise chose to illustrate their moral points or their observations on human character with reference to cultic activities. But it is interesting that such images are used, and it shows that the wise were well aware of the cult and not divorced from it. As Perdue writes, 'almost every major element of cult is mentioned by the wise' (1977: 347). He makes the point in a footnote (1977: 238, n. 93) that cultic reference could be to the ancient Near East and is not necessarily to the Israelite cult. It also shows that the wise saw the cult as part of the 'order' of the world, both social and cosmic; and it indicates, finally, that the emphasis of wisdom was always going to be on moral integrity over the ritual requirements of sacrifice and prayer, rather in the same mode as the prophets and yet in wisdom's own context of the doctrine of retribution. These observations might suggest some link-up of wisdom with the wider thought-world of the cult in ancient Israel. And the cult is not subject to influence from the Psalms alone, but links up with other areas of Israelite life, such as has been represented from legal and prophetic circles.

It is significant that these examples come from the main body of Proverbs and not from chapters 1–9. It is often held by scholars that it is chapters 1–9 that come into closer contact with other areas of Israelite life; that this has been true especially in relation to Deuteronomy and some prophetic texts; and that this is, in itself, a sign of later redaction – but this second point does not necessarily follow. The fact that the examples come from Proverbs 10–31, however, suggests that the links are primary and cannot be dismissed as later additions. The main example from Proverbs 1–9 is of course Proverbs 3:9–10: 'Honour the Lord with your substance and with the first fruits of all your produce; then your barns will be filled with plenty, and your vats will be bursting with wine.' This looks, at face value, like a straightforward cultic stipulation, and yet the link between action and reward, in true proverbial style, is clearly there. There is a communal aspect to this exhortation which is rare in the individualistic world of the proverbs; it assumes, in fact, that the one addressed is a member of a cultic community. Worshipping God is not just a private matter, but a ceremonial and ritual matter too. It will lead to material blessings (cf. Deut. 7:13; 28:8) but not, I think (contra Whybray), as an alternative to piety. Although it is just one reference to cultic matters, its presence in Proverbs 1–9 is significant in the link-up with other areas of life, not least with the legal portions of the Old Testament which include such cultic injunctions.

As well as the cult *per se*, one might ask whether there is influence on Proverbs from the Psalms generally, so as to assess whether there is further evidence of a formative influence on wisdom from the world of worship and praise. There are some proverbs where instruction turns into praise, notably in praise of the natural world and in praise of Yahweh. I have already found several echoes of ideas in the Psalms when discussing the Deuteronomic influences.

In Proverbs 1–9 there is shared vocabulary with some psalms; for instance 'equity' (מישרים; Prov. 1:3) in Psalms 9:8; 96:10; and 98:9. In the Wisdom poem in Proverbs 8, Wisdom was God's 'delight' (שעשעים, pl. here; verse 30); compare 'delight' in God's word or teaching, as in Psalm 119:24, 77, 92, 143, 174. The language of weaving applied to God's crafting of human beings in the womb (verse 23) is familiar from Psalm 139:13. In verse 24, 'brought forth' echoes God's bringing the mountains to birth in the context of God's existence before creation in Psalm 90:2. There are parallel motifs, such as the expression 'How long?' (עד־מתי) in Proverbs 1:22, the first speech of Wisdom, found in Psalms 6:4; 74:9–10; 80:5; 82:2; 90:13; and 94:3. There are more thematic links, such as the parallels between Proverbs 3:32–4, which stresses God's protection of the righteous and punishment of the wicked, with Psalm 91:3, 5, 8, 11. In Proverbs 6:23, teaching and commandment are likened to lamp and light. In Psalm 119:105, God's word is a lamp to the psalmist's feet and light for his path. Parallel genres are used, as in Proverbs 4:1–2, which appeals to tradition as does Psalm 78:2–6.

In the section Proverbs 10:1—22:16, it has already been noted that the 'fountain of life' (10:11), which is not associated with Yahweh here, is in fact associated with him in texts such as Psalm 36:9. And in 10:22 the sentiment that good things come from God is stressed more fully in Psalm 127:1–2. Proverbs 10:30, on the righteous and wicked and their dwelling in the land, is echoed, with different emphases, in Psalms 10:6; 37:3; 62:2, 6–7; and 112:6. In 11:7–8 there are echoes of psalmic sentiments (e.g. Pss. 49:12; 7:16) as well as parallels with Proverbs 26:27 and 28:10, in which the wicked fall into their own pit. In 12:3, the phrase 'established/not be moved' recalls Psalms 93:1 and 96:10 (cf. 1 Chron. 16:30). The motif of the soul thirsting for God in 13:4 recalls passages in the Psalms such as 42:2 and 63:1. In chapter 15, as already mentioned, there are echoes of Psalm 139:8 in the sentiment (verse 11) that nothing is hidden from God; and there are echoes of Psalm 37:16 in verse 16, on the fear of the Lord. In chapter 16, verses 2–3 echo Psalm 90:17 (cf. Ps. 37:5), and verse 4 echoes Psalm 11:4–7. Verse 10, in its stress on the king's juridical role, echoes Psalm 72:2; and verse 12, on the king's duties, echoes Psalm 101. Verse 24 has connections in sentiment to Psalm 19:10, while verse 27, in its reference to 'digging a pit', recalls Psalms 7:15; 57:6; 119:85; and Jeremiah 18:20, 22. In 17:1–3, God 'tries the hearts', a phrase which has overtones of purifying as well as of

judgement (cf. Pss. 26:2; 66:10; Jer. 9:6). Proverbs 17:10 recalls
Psalm 38:2. Proverbs 18:3, on wickedness, is paralleled in Psalm
119:22, and verse 6, on the fool's mouth, in Psalm 73:9. In Proverbs
18:10–11, the name of the Lord is a strong tower and the wealth of a
rich man his stronghold; the same imagery is found in Psalm 61:3
(cf. Judg. 9:51). In Proverbs 20:9, a statement on the sinfulness of
humankind is made (cf. Pss. 51:5; 143:2; Job 4:17). In Proverbs 20:12,
God has made eye and ear (cf. Ps. 94:9). In 20:24, the stress on God
as the director of human destinies is echoed in Psalm 37:23. In 20:28,
there is a pairing of loyalty and faithfulness in reference to the king
(cf. Ps. 89:24). In 21:1, 'streams of water' recall Psalm 1:3, where the
psalmist is under Yahweh's protection; and in verse 3 the mention of
righteousness and justice recalls Psalms 33:5; 51:18–19, although there
is no mention of their being better than sacrifice in these examples.
In 21:4, the reference to arrogance recalls Psalm 101:5b (cf. Prov.
6:17). Proverbs 21:13 finds a parallel in Psalm 41:12; and verse 16, in
the reference to the assembly of the dead, echoes Psalm 88:11.
Proverbs 22:11 contains echoes of Psalm 21:2.

In Proverbs 23:12, references to 'ear' and 'mind' parallel Deuteronomy 29:4 and Psalm 10:17 (cf. Prov. 18:15). Psalm 37:1 finds an
echo in Proverbs 23:17 and 24:19–20. Proverbs 24:13 also reminds
one of Psalm 119:103, in which God's word is sweeter than honey on
the palate (cf. Ps. 19:10; Ezek. 3:3). Here honey is as sweet and life-
giving as wisdom. I find no echoes of psalmic texts in the small
section 24:23–34.

In Proverbs 25–9, the situation is rather different. In 25:4, the
same analogy of taking dross from silver is used, in part, in Psalm
119:119. Proverbs 25:14 can be compared to Psalm 135:7. Verse 20
recalls the heavy-hearted songs of Psalm 137:3. 'Coals of fire' in verse
22 usually denote punishment (Pss. 18:8; 140:10). Verse 26 speaks of
the righteous giving way to the wicked and hence polluting themselves; compare Psalm 55:22, which expresses the opposite, namely
that the righteous can never be swayed in such a way (cf. Pss. 15:5;
16:8). Proverbs 26:3 can be compared to Psalm 32:9. In 26:22, the
same metaphor is used as in Psalm 7:15; and in verse 27 the same as
is used in Psalms 7:16 and 9:15. With Proverbs 28:2 compare Psalm
82:7. In 28:8, lending at interest to fellow Israelites is forbidden (cf.
Ps. 15:5). Verse 13 recalls Psalm 32:1–5 in the reference to confessing.

Although this evidence is somewhat piecemeal, it does suggest that there are more echoes of psalms in the older proverbial material (10–22:16; 24:23–30; 25–9) than in Proverbs 1–9. This might suggest early psalmic links as the material was in the process of formation; while later redaction is possible, it is, in my view, less likely. If there were early links with the cult itself, and possibly with certain psalmic texts, that would explain the presence of such language. Of course, wisdom literature soon developed its own distinctive character, but these connections are hints of a wider interaction at a formative stage.

Perhaps the most compelling evidence of mutual influence is the existence of the wisdom psalms. The opening psalm of the psalter (Ps. 1) places moral integrity above all things and sorts people into righteous and wicked. One is led to ask whether there is evidence here of cross-cultural influence, or whether the links can be dismissed as merely late editing in either the Psalms or wisdom.[18] If one accepts the view that the wisdom psalms are not all necessarily late and post-exilic, but that they may contain wisdom influence at an earlier stage in their development, this might too suggest some early cross-fertilization between the two genres, on the level both of textual echoes and of actual setting, at least for the wisdom psalms, in the cult. Given that both the Psalms and wisdom are on what might be characterized as the 'non-historical' axis of Israelite thought and faith, and that many psalms share with wisdom an interest in creation, order, kingship and human relationship, maybe this kind of connection is hardly surprising (as discussed in Chapter 4). Could it be that we are hearing echoes, albeit faint, of an original cultic tradition lying behind the earliest wisdom material in Proverbs?

Many of the proverbs simply express the joy of observation, of wonder at the world, at human experience and relationships, and at the natural world too. In this they have a quality of praise about them that seems to have gone unnoticed by scholars. Could this suggest a link-up with the worshipping life of Israel? There is in fact no reason why proverbs (particularly those circulating independently

---

[18] See Dell, 2004b.

and orally, as arguably in Prov. 10:1—22:16; 24:23–34; and 25–9, in particular) could not have been used in worship, particularly where proverbs break out into praise of the natural world or of the relationship between God and man, notably in those proverbs that do not contain a negative contrast. For example, 'To make an apt answer is a joy to anyone, and a word in season, how good it is!' (Prov. 15:23), or 'Pleasant words are like a honeycomb, sweetness to the soul and health to the body' (Prov. 16:24).[19] However, this context is possible even when the proverb is more negative in sentiment, along lines more similar to psalms of lament; for instance, 'Even in laughter the heart is sad and the end of joy is grief' (Prov. 14:13). Scholars have perhaps been too used to trying to match a social context to a genre of material, and the present work has attempted to open that discussion out so that wisdom maxims can be seen to belong to other circumstances: ethics belongs to the law as well as to wisdom's moralizing; prophecy inspires, as Wisdom does; education in wisdom is matched by education in all areas of life. Seeing such interconnections frees the proverbs from a contextual straitjacket in which they have been traditionally confined.

CONCLUSION

I have explored three areas of possible influence on Proverbs from the wider Israelite thought-world. I looked first at the prophetic echoes, and found the most compelling evidence of possible influence from prophetic ideas on wisdom in the poetry of Proverbs 1–9, notably in the shaping of the figure of woman Wisdom. I then looked at Deuteronomic links and noted that those were most extensive in the instruction texts of Proverbs 1–9 (with a few interesting echoes in Prov. 22:17—24:22). This might well suggest influence on the shaping of these instruction texts from the Deuteronomic worldview, although the opposite is also possible,

---

[19] Other contenders for this category (apart from the three cited above) are numerous: e.g. Prov. 11:25; 12:14, 28; 14:4; 26–7; 15:3, 11, 15, 30–2; 16:1, 3, 7, 9, 10, 11, 13, 15, 16, 17, 20, 21, 23, 26, 31, 33; 17:6, 17; 18:4, 10, 15, 20, 22; 19:8, 17, 20, 21, 23; 20:5, 7, 12, 27–8; 21:1, 21; 22:4; 23:24, 25, 26; 25:2–3, 11–12, 13, 15; 25:25; 26:14; 27:18–19. In 30:15ff. the sayings involving animals and numerical heightening techniques would also lend themselves to a worshipping context.

depending on when one dates this section. It may be that we are seeing parallel developments of very different texts in the same cultural milieu. It is clear that Deuteronomy has a prime teaching focus, which suits the more didactic purpose of these instruction texts in Proverbs; and similarly the language of instruction suits the worldview of a more nationalistic text which nevertheless broadens out in its didactic role. So I have found echoes in Proverbs 1–9 from mainly prophetic and legal thought-worlds, especially where those worlds are influenced by Deuteronomic language and concerns. These echoes are not extensive, but are clearly present, and indicate that those who composed this section of Proverbs were not isolated in thought from other aspects of Israelite life. This observation may have implications for the social setting of this material. The question remains: when did these influences come into the material? Was it at a formative stage of the idea, at the time the material was written, or part of a later recontextualization or redaction? Some influences have the character of being more formative, such as the prophetic overtones of the Wisdom figure in Proverbs 1:20–33, but this remains an open question.

I have, thirdly, pointed to cultic influence and echoes of psalmic texts. I have evaluated this also as a formative influence upon the material. This time, though, the weight of evidence for influence falls in the earlier sections of Proverbs, so indicating an earlier stage of the development of Proverbs. So, when we turn to Proverbs 10:1—22:16, which is likely to represent the wisdom literature at its earliest stage, it is clear that there is more influence from psalmic texts than from other thought-worlds. This might have implications for social context, linking up with Perdue's ideas about the cult. I also noted (in Chapter 4) the link between Yahweh references and those to the king. Is it likely that there was a closer connection between social order and cultic order, between the king in society and the king in the cult, and ultimately between God, the king, society, ethics and worship? Ahlström (1982) stresses the role of the king in relation to the cult and says that it is wrong to drive a wedge between state and cult. The king is God's cultic representative; in fact, palace and temple were often walled off from the rest of the city but united geographically. The king was at the centre of cultic life, at least on certain cultic occasions. The divine order was also established through the holding of festivals (Ahlström, 1995). The cult, as has been seen, is not absent from the concern of some proverbs, and furthermore, some of the examples of echoes of psalmic texts occurred where the king was mentioned. This would in turn link up with the vertical, ahistorical theological dimension that scholars have stressed (as discussed in Chapter 5). The creation axis includes the cultic as well as wisdom literature and might suggest that originally there was more connection between the two.[20]

In its later stages, wisdom appears to have departed from any cultic link (although there are some who argue for temple schools in the post-exilic period; Doll, 1985), but the 'intellectual tradition' on which Proverbs 1–9 draws is broader, incorporating prophetic and Deuteronomic influences. The Yahwistic aspect, too, links up with this conclusion; in Chapter 4 it was clear that this is found in Proverbs 10:1—22:17 in clusters of proverbs that seem to have a cohering quality within their sections, and that mention of Yahweh was also primary in Proverbs 1–9. It is one and the same Yahweh who is being addressed in the Psalms and elsewhere in the Old Testament. My conclusion here, then, is that Proverbs is more unified with other parts of Old Testament, as shown by the evidence of echoes of other texts discussed above, than scholars have generally allowed.

[20] B. W. Anderson (1987) argues that an early creation faith and the more historical exodus faith existed side by side in Israelite worship. He sees the Davidic/Jebusite cult as having historicized the creation faith and looks at creation psalms (8; 19a; 104) that show no interest in salvation history and that could be seen to pre-date that assimilation. He also argues that wisdom is especially compatible with royal Davidic covenant theology.

Conclusion

Besides being wise, the Teacher also taught the people knowledge, weighing and studying and arranging many proverbs.
(Eccles. 12:9)

I wish to begin in this Conclusion with an overview of the argument
pursued in this book and then continue with some reflections on
fresh directions in which this study might take scholars of the
wisdom literature. Perhaps the key concerns of this book, introduced at the start, are the former marginalization of wisdom and the
need for integration with the rest of the Old Testament. In the
Introduction I identified three areas in which such marginalization
had taken place and which would provide useful categories for
dividing up the discussion. These three areas were social context,
theology, and affinities with other Old Testament material, and the
focus of concern was limited to the book of Proverbs. Under the
heading of social context, the strides made by critical study were
identified and the reasons for the tendency to hive wisdom off into a
separate category and context were noted. Signs of integration were
seen to be accompanied by certain presuppositions about wisdom as
a redactional stage influencing material later rather than earlier in its
development. Under the heading of theology, the reasons for
wisdom's separateness were noted and, in particular, its marginalization in Old Testament theologies was a matter for concern. Again
signs of integration in the recognition of the importance of creation
theology were seen to be emerging and required further investi-
gation. In relation to other parts of the Old Testament, I found
reasons for separateness similiar to those in the social context and
theology areas, and again the influence of wisdom on other material

was noted. The question was asked: was there any chance that wisdom might have had a formative influence on other Old Testament texts, rather than simply a redactional one? It was suggested here that a more integrative approach might be to look within the different sections of Proverbs for wider contextual links with other Old Testament texts and traditions.

In Chapter 1 the focus was on social context(s) in Proverbs 1–9, and it was noted that the section is generally perceived as later than others with a more developed theology. The issue was raised, however, whether older material might be contained within this section, and the need to distinguish oral and written stages was stressed as a result. In this context I looked at the kinds of approach scholars apply to texts: first, a literary one in this case meant the identification of different genres within the section; second, a developmental approach in terms of historical and theological developments was seen to lead to a later dating on theological grounds; a third approach takes full account of ancient Near Eastern parallels; and a fourth is interested in Proverbs in relation to the rest of the Old Testament, whether with its theology or with its literature. I noted how suggestions as to social context tend to differ with the different sections of Proverbs and so decided to focus on those brought specifically into the discussion of Proverbs 1–9. There was also the possibility of different stages of oral and written compilation, and suggestions were aired regarding whether an educational or theological context was foremost for this material. First, I looked at the way the family context was marginalized by the discussion based on the noting of parallels with Egyptian instructions, which led to an emphasis on teaching in a court school context as the prime one for this material. Second, the focus shifted to the possibility of a wider school context, which opened up the question of the extent of literacy and of how specialized the writing-down process would have been. The issue of dating was again raised in relation to the existence of pre- or post-exilic schools. Third, the family context came to the fore again. The issues of whether teaching was indeed the primary context of this material (and the religious context secondary) and of how far it was oral and/or literary were again raised. Four recurring matters were picked out as lying behind the discussion of social context, and these set the agenda for what followed. The first was the purpose of the material, whether educational or religious or both; the second was the oral/written question; the third was whether the instructions were to be seen as structurally unified either as a whole or in their separate parts; and the fourth was the issue of dating. I then turned to a preliminary look at the instruction texts in Proverbs 1–9 (including bridging passages) and took particular note, in this survey, of issues one and three above – especially the purpose of the material, which was found to be educational (with indicators of a school or home-teaching context) with a strong ethical component (which might or might not belong to an educational context, but, when placed in instruction texts, did seem to match that context). The issue of structural unity was aired alongside the views of scholars who sought to fragment the text. The instructions were seen to be varied in terms of subject matter and theme and hence unlikely to be from the pen of one author. However, they were each found to be structural units within themselves, with inner coherence, and hence to be more likely to be written texts than oral ones (although a few pointers to an original oral context in some instructions were found).

In Chapter 2 I continued my exploration of social context in relation to Proverbs 10:1—22:16. Similar issues were raised: oral versus written stages; the question of general ethical or more educated context; how theological the material is; and a link with the court. I looked in particular at suggestions of a family/folk/tribal setting and found this kind of context convincing for the oral stage of the individual proverbs. Fascinating parallels were drawn with tribal societies, and the possibility of a legal context or even a cultic one for some of the ethical sayings was aired alongside the educational one. The related question of oral versus literary stages was then considered and the concept of an oral/literary continuum was found to be a useful one. Court and school suggestions for this material were generally found to provide a less convincing context for the sayings as they were originating, but a possible context for their collection and writing down (possibly at the time of Hezekiah). I saw that the main purpose of this sayings collection seemed to be of a general ethical type not necessarily tied to an educational context, and that structural unity of more than small thematic clusters is hard to maintain.

In Chapter 3 I looked at Proverbs 22:17—24:22 and at the suggested links with the Egyptian *Instruction of Amenemope*, which strongly suggested a court educational context for the Proverbs material, and probably a written context, in that the Egyptian instruction was a written text copied by schoolboys. Scholarly suggestions of a courtly context, not only for this section but for Proverbs in general, were considered. This section had the best claim to a court school context in the whole of Proverbs, but the context was forced in relation to the whole book. Links between Proverbs 22:17—24:22 and Proverbs 1–9 were then considered, and the opportunity was taken to look at the chapters a little more closely; and a good number of parallels between the two sections emerged. This seemed again to confirm the educational context of this section. The question of the priority of the material was raised and it was suggested that this section might have influenced Proverbs 1–9 in that 22:17—24:22 is likely to have been an earlier written text explicitly used in fairly formal educational circles, probably in a court school. Proverbs 24:23–34, a very brief collection of sayings, was best seen as an appendix to the previous section, but showed how sayings could have circulated in independent collections that are often, but not always, thematically linked. In considering Proverbs 25–9 I distinguished between the written stage, where Hezekiah's men are indicated as having copied proverbs, and the original oral stage. I looked at the chapters in structural terms and at the subject matter of the different chapters and found that there is considerable repetition of topics and echoes of texts from Proverbs 10:1—22:17, which suggested that this section was either preceded by the main sayings collection or was an oral parallel to it. I also found hints of issues raised in Proverbs 1–9 suggesting that there may have been a relationship with both of the other main parts of Proverbs, with Proverbs 25–9 as an interim stage between the collection of sayings in 10:1—22:16 and the collecting and writing down of the instructions and poems of chapters 1–9. I looked briefly at the sections in chapters 30 and 31 and decided that these individual texts were quite fragmentary and probably belonged to different settings. Proverbs 30:1–14, which has links with a foreign king, seemed to have more in common with chapters 1–9 and 22:17—24:22 in terms of context, while 30:15–33, with its character of a series of short numerical proverbs, related better to 10:1—22:16 and chapters 25–9. Proverbs 31:1–9 very much suggests a court context, and the final section of Proverbs links up with the picture of woman Wisdom in chapters 1–9 so it was decided that both these sections linked up best with 1–9; 22:17—24:22 and 30:1–14. I concluded, therefore, in relation to social context in Proverbs as a whole, that one could subdivide the book of Proverbs into two sets of clearly different social contexts: the more overtly educational context, with possible courtly/kingly links and more emphasis on the written stage of the material (in relation to the texts just mentioned); and the family/folk/tribal context, with a more general ethical character and oral nature, in 10:1—22:16; 24:23–34; 25–9 and 30:15–33.

In Chapter 4 I asked how integral is a religious dimension, and within that a Yahwistic one, first of all to Proverbs 1–9. I identified the figure of Wisdom, the references to Yahweh and the concept of the fear of Yahweh as the three main expressions of this. The views of Whybray on redactional stages were discussed, views which saw, first, references to Wisdom and then those to Yahweh as layers of redaction and called for a more holistic approach. Related issues of whether attention to other matters such as literary genre, the educational context and ancient Near Eastern parallels had taken away from a focus on the religious elements were aired. A survey of Proverbs 1–9, including the poems this time, looked at the theological elements and their function in the structure of each section. Structural integrity was imparted by the often interchangeable figures of Yahweh and Wisdom, and religious elements were seen to exist comfortably alongside more general ethical and educational concerns. I argued that the religious elements were integral, probably belonging to a formative stage of the material rather than to a later redaction. Similar questions were then posed regarding the other sections of Proverbs. In Proverbs 10:1—22:16, clusters of Yahweh sayings were noted and the stage of their placement in the present context(s) was seen to be an important one, but one which did not exclude the possibility that the Yahweh element was formative of Proverbs at the oral stage. This was favoured over the idea that this element was a superimposed reinterpretation. I also noted the proximity of proverbs mentioning Yahweh and the king, suggesting an important link of royalty with the divine. Yahweh references were also found to be integral in 22:17—24:22 and 25–9; in the former, the religious references were integrated with the educational context; and in the latter, the number of Yahweh sayings were fewer in number but significantly placed. In Proverbs 30 and 31, most Yahweh sayings were found in 30:1–14, which is generally regarded as a later section that has more in common with Job than with Proverbs.

In Chapter 5 I looked at the way the debate about wisdom's theology has evolved in scholarly discussion and at its place in the characterization of Old Testament theology. I evaluated the relative claims of creation and order to be the keynote of wisdom and found, after examination of key texts, that Proverbs 1–9 was characterized by an emphasis on creation past and present, notably in the poems concerning Wisdom, and that Proverbs 10:1—22:16 and other sections (except 30:1–14) demonstrated closer ties to creation as linked to order in the ethical and social sphere. The significance of the integral Yahwistic element in relation to the debate about creation, and countering of ideas that the material was in any way secular or just anthropocentric, were concerns here. The work of key critical scholars whose work has shaped the debate was surveyed, notably that of von Rad, Schmid and Zimmerli; and then views were aired that sought to integrate creation faith with other parts of Old Testament faith in the context of a consideration of Old Testament theology. I suggested that creation faith was part of a wider counter-theme to the salvation-history model, with important links to monotheism and universalism. Following the analysis of texts treating creation motifs, I linked the importance of the Yahwistic emphasis (established in Chapter 4) with the wider theological debate about the character of wisdom's theology, rejecting views that argued for a different Yahweh in this material from that in the rest of the Old Testament. I noted views that try to separate and others that try to integrate wisdom and Yahwism, preferring the latter model. Hubbard's view, seeing more theological integration of the wisdom literature with other concepts in the Old Testament such as prophecy, cult and covenant, and Høgenhaven's ideas about the roots of wisdom thought as finding a place in early Israelite thought, were particularly relevant here.

In Chapter 6 the influence upon Proverbs from other genres, texts and traditions from the Old Testament was discussed. I especially considered influence *into* the text rather than influence *out*. In relation to Proverbs 1–9, the views of a small group of scholars who have been down this road were examined, and this was seen to be a neglected area, possibly because of so much focus on ancient Near Eastern parallels in relation to this section. Some scholars regarded any links as little more than common vocabulary in a different context, and others saw echoes of words and phrases as more of an intentional influence. These issues were seen to be linked to those of date and priority of influence of one text over another. In relation to the rest of Proverbs, there were significant hints that legal and cultic contexts could have provided alternative backgrounds for some sayings. I then looked specifically at prophetic links and found little evidence of the influence in Proverbs 10–31, although there was some link-up of prophetic overtones in some of the more Yahwistic passages. The main evidence was in Proverbs 1–9 and, within that, in the poems about woman Wisdom, where there were close links to prophetic language, particularly in 1:20–33. The possibility of Deuteronomic influence was then investigated in relation to echoes of texts, and the main evidence was found in the instructions of chapters 1–9. General phrases, such as the 'fear of Yahweh', and concepts such as the Torah, were found to be in harmony in their legal and wisdom usages, the fear of Yahweh also linking up with the cultic life of Israel. In other parts of Proverbs linkage with Deuteronomic thought was not strong. By contrast, I found (with Perdue) good evidence in Proverbs 10–31 of cultic observance and some illuminating echoes of psalmic texts. This is a reminder of the wisdom psalms that indicates a link between the wisdom writers and the cult. Some proverbs break out into praise, and such observations highlight the need for a wider appreciation of the overlap in possible context for proverbial wisdom.

My primary purpose in this book, then, has been to highlight the integration of wisdom as represented in the book of Proverbs. I have shown the integration of different sections of Proverbs: with one another and in relation to social context and theology, and the integration of thought with other parts of the Old Testament.[1]

---

[1] Such a discussion could be taken further to relate to other wisdom books. In Job I have argued that, such is the diversity of forms that imitate other areas of Israelite life, one is

At the end of the first three chapters on social context, I discovered that two social contexts predominate as possibilities for different groupings of sections of Proverbs. The first grouping was Proverbs 1–9; 22:17—24:22; 30:1–14; and 31. The strength of Egyptian parallels to these sections was noted, and also the cross-reference, in particular between Proverbs 1–9 and 22:17—24:22. This suggests that there was a close relationship between these sections. What they had in common with the educational context of Egyptian material was the use of the form of the instruction and the borrowing of the *Instruction of Amenemope* as a template for Proverbs 22:1—24:22. As for Proverbs 30 and 31, these sections represent the wisdom of foreigners and again serve to stress that foreign influence from wider wisdom circles. Education is the key link here, but, as seen in Chapter 4, in Israel an educational function was not separate from religious concerns. Integral to the Israelite instruction material in Proverbs 1–9 is mention of God and Wisdom.[2] The home/school/court contexts for this material are all possible, but high-level court schooling is probably most likely, the main evidence being outside Proverbs 1–9 (in the *Amenemope* parallel context for Proverbs 22:17—24:22, in the mention of kings in Proverbs 30 and 31, and in the nature of the discussion in 31:1–19). There may be evidence here of a development from one context to another, but it is probably not as simple as that, given that different social contexts existed alongside one another. However, it is possible that material was first disseminated in an oral tradition or that separate and piecemeal written instruction texts existed and that they were then collected in both school and court circles, and those two may have been inextricably linked in that the main context for schooling, and of the production of material suitable for such activity, was at the court of the king.

---

stretching the boundaries of the definition of wisdom by including the book as wisdom on a narrow form-critical definition. While I hold by that conclusion, I would add in the light of the findings here that even the most mainstream of the wisdom books, Proverbs, does not show a complete absence of linkage with wider Israelite tradition; it is simply a matter of degree. I see the book of Ecclesiastes as having closer ties with mainstream wisdom, but again echoes of other texts have been noted (especially overtones of Gen. 1–11), and it would be interesting to put these same questions to that text.

[2] The Egyptian material may also have had a divine dimension, with the Ma'at link, but it is beyond the scope of this book to discuss that issue.

The alignment of Proverbs 1–9 with these other sections serves to demonstrate the presence of early educational material in its pages. Furthermore, this influence is not to be separated from the Yahwistic nature of the material. The only parts of Proverbs 1–9 which are arguably later, on grounds of theological development, are the poems about Wisdom; but again, with the link of ideas with Ma'at and the possible goddess overtones, even within those ideas there may be earlier roots. However, perhaps at the time of compilation of the section or even of the book of Proverbs, these poems may have found an important redactional role in binding together not just the section, but the whole book (witness, too, the link with Proverbs 31 in the female portrayal which, in its positioning, balances the feminine portrayals in the book as a whole). Some of the conclusions from Chapter 6 come in here, since the wisdom poems seem to have been formulated in a world where prophecy was known, and there is some imitation of its themes in the presentation of woman Wisdom. I also found Deuteronomic links in Proverbs 1–9 that indicated some influence from the Deuteronomic movement, which also indicated a 'later' set of instruction texts from the period from the seventh century BC leading up to the exile (although again, with the instruction genre being an old one, these might have had earlier roots). I would argue here, though, that nothing from Proverbs 1–9 necessitates a date well after the exile, and I would put that as the *terminus ad quem* for the production of this section and possibly of the whole book. It is perhaps unlikely that the section was composed before the time of Hezekiah, and the interaction with Deuteronomic concerns may indicate a dating concurrent with the work of that movement. Perhaps this sheds light on the reference to the 'men of Hezekiah' in Proverbs 25:1, in that their remit may have included gathering proverbs as well as being involved in the thought-world of Deuteronomic ideas.

The other main group of 'sections' from Proverbs was 10:1—22:16; 24:23–4; 25–9; and 30:15–33. This seemed to represent the older tradition of sayings that circulated, chiefly orally. The material here was not seen to be confined to an educational context in any formal sense, but rather was part of a broader ethical concern to attempt to order life and to understand God in his role as creator. It was seen in Chapter 4 how there was more extensive mention of

God here than has commonly been acknowledged, and it was noted in Chapter 5 that, although God is primarily portrayed as creator, that portrayal does not diminish his distinctiveness as the same Yahweh of the Israelite nation that we find elsewhere in the Old Testament. I observed in Proverbs 30:15–33 a type of nature wisdom that would seem to link back to Solomon himself in 1 Kings 5 and which forms an important strand of the oldest wisdom tradition. The elements of cross-reference and borrowing between sections, notably the borrowing from 10:1—22:16 in chapters 25–9 were also of interest. This suggests that, by the time of the formation of the collection in chapters 25–9 at the hands of Hezekiah's men, the main section of Proverbs (10:1—22:16) already had wide currency, and that while the collection of proverbs was done in more elevated courtly circles, that may represent only one stage of the formation of the material. The Hezekian context is clearly a very important one for the formation of the book of Proverbs – the 'collection of collections' was taking shape.

One is being given a window here into the final stage of a longer process, and there is an important distinction to be made between ideas as they are conceived and coined and the writing process that ultimately leads to the written text we have today. I have chosen to place the stress in this section on the oral stage and on possible contexts for the proverbs outside wisdom alone, particularly in cultic life. So, in Chapter 6 I noted links with cultic concerns, indicating a possible early psalmic tradition that linked up with wisdom.[3] This might provide a wider clue regarding context: the proverbs were clearly used in many situations in society, to give force to an argument, simply to make an observation, to teach from experience, and to warn others not to fall into similar traps and make similar mistakes. They could also have been used in worship, particularly where proverbs break out into praise of the natural world or of the relationship between God and man. The emphasis on God as creator in many proverbs, too, may help to confirm this link.

---

[3] This may also be evidenced in some wisdom psalms (see Dell, 2004).

In this grouping of texts,[4] a unique glimpse is given into the important role wisdom undoubtedly had in the pre-exilic period, in the formation of ideas and in the shaping of a whole dimension of life in which people lived. It shaped ethical concerns, it described God, and it sought to understand the world in an ordered framework. It was used educationally, but also as part of a wider cultic concern to wonder at the world in which people found themselves. It could be used by all – by people in the home, in school, in the temple, and in the courts of kings. It was an expression of a fundamental element of Yahwism and, as such, takes its place alongside the more historical recitation of the faith in a dynamic synthesis.

Being such an important and integrated area of Israelite life, then, wisdom should proudly take its place alongside other traditions and other genres of material within the canon and should be evaluated with much more prominence in the overall discussion of Old Testament theology. The two dimensions of ethics and education as demonstrable social contexts for proverbial material, combined with its distinctive theological approach, give wisdom literature an entrance into the heartland of Israelite concern. Subtle connections with texts from outside in Proverbs 1–9, in particular, give it a role within a broader intellectual tradition in which priests, lawyers, poets and sages were united in the quest to understand Yahweh from whichever angles they chose. These links with other texts tell us both about the period of formation of the text and the earliest roots of ideas, and it is demonstrable that both stages exist in the texts under discussion.[5] I have shown how it is likely that there was a

---

[4] It should be noted that in Chapter 6, when I was looking for echoes of other texts in Proverbs, these groupings that I had made under the heading of social context did not align in the same way. Proverbs 1–9 showed the greatest links with other texts, although there were hints of wider engagement also in Prov. 22:17—24:22. The other sections really had to be ranged together in a group as showing less influence, except in the cultic sphere. This may have implications for my conclusions over social context, but not profound ones, I think.

[5] In relation to the earliest proverbial material, it can be demonstrated that the theological ideas contained in the proverbs influenced other material in the Old Testament as it was in the process of formation. There is influence of wisdom – in forms, content and context – on other material, such as the eighth-century prophets, as has been well demonstrated by other scholars. Had this study been longer, I might have gone into those connections in more depth.

close relationship with the cultic context in the earliest proverbial material and how prophetic and Deuteronomic language was not unknown to those who either shaped or wrote down key parts of Proverbs 1–9. The context of faith in Yahweh is the fundamental, overarching theological perspective behind the material, even in sections where God is very much behind the scenes and although those references become more numerous in Proverbs 1–9, adding weight to the idea of some further theological development (mainly evidenced in the development of the woman Wisdom concept). Yahweh is by no means absent from the main body of the proverbial material. While Yahweh is portrayed as creator and orderer in this material, rather than as covenant partner with Israel, he is the same Yahweh who manifests himself in different ways. To reiterate again, there is an important difference between the view of God as creator in chapters 10–31 and 1–9, in that I found more of an emphasis on God as orderer in the former section, and more of a stress on creation as past and present event in the latter (and in 30:1–14). This is another indicator of a later, more profound musing on God's creative role in the Proverbs 1–9 text, possibly influenced by other parts of the canon.[6] It also suggests that, in Proverbs, the more basic view of God as creator is of him as orderer of the whole of life: the created world, the natural order, human society and hierarchy, the path of human life, and finding sense in human experience. The figure of Wisdom provides a bridge between the divine and the human realms, and interchangeable mention in, Proverbs, 1–9 of Yahweh and Wisdom, Yahweh and the king (as also in 10:1—22:16), and Yahweh and father, teacher, path and way show that this alignment does not disappear in the more educational material.

In conclusion, it is perhaps sufficient to say that in the book of Proverbs the wisdom tradition is truly integrated with its canonical bedfellows, not just in its perception of God and not just within the corpus of other wisdom literature, but throughout the Old

---

[6] This would be an interesting area to explore further. Again, in this conclusion I found less of a link with the divisions of material in relation to social context; but then, if the divisions in Proverbs could be too neatly organized, there would have been no need for scholars to discuss them!

Testament. As such, wisdom represents a mainstream tradition within Old Testament life and thought. Both the social context(s) and theology of the book of Proverbs can be successfully integrated in relation to other known contexts of social functions and theological expression, and hence I maintain that wisdom should be integrated fully into scholarly consideration of Old Testament theology and no longer regarded as an outsider to more mainstream concerns.

Bibliography

Ahlström, G. W. (1982), *Royal Administration and National Religion in Ancient Palestine*, Studies in the History of the Ancient Near East 1, Leiden: Brill

—— (1995), 'Administration of the state in Canaan and ancient Israel', *Civilizations of the Ancient Near East*, 1, J. M. Sasson, J. Baines, G. Beckman, K. S. Rubinson (eds.), New York: Charles Scribner's Sons: 587–603

Albertz, R. (1974), *Weltschöpfung und Menschenschöpfung*, Calwer Theologische Monographien, Reihe A, Bibelwissenschaft 3, Stuttgart: Calwer

Albreckson, B. (1967), *History and the Gods*, CB 1, Lund: C. W. K. Gleerup

Alonso-Schökel, L. (1968), *Proverbios y Eclesiástico: Traducción y Commentario*, Madrid: Cristiandad

Alt, A. (1955), 'Zur literarische Analyse des Amenemope', VTS 3: 16–25

—— (1976), 'Solomonic wisdom', *Studies in Ancient Israelite Wisdom*, J. L. Crenshaw (ed.), New York: KTAV, 102–12 (Ger. 1951)

Anderson, B. W. (1987), *Creation versus Chaos: The Reinterpretation of Mythical Symbolism in the Bible*, Philadelphia: Fortress Press

—— (1994), *From Creation to New Creation: Old Testament Perspectives*, OBT, Minneapolis: Augsburg Fortress

—— (1999), *Contours of Old Testament Theology*, Minneapolis: Augsburg Fortress

—— (ed.) (1984), *Creation in the Old Testament*, Philadelphia: Fortress Press; London: SPCK

Anderson, R. T. (1960), 'Was Isaiah a scribe?', *JBL* 79: 57–8

Anthes, R. (1933), *Lebensregeln und Lebensweisheit der alten Ägypter*, Der Alte Orient 32/2, Leipzig: J. C. Hinrichs'sche Buchhandlung

Audet, J.-P. (1960), 'Origines comparés de la double tradition de la loi et de la sagesse dans le proche-orient ancien', *Trudy* xxv, Moscow: Tsd-vo Vostochnoi lit-ry: 352–57

Baines, J. (1983), 'Literacy and ancient Egyptian society', *Man* 18: 572–99

Barr, J. (1993), *Biblical Faith and Natural Theology*, Oxford: Clarendon Press

Barré, M. L. (ed.) (1997), *Wisdom, You are My Sister: Studies in Honour of R. E. Murphy O. Carm on the Occasion of his 80th Birthday*, CBQMS 29, Washington, DC: Catholic Biblical Association of America

Barton, J. (1984), 'Gerhard von Rad on the world-view of early Israel', *JTS* NS 35/2: 301–23

Barucq, A. (1964), *Le Livre de Proverbes*, Sources Bibliques, Paris: Gabalda

Baumann, G. (1966), *Die Weisheitsgestalt in Proverbien 1–9: Traditions-geschichte und theologische Studien*, FAT 16, Tübingen: Mohr (Siebeck)

Baumgartner, W. (1933), *Israelitische und Altorientalische Weisheit*, Tübingen: J. C. B. Mohr

(1951), 'The Wisdom Literature', *The Old Testament and Modern Study: A Generation of Discovery and Research*, H. H. Rowley (ed.), Oxford: Clarendon Press: 210–37

Becker, J. (1965), *Gottesfurcht im Alten Testament*, AB 25, Rome: Biblical Institute

Blank, S. H. (1962), 'Wisdom', *IDB* 4, New York: Abingdon Press: 852–61

Blenkinsopp, J. (1991), 'The social context of the "outsider woman" in Proverbs 1–9', *Biblica* 72: 457–73

(1995a), *Wisdom and Law in the Old Testament: The Ordering of Life in Israel and Early Judaism*, Oxford: Oxford University Press. 2nd edition

(1995b), *Sage, Priest, Prophet: Religious and Intellectual Leadership in Ancient Israel*, Louisville: Westminster John Knox Press

(1997), 'The family in first temple Israel', *Families in Ancient Israel*, L. G. Perdue, J. Blenkinsopp, J. J. Collins and C. Meyers, Louisville: Westminster John Knox Press: 48–103

Boer, P. A. H. de (1960), 'The Counsellor', *Wisdom in Israel and the Ancient Near East*, M. Noth and D. W. Thomas (eds.), Leiden: Brill: 42–71

Boström, L. (1990), *The God of the Sages: The Portrayal of God in the Book of Proverbs*, CB 29, Stockholm: Almqvist & Wiksell International

Bright, J. (1967), *The Authority of the Old Testament*, London: SCM Press

Brown, W. P. (1996), *Character in Crisis: A Fresh Approach to the Wisdom Literature of the Old Testament*, Grand Rapids: Eerdmans

Brueggemann, W. A. (1970a), 'The triumphalist tendency in exegetical history', *JAAR* 38: 367–80

(1970b), 'Scripture and an ecumenical lifestyle: a study in wisdom theology', *Interpretation* 24/1, 3–19

(1972) *In Man We Trust*, Atlanta: John Knox Press

(1980), 'A convergence in recent Old Testament theologies', *JSOT* 18: 2–18

(1990), 'The social significance of Solomon as a patron of wisdom', *The Sage in Israel and in the Ancient Near East*, J. G. Gammie and L. G. Perdue (eds.), Winona Lake: Eisenbrauns, 117–32

(1996), 'The loss and recovery of creation in Old Testament theology', *Theology Today* 53: 177–90

(1997), *Theology of the Old Testament: Testimony, Dispute, Advocacy*, Minneapolis: Augsburg Fortress

Brunner, H. (1963), 'Der frei Wille Gottes in der ägyptischen Weisheit', *Les Sagesses du Proche-Orient ancien: Colloque de Strasbourg 17–19 Mai 1962*, Paris: Presses universitaires de France: 102–20

Bryce, G. E. (1979), *A Legacy of Wisdom*, Lewisburg: Bucknell University Press

Budge, E. A. W (1922), *Second Series of Facsimiles of Egyptian Hieratic Papyri in the British Museum*, London: British Museum

(1924), *The Teaching of Åmen-em-àpt, Son of Kanekht: The Egyptian Hieroglyphic Text and an English Translation*, London: Hopkinson

Camp, C. V. (1985), *Wisdom and the Feminine in the Book of Proverbs*, Sheffield: Almond Press

Carmichael, C. M. (1974), *The Laws of Deuteronomy*, Ithaca: Cornell University Press

Cazelles, H. (n.d.), *Sagesses antérieures aux Proverbes*, Paris, Institut Catholique: 109–44

(1963), 'Les Débuts de la sagesse en Israel', *Les Sagesses du Proche-Orient ancien: Colloque de Strasbourg 17–19 Mai 1962*, Paris, Presses universitaires de France: 27–39

Ceresko, A. (1994) *Psalmists and Sages: Studies in Old Testament Poetry and Religion*, Indian Theological Studies Supplements 2, Bangalore, India: Institute Publications

Childs, B. S. (1979), *Introduction to the Old Testament as Scripture*, London: SCM Press

(1985), *Old Testament Theology in a Canonical Context*, London: SCM Press

(1992), *Biblical Theology of the Old and New Testaments: Theological Reflection on the Christian Bible*, London: SCM Press

Clements, R. E. (1992), *Wisdom in Theology*, Carlisle: Paternoster Press; Grand Rapids: Eerdmans

Clifford, R. J. (1985), 'The Hebrew scriptures and the theology of Creation', *TS* 46: 507–23

(1988), 'Creation in the Hebrew Bible', *Physics, Philosophy and Theology: A Common Quest for Understanding*, R. J. Russell, W. R. Stoeger and G. V. Coyne (eds.), Vatican City State: Vatican Observatory, 151–70

(1992), 'Creation in the Psalms', *Creation in the Biblical Traditions*, R. J. Clifford and J. J. Collins (eds.), CBQMS 24, Washington, DC: Catholic Biblical Association of America: 57–69

(1999), *Proverbs: A Commentary*, OTL, Louisville: Westminster John Knox Press

Coats, G. W., and Long, B. O. (eds.) (1977), *Canon and Authority*, Philadelphia: Fortress Press

Collins, J. J. (1977), 'The biblical precedent for natural theology', JAARS 45: 35–62

(1980), 'Proverbial wisdom and the Yahwist vision', *Gnomic Wisdom*, J. D. Crossan (ed.), *Semeia* 17: 1–18

Conzelmann, H. (1971), 'The mother of wisdom', *The Future of Our Religious Past: Essays in Honour of Rudolf Bultmann*, J. M. Robinson (ed.), London: SCM Press

Crenshaw, J. L. (1976), 'Prologomenon', *Studies in Ancient Israelite Wisdom*, J. L. Crenshaw (ed.), New York: KTAV: 1–60. Reprinted in Crenshaw (1995a): 90–140

(1981a), 'Wisdom and authority: sapiential rhetoric and its warrants', VTS 32: 10–29. Reprinted in Crenshaw (1995a): 326–43

(1981b), *Old Testament Wisdom: An Introduction*, Atlanta: John Knox Press, 1981. Reprinted London: SCM Press, 1982; revised edition Louisville: Westminster John Knox Press, 1998

(1985), 'Education in ancient Israel', *JBL* 104, 1985: 601–15. Reprinted in Crenshaw (1995a): 235–49

(1992), 'Prohibitions in Proverbs and Qohelet', *Priests, Prophets and Scribes: Essays on the Formation and Heritage of Second Temple Judaism in Honour of Joseph Blenkinsopp*, E. Ulrich, J. W. Wright, R. P. Carroll (eds.) Sheffield: JSOT Press: 115–24. Reprinted in Crenshaw (1995a): 417–25

(1995a), *Urgent Advice and Probing Questions: Collected Writings on Old Testament Wisdom*, Macon: Mercer University Press

(1995b), 'The perils of specializing in wisdom: what I have learned from thirty years of teaching', Crenshaw (1995a): 586–96

(1998), *Education in Ancient Israel: Across the Deadening Silence*, New York: Doubleday

(2000), 'Unresolved issues in wisdom literature', *An Introduction to Wisdom Literature and the Psalms: Festschrift Marvin E. Tate*, H. W. Ballard Jr and W. D. Tucker Jr (eds.), Macon: Mercer University Press

Crook, M. B. (1954), 'The Marriageable Maiden of Proverbs 31:10–31', *JNES* 13: 137–40

Cross, F. M., Jr (1973), *Canaanite Myth and Hebrew Epic*, Cambridge, MA: Harvard University Press

Culpepper, R. A. (1987), 'Education', *The International Standard Bible Encyclopaedia*, Grand Rapids: Eerdmans

Davidson, A. B. (1904), *The Theology of the Old Testament*, Edinburgh: T. & T. Clark

Davidson, R. (1990), *Wisdom and Worship*, London: SCM Press; Philadelphia: Trinity Press International

Davies, G. I. (1995), 'Were there schools in ancient Israel?', *Wisdom in Ancient Israel: Essays in Honour of J. A. Emerton*, J. Day, R. P. Gordon and H. G. M. Williamson (eds.), Cambridge: Cambridge University Press: 199–211

Davies, P. R. (1998), *Scribes and Schools: The Canonization of the Hebrew Scriptures*, Louisville: Westminster John Knox Press

Day, J., Gordon, R. P., and Williamson, H. G. M. (eds.) (1995), *Wisdom in Ancient Israel: Essays in Honour of J. A. Emerton*, Cambridge: Cambridge University Press

Dell, K. J. (1998), 'The king in the wisdom literature', *King and Messiah in Israel and the Ancient Near East*, J. Day (ed.), JSOTS 270, Sheffield: Sheffield Academic Press: 163–86

— (1991), *The Book of Job as Sceptical Literature*, BZAW 197, Berlin and New York: Walter de Gruyter

— (1997), 'On the development of wisdom in Israel', *Congress Volume, Cambridge 1995*, VTS 66: 135–51

— (2000), *Get Wisdom, Get Insight: An Introduction to Israel's Wisdom Literature*, London: Darton, Longman & Todd

— (2003), 'Covenant and creation in relationship', *Covenant as Context: Essays in Honour of E. W. Nicholson*, A. D. H. Mayes and R. B. Salters (eds.), Oxford: Oxford University Press: 111–33

— (2004a), 'How much wisdom literature has its roots in the pre-exilic period?', *In Search of Pre-exilic Israel*, J. Day (ed.), London and New York: T. & T. Clark International: 251–71

— (2004b) '"I will solve my riddle to the music of the lyre" (Psalm 49:4[5]): A cultic setting for wisdom psalms?', *VT* 54/4: 445–58

— (2005) 'Does the Song of Songs have any connections to wisdom?', *Perspectives on the Song of Songs*, A. C. Hagedorn (ed.), BZAW 346, Berlin and New York: Walter de Gruyter: 8–26

— (forthcoming, 2006), 'God, Creation and the Contribution of Wisdom', *The God of Israel*, R. P. Gordon (ed.), Cambridge: Cambridge University Press

Demsky, A. (1971), 'Education in the Biblical Period', *EJ* vi, Jerusalem: cols. 382–98

(1997), 'Literacy', *The Oxford Encyclopaedia of Archaeology in the Near East*, E. M. Meyers (ed.), New York and Oxford: Oxford University Press: 111: 362–9

Dentan, R. C. (1968), *The Knowledge of God in Ancient Israel*, New York: Seabury Press

Doll, P. (1985), *Menchenschöpfung und Weltschöpfung in der alttestamentlichen Weisheit*, SBS 117, Stuttgart: Katholisches Bibelwerk

Driver, S. R. (1891), *An Introduction to the Literature of the Old Testament*, Edinburgh: T. & T. Clark

Drubbel, A. (1936), 'Le Conflit entre la sagesse profane et la sagesse religieuse', *Biblica* 17: 45–70

Dürr, L. (1932), *Das Erziehungswesen im alten Testament und im Antiken Orient*, Leipzig: J. C. Hinrichs

Eakin, F. E., Jr (1977), 'Wisdom, creation and covenant', *Perspectives in Religious Studies* 4: 218–32

Eaton, J. (1989), *The Contemplative Face of Old Testament Wisdom*, London: SCM Press; Philadelphia: Trinity Press International

Eichrodt, W. (1951), *Man in the Old Testament*, London: SCM Press (Ger. 1947)

(1961–7), *Theology of the Old Testament*, 2 vols., London: SCM Press (Ger. 1933–9)

Eissfeldt, O. (1913), *Der Maschal: eine wortgeschichtliche Untersuchung nebst einer literargeschichtlichen Untersuchung der mashal genannten Gattungen 'Volkssprichwort' und 'Spottlied' im Alten Testament*, BZAW 24, Giessen: Alfred Töpelmann

Emerton, J. A. (1966), ' "Spring and torrent" in Psalm lxxiv. 15', VTS 15: 122–33

(2001), 'The Teaching of Amenemope and Proverbs XXII 17 – XXIV 22: Further reflections on a long-standing problem', *VT* 51: 431–65

Engnell, I. (1967), *Studies in Divine Kingship in the Ancient Near East*, Oxford: Basil Blackwell

Erman, A. (1924), 'Eine ägyptische Quelle der "Sprüche Salomos" ', SPAW zu Berlin, Phil.-hist. Klasse 15: 86–93

Fichtner, J. (1933), *Die altorientalische Weisheit in ihrer israelitisch-jüdischen Ausprägung*, BZAW 62, Giessen: Alfred Töpelmann

(1976), 'Isaiah among the wise', *Studies in Ancient Israelite Wisdom*, J. L. Crenshaw (ed.), New York, KTAV (Ger. 1949)

Finnegan, R. (1970), *Oral Literature in Africa*, Oxford: Oxford University Press

Fishbane, M. (1985), *Biblical Interpretation in Ancient Israel*, Oxford: Clarendon Press

Fontaine, C. R. (1982), *Traditional Sayings in the Old Testament: A Contextual Study*, Bible Literature 5, Sheffield: Almond Press

(1990), 'The sage in family and tribe', *The Sage in Israel and the Ancient Near East*, J. G. Gammie and L. G. Perdue (eds.), Winona Lake: Eisenbrauns: 155–64

(1993), 'Wisdom in Proverbs', *In Search of Wisdom: Essays in Memory of John G. Gammie*, L. G. Perdue, B. B. Scott and W. J. Wiseman (eds.), Louisville: Westminster John Knox Press, 1993

Fox, M. V. (1968), 'Aspects of the religion of the book of Proverbs', *HUCA* 39: 55–69

(1980), 'Two decades of research in Egyptian wisdom literature', *ZÄS* 107: 120–35

(1986), 'Egyptian onomastica and biblical wisdom', *VT* 36: 302–10

(1994), 'The pedagogy of Proverbs 2', *JBL* 113: 233–43

(1996), 'The social location of the book of Proverbs', *Texts, Temples and Traditions: A Tribute to M. Haran*, M. V. Fox, V. Hurowitz, A. Hurvitz, M. Klein, B. Schvatz and N. Shupak (eds.), Winona Lake: Eisenbrauns: 227–39

(2000), *Proverbs 1–9*, Anchor Bible 18a, New York: Doubleday

Frankfort, H. (1948), *Kingship and the Gods*, Chicago: University of Chicago Press

(1949), *Ancient Egyptian Religion: An Interpretation*, New York: Columbia University Press

Frankfort, H. A., and Jacobsen, T. (1946), *The Intellectual Adventure of Ancient Man (Before Philosophy)*, Chicago: University of Chicago Press

Frick, F. S. (1985), *The Formation of the State in Ancient Israel: A Survey of Models and Theories*, Sheffield: Almond Press

Frizzell, L. E. (ed.) (1980), *God and His Temple: Reflections on Prof. S. Terrien's The Elusive Presence: Towards a New Biblical Theology*, South Orange: Seton Hall University Institute of Judaeo-Christian Studies

Gammie, J. G. and Perdue, L. G., (1990), *The Sage in Israel and in the Ancient Near East*, Winona Lake: Eisenbrauns

Gemser, B. (1938), *Sprüche Salomos*, HAT 16

(1960) 'The spiritual structure of biblical aphoristic wisdom', VTS 7: 102–28. Reprinted in *Studies in Ancient Israelite Wisdom*, J. L. Crenshaw (ed.), New York: KTAV, 1976: 208–19

Gerstenberger, E. (1965a), 'Wesen und Herkunft des "apodiktischen Rechts"', *WMANT* 20, Neukirchen-Vluyn: Neukirchener Verlag

(1965b), 'Covenant and commandment', *JBL* 84: 49–51

Gese, H. (1958), *Lehre und Wirklichkeit in der alten Weisheit*, Tübingen: J. C. B. Mohr

(1984), 'Wisdom literature in the Persian period', *The Cambridge History of Judaism* 1, W. D. Davies and L. Finkelstein (eds.), Cambridge: Cambridge University Press

Gilbert, M. (1979), 'Le Discours de la sagesse en Proverbs 8: structure et cohérence', *La Sagesse de l'Ancien Testament*, M. Gilbert (ed.), BETL 52, Gembloux: Duculot: 202–18

(1991), Le Discours menaçant de sagesse en Proverbes 1:20–33', *Storia e Tradizioni di Israele scritti in onore di J. Alberto Soggin*, D. Garrone, and F. Israel (eds.), Brescia: Paideia: 99–119

Goldingay, J. (1979), 'The "salvation history" perspective and the "wisdom" perspective within the context of biblical theology', *EQ* 51: 194–207

Golka, F. (1983), 'Die israelitische Weisheitsschule oder "des Kaiser neue Kleider"', *VT* 33: 257–70

(1986), 'Die Konigs und Hofspruche und der Ursprung der israelitischen Weisheit', *VT* 36: 13–36

(1993), *The Leopard's Spots: Biblical and African Wisdom in Proverbs*, Edinburgh: T. & T. Clark

Gottwald, N. (1980), *The Tribes of Yahweh: A Sociology of the Religion of Liberated Israel 1250–1050 BCE*, London: SCM Press

Greenfield, J. C. (1995), 'The Wisdom of Ahiqar', J. Day, R. P. Gordon and H. G. M. Williamson (eds.), *Wisdom in Ancient Israel: Essays in Honour of J. A. Emerton*, Cambridge: Cambridge University Press: 43–54

Gressmann, H. (1924), 'Die neugefundene Lehre des Amen-em-ope und die vorexilische Spruchdichtung Israels', *ZAW* 44: 272–96

Gunkel, H. (1967), *The Psalms: A Form-critical Introduction*, Philadelphia: Fortress Press (Ger. 1926)

Hamutyinei, M. A., and Plangger, A. B., *Tsumo-Shumo: Shona Proverbial Lore and Wisdom*, Zimbabwe: Mambo Press, 1987

Hanson, P. (1977), 'The theological significance of contradiction within the book of the covenant', *Canon and Authority*, G. W. Coats and B. O. Long (eds.), Philadelphia: Fortress Press

(1978), *Dynamic Transcendence: The Correlation of Confessional Heritage and Contemporary Experience in a Biblical Model of Divine Activity*, Philadelphia: Fortress Press

Haran, M. (1978), *Temples and Temple-service in Ancient Israel: An Inquiry into Biblical Cult Phenomena and the Historical Setting of the Priestly School*, Oxford: Clarendon Press

(1988), 'On the diffusion of literacy and schools in ancient Israel', *Congress Volume: Jerusalem, 1986*, J. A. Emerton (ed.), VTS 40, Leiden: 87–91

Harner, P. B. (1967), 'Creation faith in Deutero-Isaiah', *VT* 17: 298–306

Harrelson, W. (1970), *From Fertility Cult to Worship*, Garden City, New York: Doubleday

(1980), *The Ten Commandments and Human Rights*, Philadelphia: Fortress Press

Harris, S. L. (1996), *Proverbs 1–9: A Study of Inner-biblical Interpretation*, Alpharetta: Scholars Press

Harris, W. V. (1989), *Ancient Literacy*, Cambridge, MA, and London: Harvard University Press

Harvey, J. (1971), 'Wisdom literature and biblical theology', *BTB* 1: 308–19

Hasel, G. (1991), *Old Testament Theology: Basic Issues in the Current Debate*, 4th edition, Grand Rapids: Eerdmans

Hayes, J. H. (1980), *Introduction to Old Testament Study*, Nashville: Abingdon Press

Hayes, J. H., and Prussner, F. (1985), *Old Testament Theology: Its History and Development*, London: SCM Press

Heaton, E. W. (1974), *Solomon's New Men*, London and New York: Pica Press

(1993), 'Memory and encounter: an educational ideal', *Of Prophets' Visions and the Wisdom of Sages: Essays in Honour of R. Norman Whybray on his Seventieth Birthday*, H. A. McKay and D. J. A. Clines (eds.), JSOTS 162, Sheffield: Sheffield Academic Press: 179–91

(1995), *The School Tradition of the Old Testament*, Oxford: Clarendon Press, 1995

Heim, K. M. (2001), *Like Grapes of Gold Set in Silver: Proverbial Clusters in Proverbs 10:1—22:16*, BZAW 273, Berlin and New York: Walter de Gruyter

Hermisson, H.-J. (1965), *Sprache und Ritus im Altisraelitischen Kult*, WMANT 19, Neukirchen: Neukirchener Verlag

(1968), *Studien zur israelitischen Spruchweisheit*, WMANT 28, Neukirchen-Vluyn: Neukirchener Verlag

(1978), 'Observations on the creation theology in wisdom', *Israelite Wisdom: Essays in Honor of Samuel Terrien*, J. G. Gammie, W. A. Brueggemann, W. L. Humphreys and J. M. Ward (eds.), Missoula: Scholars Press: 43–57; Reprinted in B. W. Anderson (ed.), *Creation in the Old Testament*, London: SCM Press; Philadelphia: Fortress Press, 1984: 118–34

Hildebrandt, T. (1988), 'Proverbial Pairs: Compositional Units in Proverbs 10–29', *JBL* 197: 207–24

Hillers, D. R. (1969), *Covenant: The History of a Biblical Idea*, Baltimore: Johns Hopkins University Press

Høgenhaven, J. (1987), *Problems and Prospects of Old Testament Theology*, Sheffield: JSOT Press

Hooke, S. H. (1958), *Myth, Ritual and Kingship: Essays on the Theory and Practice of Kingship in the Ancient Near East and in Israel*, Oxford: Clarendon Press

Hoppe, L. J. (1979), 'Biblical wisdom: a theology of creation', *Listening* 14: 196–203

Horwitz, W. J. (1979), 'The Ugaritic scribe', *UF* 11: 389–94

Hubbard, D. A. (1966), 'The wisdom movement and Israel's covenant faith', *TB* 17: 3–33

Humbert, P. (1935), 'La Relation de Genèse 1 et du Psaume 104 avec la liturgie du Nouvel-An israélite', *RHPhR* 15: 1–27

Humphreys, W. L. (1978), 'The motif of the wise courtier in the book of Proverbs', *Israelite Wisdom: Theological and Literary Studies in Honor of Samuel Terrien*, J. G. Gammie (ed.), Missoula: Scholars Press: 177–90

Jacob, E., (1971), 'Sagesse et alphabet: á propos de Proverbes 31.10–31', *Hommages à André Dupont-Sommer*, Paris: Librairie d'Amérique et d'Orient Adrien Maisonneuve: 287–95

(1975), 'Principe canonique et la formation de l'Ancien Testament', VTS 28 (Congress Volume, Leiden: Brill, 1975): 101–22

Jamieson-Drake, D. (1991), *Scribes and Schools in Monarchic Judah: A Socio-archaeological Approach*, JSOT 109, Sheffield: Sheffield Academic Press

Jenks, A. W. (1985), 'Theological presuppositions of Israel's wisdom literature', *HBT* 7: 43–75

Kalugila, L. (1980), *The Wise King: Studies in Royal Wisdom as Divine Revelation in the Old Testament and Its Environment*, CB 15, Uppsala, Lund: C. W. J. Gleerup

Kaufmann, Y. (1966), *Religion of Israel: From its Beginning to the Babylonian Exile*, translated and abridged by M. Greenberg, Chicago: University of Chicago Press

Kayatz, C. B. (1966), *Studien zu Proverbien 1–9: eine form- und motivgeschichtliche Untersuchung unter Einbeziehung ägyptischen Vergleichmaterials*, WMANT 22, Neukirchen-Vluyn: Neukirchener Verlag

(1969), *Einführung in die alttestamentliche Weisheit*, Biblische Studien 55, Neukirchen-Vluyn: Neukirchener Verlag

Klostermann, A. (1908), 'Schulwesen im alten Israel', *Th. Zahn, Festschrift*, Leipzig: A. Deichert (Georg Böhme): 193–232

Knierim, R. P. (1981), 'Cosmos and history in Israel's theology', *HBT* 3: 59–123

(1984), 'The task of Old Testament theology', *HBT* 6: 25–57

Koch, K. (1955), 'The Old Testament view of nature', *ZTK* 52: 1–42

(1983), 'Is there a doctrine of retribution in the Old Testament?', *Theodicy in the Old Testament*, J. L. Crenshaw (ed.), Philadelphia: Fortress Press, 57–87 (Ger. 1955)

Köhler, L. H. (1936), *Theologie des Alten Testaments*, Tübingen: J. C. B. Mohr

Kovacs, B. W. (1974), 'Is there a class ethic in Proverbs?', *Essays in Old Testament Ethics*, J. L. Crenshaw and J. T. Willis (eds.), New York: KTAV

Kramer, S. N. (1958), *History Begins at Sumer*, London: Thames & Hudson (1961), *The Sumerians*, Chicago and London: University of Chicago Press

Kraus, H.-J. (1951), *Die Verhündigung der Weisheit: Eine Auslegung des Kapitels Sprüch*, Biblische Studien 2, Giessen
(1979), *Theologie der Psalmen*, Neukirchen-Vluyn: Neukirchener Verlag, 1979

Lambert, W. G. (1960), *Babylonian Wisdom Literature*, Oxford: Clarendon Press

Landes, G. M. (1974), 'Creation tradition in Proverbs 8:22–31 and Genesis 1', *A Light Unto My Path: Old Testament Studies in Honor of Jacob M. Myers*, H. N. Bream, R. D. Heim and C. A. Moore (eds.), Philadelphia: Temple: 279–93
(1978), 'Creation and Liberation', *Union Seminary Quarterly Review* 33: 79–89

Landsberger, B. (1960), 'Scribal concepts of education', *City Invincible: A Symposium on Urbanization and Cultural Development in the Ancient Near East*, Chicago: University of Chicago Press

Lang, B. (1972), *Die Weisheitliche Lehrrede*, SBS 54, Stuttgart
(1979), 'Schule und Unterricht im alten Israel', *La Sagesse de L'Ancien Testament*, M. Gilbert (ed.), BETL 51, Leuven: Leuven University Press; Gembloux: Duculot: 186–201

Lang, B. (1986), *Wisdom and the Book of Proverbs: An Israelite Goddess Redefined*, New York: Pilgrim Press

Leeuwen, R. C. van (1988), *Context and Meaning in Proverbs 25–27*, SBLDS 96, Atlanta: Scholars Press

Lemaire, A. (1981), *Les Ecoles et la formation de la Bible dans l'ancien Israël*, OBO 39, Fribourg, Switzerland: Editions Universitaires; Göttingen: Vandenhoeck & Ruprecht

Lemaire, A. (1984), 'Sagesse et écoles', *VT* 34: 270–81
(1992), 'Writing and writing materials', *Anchor Bible Dictionary*, VI, D. N. Freedman (ed.), New York: Doubleday, 999–1008

Levenson, J. (1994), *Creation and the Persistence of Evil: The Jewish Drama of Divine Omnipotence*, San Francisco: Harper & Row, 1988. Reprinted Princeton: Princeton University Press

Lichtheim, M. (1980), *Ancient Egyptian Literature: A Book of Readings* II, Berkeley, Los Angeles and London: University of California Press

Lindblom, J. (1962), *Prophecy in Ancient Israel*, Oxford: Basil Blackwell

Lindeskog, G. (1953), 'The theology of creation in the Old and New Testaments', *The Root of the Vine: Essays in Biblical Theology*, A. Fridrichsen (ed.), Westminster: Dacre Press: 1–22

Lohfink, N. (1991), 'Poverty in the laws of the ancient Near East and of the Bible', *TS* 52: 34–50

Ludwig, T. M. (1973), 'The traditions of the establishing of the earth in Deutero-Isaiah', *JBL* 92: 345–57

McCreesh, T. (1985), 'Wisdom as wife: Proverbs 31:10–31', *RB* 92: 25–46

McKane, W. (1965), *Prophets and Wise Men*, SBT 44, London: SCM Press
  (1970), *Proverbs: A New Approach*, OTL, London: SCM Press
  (1986–96), *A Critical and Exegetical Commentary on Jeremiah* (2 vols.), ICC, Edinburgh: T. & T. Clark

Mack, B. L. (1970), 'Wisdom myth and mythology', *Interpretation* 24: 46–60

Malamat, A. (1965), 'Organs of statecraft in the Israelite monarchy', *Biblical Archaeologist* 28: 34–65

Malchow, B. (1938), 'A manual for future monarchs', *CBQ* 47: 238–45

Malfoy, J. (1965), 'Sagesse et loi dans le Deuteronomie', *VT* 15: 49–65

Martens, E. A. (1992), 'The Multicolored Landscape of Old Testament Theology', *The Flowering of Old Testament Theology*, B. C. Ollenburger, E. A. Martens and G. F. Hasel, Winona Lake: Eisenbrauns, 43–57

Meinhold, A. (1991), *Die Sprüche*, ZB 16 (2 vols.), Zurich: Theologischer Verlag

Meinhold, J. (1908), *Die Weisheits Israels in Spruch, Sage und Dichtung*, Leipzig: Quelle & Meyer

Mettinger, T. N. D. (1988), *In Search of God: The Meaning and Message of the Everlasting Names*, Philadelphia: Fortress Press

Michel, D. (1992), 'Proverbia 2 – ein Dokument der Geschichte der Weisheit', *Alttestamentlicher Glaube und Biblische Theologie: Festschrift für Horst Dietrich Preuss*, J. Hausmann et al. (eds.), Stuttgart: Kohlhammer: 233–43

Millard, A. (1985), 'An assessment of the evidence of writing in ancient Israel', *Biblical Archaeology Today: Proceedings of the International Congress on Biblical Archaeology*, Jerusalem, April 1984, Jerusalem: Israel Exploration Society

Minear, P. S. (1948), *Eyes of Faith: A Study in the Biblical Point of View*, London: Redhill

Moore, R. D. (1994), 'A home for the alien: worldly wisdom and covenantal confession in Proverbs 30:1–9', *ZAW* 106: 96–107

Morgan, D. F. (1981), *Wisdom in the Old Testament Traditions*, Atlanta, John Knox Press

Murphy, R. E. (1966), 'The kerygma of the book of Proverbs', *Interpretation* 20: 3–14

(1967), 'Assumptions and problems in Old Testament wisdom research', *CBQ* 29: 101–12

(1975), 'Wisdom and Yahwism', *No Famine in the Land: Studies in Honor of John L. McKenzie*, J. W. Flanagan and A. W. Robinson (eds.), Missoula: Scholars Press

(1978), 'Wisdom: theses and hypotheses', *Israelite Wisdom: Essays in Honor of Samuel Terrien*, J. G. Gammie (ed.), Missoula: Scholars Press: 35–42

(1981a), 'The faces of wisdom in the book of Proverbs', *Mélanges bibliques et orientaux en l'honneur de M. H. Cazelles*, A. Caquot and M. Delcor (eds.), AOAT 212, Neukirchen-Vluyn: Neukirchener Verlag: 337–45

(1981b), *Wisdom Literature*, The Forms of the Old Testament Literature 13, R. Knierim and G. M. Tucker (eds.), Grand Rapids: Eerdmans

(1985), 'Wisdom and creation', *JBL* 104: 3–11

(1986), 'Proverbs and Theological Exegesis', *The Hermeneutical Quest: Essays in Honor of James Luther Mays on His Sixty-fifth Birthday*, D. G. Miller (ed.), PTMS 4, Allison Park: Pickwick Publications: 87–95

(1987), 'Religious dimensions of Israelite wisdom', *Ancient Israelite Religion*, P. D. Miller Jr, P. D. Hanson and S. D. McBridge (eds.), Philadelphia: Fortress Press: 452–6

(1988), 'Wisdom and eros in Proverbs 1–9', *CBQ* 50: 600–3

(1990) *The Tree of Life: An Exploration of Biblical Wisdom Literature*, New York: Doubleday. Revised edition, Grand Rapids: Eerdmans, 2002

(1994a) 'Wisdom literature and biblical theology', *BTB* 24: 4–7

(1994b), 'Israelite wisdom and the home', *'Où demeures tu?' (Jn. 1:38): La Maison depuis le monde biblique: Festschrift Guy Coutourier*, J.-C. Petit (ed.), Montreal: Fides: 199–212

(1998), *Proverbs*, Word Biblical Commentary 22, Nashville: Thomas Nelson

(2000), 'Wisdom and Yahwism revisited', *Shall Not the Judge of all the Earth Do What is Right?: Studies on the Nature of God in Tribute to James L. Crenshaw*, D. Penchansky and P. L. Redditt (eds.), Winona Lake: Eisenbrauns: 191–200

Napier, B. D. (1962), 'On creation-faith in the Old Testament: a survey', *Interpretation* 16: 21–42

Naré, L. (1986), *Proverbes salomoniens et proverbes mossi: étude comparative à partir d'une nouvelle analyse de Pr 25–29*, Publications Universitaires Européannes, série xxiii, vol. 283, Frankfurt: Peter Lang

Nel, P. J. (1981), 'The genres of biblical wisdom literature', *JNWSL* 9: 129–142

(1982), *The Structure and Ethos of the Wisdom Admonitions in Proverbs*, BZAW 158, Berlin: Walter de Gruyter

Neufeld, C. (1960), 'The emergence of a royal-urban society in ancient Israel', *HUCA* 31: 31–52

Niditch, S. (1996), *Oral World and Written Word: Ancient Israelite Literature*, Louisville: Westminster John Knox Press

Newsome, C. A. (1989), 'Woman and the discourse of patriarchal wisdom: a study of Proverbs 1–9', *Gender and Difference in Ancient Israel*, P. L. Day (ed.), Minneapolis: Fortress Press: 142–60

Oesterley, W. O. E. (1929), *The Book of Proverbs*, Westminster Commentaries, London: Methuen

Oppenheim, A. L. (1975), 'The position of the intellectual in Mesopotamian society' *Daedalus: Journal of the American Academy of Arts and Sciences* 104: 237–46

Östborn, G. (1950), *Cult and Canon: A Study of the Canonization of the Old Testament*, Uppsala Universitets Arsskrift, Uppsala: Lundequistska bokhandeln

Otzen, B., Gottlieb, H., and Jeppensen, K. (1980), *Myths in the Old Testament*, London: SCM Press

Perdue, L. G. (1977), *Wisdom and Cult: A Critical Analysis of the Views of Cult in the Wisdom Literatures of Israel and the Ancient Near East*, SBLDS 30, Missoula: Scholars Press

(1981), 'Liminality as a social setting for wisdom instruction', *ZAW* 93: 114–26

(1990), 'The social character of Paraenesis and Paranetic Literature', *Semeia* 50: 5–39

(1991), *Wisdom in Revolt*, Sheffield: Almond Press

(1994a), *The Collapse of History: Reconstructing Old Testament Theology*, Minneapolis: Fortress Press

(1994b), *Wisdom and Creation*, Nashville: Abingdon Press

(1997), 'Wisdom Theology and Social History in Proverbs 1–9' *Wisdom, You Are My Sister: Studies in Honor of Roland E. Murphy, O. Carm., on the Occasion of His Eightieth Birthday*, M. L. Barré, (ed.), CBQMS 29, Washington: Catholic Biblical Association of America: 78–101

Perdue, L. G., Blenkinsopp, J., Collins, J. J., and Meyers, C. (1997), *Families in Ancient Israel*, Louisville: Westminster John Knox Press

Pleins, J. D. (1987), 'Poverty in the social world of the wise', *JSOT* 37: 61–78

Plöger, O. (1984), *Sprüche Salomos* (Proverbia), BKAT 17, Neukirchen-Vluyn: Neukirchener Verlag, 1984

Polk, T. (1983), 'Paradigms, parables and mešālîm: On reading the māšāl in scripture', *CBQ* 45: 564–83

Preuss, H. D. (1970), 'Erwagungen zum theologischen Ort alttestamen-
tliche Weisheitsliteratur', *EvTh* 30: 393–417
    (1972), 'Das Gottesbild der älteren Weisheit Israels', *Studies in the
Religion of Ancient Israel*, VTS 23, Leiden: Brill: 117–45
    (1987), *Einführung in die alttestamentliche Weisheitsliteratur*, Urban-
Taschenbücher 383, Stuttgart: Kohlhammer
    (1995–6), *Old Testament Theology* (2 vols.), Louisville: Westminster John
Knox Press; Edinburgh: T. & T. Clark (Ger. 1991)
Puech, E. (1988), 'Les Ecoles dans l'Israël préexiliques: données épigraphi-
ques', *Congress Volume: Jerusalem, 1986*, VTS 40, Leiden: Brill,
189–203
Rad, G. von (1966a), 'The beginnings of historical writing in ancient
Israel', *The Problem of the Hexateuch and Other Essays*, Edinburgh
and London: Oliver & Boyd: 166–204 (Ger. 1953)
    (1966b), 'Some aspects of the Old Testament world view', *The Problem
of the Hexateuch and Other Essays*, Edinburgh and London: Oliver and
Boyd: 144–65 (Ger. 1953)
    (1972), *Wisdom in Israel*, London: SCM Press (Ger. 1970)
    (1975), *Old Testament Theology* (2 vols.), London: SCM Press. (Ger.
1958–61; ET 1962–5)
Rainey, A. F. (1969), 'The scribe at Ugarit: his position and influence',
Proceedings of the Israel Academy of Sciences and Humanities, 3:
126–47
Ranston, H. (1930), *The Old Testament Wisdom Books and Their Teaching*,
London: Epworth Press
Redford, D. B. (1992), *Egypt, Canaan and Israel in Ancient Times*, Princeton:
Princeton University Press
Reventlow, H. Graf (1985), *Problems of Old Testament Theology in the
Twentieth Century*, London: SCM Press
    (1985), 'The world horizon of Old Testament theology', *Problems of
Old Testament Theology in the Twentieth Century*, London: SCM
Press
Richter, W. (1966), *Recht und Ethos: versuch einer Ortung des Weisheitlichen
Mahnspruches*, Studien zum Alten und Neuen Testament 15, Munich:
Kösel
Ringgren, H. (1963), *The Faith of the Psalmists*, London: SCM Press
    (1966), *Israelite Religion*, London: SPCK (Ger. 1963)
Robert, A. (1934–5), 'Les Attaches littéraires bibliques de Proverbes I–IX',
RB 43 (1934): 42–68, 172–204, 374–84; 44; (1935): 344–65, 512–25
Rogerson, J. W. (1977), 'The Old Testament view of nature: some prelim-
inary questions', *OTS* 20: 67–84
Roth, W. M. W. (1965), *Numerical Sayings in the Old Testament: A Form-
critical Study*, VTS 13, Leiden: Brill

Schmid, H. H. (1966), *Wesen und Geschichte der Weisheit*, BZAW 101, Berlin: Töpelmann

    (1968), *Gerechtigkeit als Weltordnung*, BHT 40, Tübingen: J. C. B. Mohr

    (1974), *Altorientalische Welt in der alttestamentlichen Theologie*, Zurich: Theologischer Verlag

    (1984), 'Creation, righteousness and salvation as the broad horizon of biblical theology', *Creation in the Old Testament*, B. W. Anderson (ed.), London: SCM Press; Philadelphia: Fortress Press: 102–117 (Ger. 1973)

Scott, R. B. Y. (1961), 'Folk proverbs of the ancient Near East', *Transactions of the Royal Society of Canada* 55: 47–56. Reprinted in J. L. Crenshaw (ed.), *Studies in Ancient Israelite Wisdom*, New York: KTAV, 1976: 417–26

    (1965), 'Solomon and the Beginnings of Wisdom in Israel', *Wisdom in Israel and the Ancient Near East*, M. Noth and D. Winton Thomas (eds.),VTS 3, Leiden: Brill: 262–79

Sellin, E. (1924), 'Die neugefundene "Lehre des Amen-em-ope" in ihrer Bedeutung für die jüdische Literatur- und Religionsgeschichte', *DLZ* 45: cc. 1873–84

Sheppard, G. T. (1980), *Wisdom as a Hermeneutical Construct: A Study in the Sapientializing of the Old Testament*, BZAW 151, Berlin and New York: Walter de Gruyter

Shupak, N. (1987), 'The *Sitz im Leben* of the book of Proverbs', *RB* 94: 98–119

    (1993), *Where Can Wisdom be found? The Sage's Language in the Bible and Ancient Near Eastern Literature*, Fribourg: University Press; Göttingen: Vandenhoeck & Ruprecht

Sjöberg, A. W. (1975), 'The Old Babylonian Edubba', *Sumeriological Studies in Honor of T. Jacobsen, Assyriological Studies* 20, Chicago: University of Chicago Press, 159–79

Skehan, P. W. (1967), 'Wisdom's house', *CBQ* 29: 162–80. Revised version in Skehan, P. W. (1971), *Studies in Israelite Poetry and Wisdom*, CBQMS 1, Washington, DC: Catholic Biblical Association of America

    (1971) 'A single editor for the whole book of Proverbs', *Studies in Israelite Poetry and Wisdom*, CBQMS 1, Washington, DC: Catholic Biblical Association of America: 15–26

Skladny, U. (1962), *Die ältesten Spruchsammlungen in Israel*, Göttingen: Vandenhoeck & Ruprecht.

Smith, M. (1971), *Palestinian Parties and Politics that Shaped the Old Testament*, New York: Columbia University Press

Stager, L. (1985), 'The archaeology of the family in ancient Israel', *Bulletin of the American Schools of Oriental Research* 260: 1–35

Steiert, F.-J. (1990), *Die Weisheit Israels - ein Fremdkörper im Alten Testament? Eine Untersuchung zum Buch der Sprüche auf dem Hintergrund der ägyptischen Weisheitslehren*, FTS 143, Freiburg: Herder, 1990

Terrien, S. (1966), 'Creation, cultus and faith in the Psalter', *Theological Education* 2: 116–28

(1980), 'The pursuit of a theme', *God and His Temple: Reflections on Professor Terrien's The Elusive Presence: Toward a New Biblical Theology*, South Orange: Seton Hall University Institute of Judaeo-Christian Studies

(1981), 'The play of wisdom: turning point in biblical theology', *HBT* 3: 125–53

Toombs, L. E. (1955), 'Old Testament theology and the wisdom literature', *JBR* 23:193–6

Towner, W. S. (1977), 'The renewed authority of Old Testament wisdom for contemporary faith', *Canon and Authority: Essays in Old Testament Religion and Theology*, G. W. Coats and B. O. Long (eds.), Philadelphia: Fortress Press, 132–47

Toy, C. H. (1899), *Proverbs*, ICC, Edinburgh: T. & T. Clark

Tracy D., and Lash, N. (eds.) (1983), *Cosmology and Theology*, New York and Edinburgh: T. and T. Clark

Ulrich, E. (1992), *Priests, Prophets and Scribes: Essays on the Formation and Heritage of Second Temple Judaism in Honour of Joseph Blenkinsopp*, JSOTS 149, Sheffield: JSOT Press

Vanstiphout, H. L. J. (1979), 'How did they learn Sumerian?' *JCS* 31: 118–26

Vaux, R. de (1961), *Ancient Israel: Its Life and Institutions*, London: Darton, Longman & Todd

Vawter, B. (1986), 'Prov. 8:22, wisdom and creation', *The Path of Wisdom: Biblical Investigations*, Wilmington: Michael Glazier: 161–77

Voort, A. van der (1951), 'Genèse 1:1 à 2:4a et la Psaume 104', *RB* 58: 321–47

Waltke, B. K. (1979), 'The book of Proverbs and Old Testament theology', *BS* 136: 302–17

(1996), 'Does Proverbs promise too much?', *Andrews University Seminary Studies* 34, nos. 1–2: 319–36

(2004), *The Book of Proverbs: Chapters 1–15*, Grand Rapids: Eerdmans

Weeks, S. (1994), *Early Israelite Wisdom*, Oxford: Clarendon Press

Weinfeld, M. (1977), *Deuteronomy and the Deuteronomic School*, Oxford: Oxford University Press

(1991), *Deuteronomy 1–11*, Anchor Bible 5, New York, London: Doubleday

Westermann, C. (1971a), 'Weisheit im Sprichwort', *Schalom: Studien zu Glaube und Geschichte Israels* (A. Jepson Festschrift), K.-H Bernhardt (ed.), Arbeiten zur Theologie I/46, Stuttgart: Calwer Verlag: 73–85.

Reprinted in *Forschung am Alten Testament: Gesammelte Studien* 11, TBAT 55, Munich: Kaiser Verlag, 1974: 149–61

Westermann, C. (1971b), 'Creation and History in the Old Testament', *The Gospel and Human Destiny*, V. Vajta (ed.), Minneapolis: Augsburg Press, 11–23

(1972), *Beginning and End in the Bible*, Philadelphia: Fortress Press

(1974), *Creation*, London: SPCK (Ger. 1971)

(1978a), *Theologie des Alten Testaments in Grundzügen*, Grundrissse zum Alten Testament 6, Göttingen: Vandenhoeck & Ruprecht

(1978b), *Blessing in the Bible and the Life of the Church*, Philadelphia: Fortress Press (Ger. 1968)

(1979), *What Does the OT Say about God?*, Atlanta: John Knox Press; London: SPCK

(1982), *Elements of Old Testament Theology*, Atlanta: John Knox Press (Ger. 1978)

(1991), *Forschungsgeschichte zur Weisheitsliteratur 1950–1990*, Arbeiten zur Theologie 71, Stuttgart: Calwer Verlag

(1995), *Roots of Wisdom: The Oldest Proverbs of Israel and Other Peoples*, Louisville: Westminster John Knox Press (Ger. 1990)

Whedbee, J. W. (1971), *Isaiah and Wisdom*, New York: Abingdon Press

Wheeler Robinson, H. (1946), *Inspiration and Revelation in the Old Testament*, Oxford: Clarendon Press

Whybray, R. N. (1965), *Wisdom in Proverbs*, SBT 45, London: SCM Press

(1974), *The Intellectual Tradition in the Old Testament*, BZAW 135, Berlin and New York: Walter de Gruyter

(1979), 'Yahweh-sayings and their contexts in Proverbs 10:1–22:16', M. Gilbert (ed.), *La Sagesse de l'ancien Testament*, BETL 51, Leuven: Leuven University Press; Gembloux: Duculot: 153–65. Reprinted in *Wisdom: The Collected Articles of Norman Whybray*, K. J. Dell and M. Barker (eds.), SOTS Monograph Series, Aldershot and Burlington: Ashgate, 2005: 45–57

(1982), 'Wisdom literature in the reigns of David and Solomon', *Studies in the Period of David and Solomon and Other Essays*, T. Ishida (ed.), Winona Lake: Eisenbrauns, 13–26. Reprinted in *Wisdom: The Collected Articles of Norman Whybray* (see Whybray, 1979): 223–36

(1989), 'The social world of the wisdom writers', *The World of Ancient Israel*, R. E. Clements (ed.), Cambridge: Cambridge University Press: 227–50. Reprinted in *Wisdom: The Collected Articles of Norman Whybray* (see Whybray, 1979): 227–60

(1990), *Wealth and Poverty in the Book of Proverbs*, Sheffield: JSOT Press

(1994a), *The Composition of the Book of Proverbs*, JSOTS 168, Sheffield: Sheffield Academic Press

(1994b), 'The structure and composition of Proverbs 22:17—24:22', *Crossing the Boundaries: Essays in Biblical Interpretation in Honour of Michael D. Goulder*, S. E. Porter, P. Joyce and D. E. Orton (eds.), Leiden: Brill: 83–96. Reprinted in *Wisdom: The Collected Articles of Norman Whybray* (See Whybray, 1979): 76–89

(1994c), *Proverbs*, New Century Bible Commentary, London: Marshall Pickering; Grand Rapids: Eerdmans

(1996), *Reading the Psalms as a Book*, JSOTS 222, Sheffield: Sheffield Academic Press

Widengren, G. (1959), 'Oral tradition and written literature in the light of Arabic evidence with special regard to prose narratives', *Acta Orientalia* 23: 201–62

Wilcoxen, J. (1968), 'Some anthropocentric aspects of Israel's sacred history', *JR* 48: 333–50

Williams, J. G. (1969), 'The social location of Israelite prophecy', *JAAR* 37: 153–165

(1980), 'The power of form: a study of biblical Proverbs', *Semeia* 17: 35–58

(1981), *Those who Ponder Proverbs: Aphoristic Thinking and Biblical Literature*, Sheffield: Almond Press

Williams, R. J. (1972), 'Scribal training in ancient 'Egypt'', *JAOS* 92: 214–21

Willis, J. (1969), *A Rigid Scrutiny: Essays by Ivan Engnell*, Nashville: Vanderbilt University Press

Wilson, G. H. (1985), *The Editing of the Hebrew Psalter*, SBLDS 76, Chico: Scholars Press

Wolff, H. W. (1973), *Amos the Prophet: The Man and His Background*, Philadelphia: Fortress Press (Ger. 1964)

(1974), *Hosea*, Hermeneia, Philadelphia: Fortress Press (Ger. 1961)

(1977), *Joel and Amos*, Hermeneia, Philadelphia: Fortress Press (Ger. 1975)

(1981), *Micah the Prophet*, Hermeneia, Philadelphia: Fortress Press (Ger. 1978)

Wolters, A. (1988), 'Proverbs xxxi: 10–31 as heroic hymn: a form-critical analysis', *VT* 38: 446–57

Wright, G. E. (1952), *God Who Acts: Biblical Theology as Recital*, SBT 8, London: SCM Press

(1957), *The Old Testament against its Environment*, SBT 2, London: SCM Press

(1969), *The Old Testament and Theology*, New York: Harper & Row

Wurthwein, E. (1960), *Das Weisheit Aegyptens und das Alte Testament*, Marburg: Elwert

Yee, G. A. (1982), 'An analysis of Proverbs 8:22–31 according to style and structure', *ZAW* 94: 58–66

(1989), 'I have perfumed my bed with myrrh': The foreign woman (*'iššâ zārâ*) in Proverbs 1–9', *JSOT* 43: 53–68

(1992), 'The theology of creation in Proverbs 8:22–31', *Creation in the Biblical Traditions*, R. J. Clifford and J. J. Collins (eds.), CBQMS 24, Washington, DC: Catholic Biblical Association of America: 85–96

Zimmerli, W. (1933), 'Zur Struktur der alttestamentlichen Weisheit,' *ZAW* 51:177–204

(1964), 'The place and limit of wisdom in the framework of Old Testament theology', *SJT* 17: 146–58

(1971), 'Alttestamentliche Traditionsgeschichte und Theologie', *Probleme Biblischer Theologie: Gerhard von Rad zum 70. Geburtstag*, H. W. Wolff (ed.), Munich: C. Kaiser: 632–47

(1974), 'Considerations about the form of an Old Testament theology', *Studien zur alttestamentlichen Theologie und Prophetie: Gesammelte Aufsätze* 11, TBAT 51, Munich: C. Kaiser, 27–54

(1976), *The Old Testament and the World*, London: SPCK

(1978), *Old Testament Theology in Outline*, Edinburgh: T. & T. Clark; Atlanta: John Knox Press (Ger. 1972)

Zuck, R. B. (1995), *Learning from the Sages: Selected Studies on the Book of Proverbs*, Grand Rapids: Eerdmans

Index